Selfish Whining Monkeys

How We Ended Up Greedy, Narcissistic and Unhappy

ROD LIDDLE

FOURTH ESTATE · London

First published in Great Britain in 2014 by
Fourth Estate
An imprint of HarperCollins*Publishers*
77–85 Fulham Palace Road,
Hammersmith, London W6 8JB
www.4thestate.co.uk

2

A catalogue record for this book is
available from the British Library

ISBN 978-0-00-735127-5

Printed and bound in Spain by
Graficas Estella

MIX
Paper from
responsible sources
FSC
www.fsc.org
FSC C007454

For Alicia

Contents

... remember that I am an ass; though it be not written down, yet forget not that I am an ass.

William Shakespeare, *Much Ado About Nothing*

I

Aeroplanes

Home is so sad. It stays as it was left,
Shaped to the comfort of the last to go
As if to win them back.

Philip Larkin

I got an aeroplane for Christmas when I was six years old. Not a real one, but a heavy tinplate thing with chunky red flashing plastic lights on the wings and some sort of noise box which made a sound like one of those heaving 1950s vacuum cleaners, a piercing shriek like it was undergoing a hysterectomy without anaesthetic. I'd seen it in, I think, the toy department of Selfridges in Oxford Street on the annual trip to town where I got to visit Santa's grotto and choose my present for the year. I can remember right now standing by the counter piled up with all these unimagined and beguiling toys and seeing the aeroplane up on top, lights flashing, screaming away – a big BOAC passenger liner – and being utterly, if momentarily, captivated by it.

'Why would you want a plane?' my mum asked with a sort of perplexed distaste as we stood there. None of us had ever been on one, nor were likely to. Aside from the unimaginable cost and the fear of flying, my family didn't really hold with abroad on account of it being too hot and full of wogs. My dad had been abroad only once, briefly, to shell bits of Belgium during those interminable, drawn-out final stages of the Second World War. I still have a replica of the MTB he served on, carved with rough approximation to detail out of the brass casing of a German shell which had hit his boat but – mercifully, for my dad and by extension me – not detonated. They shelled Belgium after it had been liberated, according to my dad, because they simply couldn't abide the Belgians, devious and bitter people and, if we're being honest, far, far, worse than the Krauts. So in early 1945 Dad's MTB anchored in some Belgian port, I forget which, and took potshots at the church tower from the stern cannon, and when they went onshore they pissed in the streets because that's what the Belgians were habituated to, apparently. Awful people, almost as bad as the French.

Many years later, when I went on a work trip to Antwerp, I kept my eyes trained upwards in case they started throwing buckets of piss out of the windows, as my dad gravely assured me they would. No proper sanitation in Belgium, you see – an echo, in my dad's mind, of John Betjeman's bitter little list of stuff which made Britain distinct:

> Free speech, free passes, class distinction,
> Democracy and proper drains.

My mum had never been abroad, not even to kill people. A little later, in the early 1970s, she said she quite fancied visiting Egypt because they were at war with Israel and she didn't much like Jews. But she never went.

So, anyway, after this short cross-examination in Selfridges I got my plane, pulled off the wrapping paper on Christmas Day and ran around the house with the thing with its lights on and the engine making that fucking demented noise, swooping down every so often to attack our amiable half-breed dog Skipper who, after a few moments of this torment, bit me deeply on the arm and then cowered behind the settee, tail wrapped underneath his arse and backbone curved almost in a semi-circle, because he knew he was in the shit, with me howling holding up my arm for all to see. And yet as it turned out Skipper was exonerated, my mother correctly assuming that the dog had been provoked beyond all reasonable limits and I had got what I deserved. So I stood there crying at the injustice of it all while Skipper – out of contrition or hunger, who knows? – licked away at the blood still pouring from the gash on my arm, the edges of the wound slightly blueish where his dumb and blunt half-Labrador teeth had merely bruised, rather than cut. But the licking was OK, because dogs' tongues were antiseptic, according to my mum. 'Better than Germolene, a dog's tongue. You don't need a bandage,' she had said. I don't know why, but I'll always remember that purple-blue colour around the wound. It seemed exotic and in some way more severe, more of a grown-up wound, than if it had just been blood.

The plane lasted maybe three days before the huge clunking batteries gave out and my interest in swooping around with it – carefully avoiding the dog now – gave out too. And I had a sense, by about tea-time on 28 December 1966, when the family at last scuttled itself gratefully back from the sitting room – which would next be used twelve months hence; hell, you could still smell the pine needles in June – to the warm cluttered chaos of the parlour, that it had been a wasted opportunity, this growling, flashing plane. One trip to London every year – we lived twelve or thirteen miles away in Bexleyheath, and my dad worked in town during the week, but aside from Christmas we never, ever, went in ourselves – and one big present every year, and I'd chosen this thing that just made a noise and flashed its lights. I wasn't sure what I should have chosen, but the plane definitely wasn't it. The plane was, I thought to myself silently, shite.

Its very shiteness, of course, is why it sticks in the memory, a forlorn disappointment and also a warning. It nags away at me now when I buy presents for my own kids and they express the mildest interest in something which I know will hold their attention only briefly and will consequently be, for them, a source of long regret. Toys which are flashy, superficial and demand nothing from their owners, like those rides at Alton Towers or Thorpe Park in which you queue for hours to be strapped down and flung somewhere for twenty seconds, maybe through water if you're lucky, and you end up wondering what the fuck it was all about, all that waiting, with the furious wasps buzzing around a thousand hideous onesies smeared with ketchup and the dried-out sugar from soft drinks and the whining, the incessant whining, about how long we have to wait for stuff.

But actually I shouldn't worry – because there are three cupboards upstairs full of discarded toys with corroded batteries, and three more full of toys which are still, intermittently, used. The occasional duff present is of absolutely no consequence to my children. The problem these days is wondering what the hell I can buy the little bastards that they haven't already got, wandering confused and desperate through Hamleys and Comet and Dixons, while they themselves are disconcertingly blasé about presents: nothing you can give them excites them, no matter how much you spend. At Christmas and on birthdays I check with the mother of my two boys – we're divorced – and she's as much at a loss as me. What can we buy them that will induce that immensely gratifying gaze of awe and delight, that look you want to see on their little faces on Christmas morning? A Ferrari, maybe, or their own country. Buy them Chad, or Belgium. Would that raise a smile, get them excited for a moment? But on Christmas morning what they really want is a lie-in, just to sleep ever onwards. And it's not their fault, any of this. They don't clamour for gifts; quite the reverse. They don't clamour like I used to clamour, back when presents were exceptional and therefore it really mattered what you were given.

The plane banks sharply to the left, too sharply for my liking. My plastic beaker of warm chemical urinous white wine and half-empty packet of bowel-racking nicotine-replacement gum slides across the plastic tray table and I see the cheerful gay cabin steward with his impeccably neat number-one cut frown suddenly halfway down the aisle as he temporarily loses grip of his big trolley of scratchcards and duty-free chavgifts and booze and the whole thing careers onto the shoulder of some placidly dozing woman to whom he copiously and noisily apologises. You watch their faces, the cabin crew, and when they look worried, when they look startled, you worry too.

I don't fly well. I have to suspend my disbelief when I get on a plane. Here we are, 38,000 feet above Paris. The weather was fine when we left Freiburg, it was predicted to be OK at Gatwick; but there's always that mysterious clear-air mischief lurking in between, up here beyond the clouds in this desolate and silent realm – a 'bad, evil and dangerous place', as some sixty-year-old American crop-duster pilot told me when we were thrown together in cattle class on a scheduled flight to San Francisco not so long ago. He never flew above 10,000 feet. Up to that level, he knew where he was; beyond it he was lost and scared – it's too cold and too weird up beyond the clouds.

So I watch the cabin crew and listen for a change in the timbre of the engine noise, which might well mean we're fucked, or – this always has me frightened – after the distinct lack of emphasis with which the landing gear supposedly locks itself into place, when the tray tables have been obediently stowed and we're nearly at the end, that prolonged muffled whirring and growling and the lack of that satisfying click.

I don't fly well. Like everyone – nearly everyone – I don't want to die, and flying all over the place seems to be tempting providence, to be tweaking the tail of death. It seems to be, you know, pushing it a bit. At least on a plane I am so terrified by the prospect of airborne death flapping its big black wings above my head that I temporarily forget the stuff that plagues me the rest of the time: the black crab in the brain, the sterol noose around the heart, the scarlet blood in the stool, the sudden lurched slump and slurred diction occasioned by rapidly detonating blood vessels, the fire in the basement, the flight of piss-stained concrete stairs, the mugger's knife.

My kids – well, the two boys – sit strapped in next to me, oblivious and insouciant, one of them reading Lord of the Flies (and identifying, I fear, with Jack), the other one trying to fashion a paper aeroplane out of his boarding-pass stub. They fly very well indeed, never a complaint from them, packet of pretzels and a Coke and they're fine for however long – an hour, thirteen hours, you name it. CAT makes them grin and take the piss out of their father for the beads of sweat which line up sentinel-like on my brow, for the suddenly gripped armrest, dry mouth and hyperventilation. They've been doing it for so long now, since they were born, I guess. Long and short haul, across the world and back in time for The Simpsons. Lucky, lucky, boys. Their mother isn't with us – we're divorced; did I mention that? – she's on a different plane, heading for New York. Their stepmum and stepsister are somewhere in the middle of the plane, where it is technically slightly safer if we land on water, but also where the stale flatus tends to congregate, I'm told. This was an Easter break, Vienna and the Black Forest. A treat for them, we explained. A bit of culture, a modicum of fun here and there, the opportunity for the kids to absorb a broader perspective on foreigners than the one with which I was raised. And it works, I think. Although the boys are still prone to say something embarrassing about Hitler very loudly in German restaurants.

My long-term memory, which used to be pretty good, has become, of late, frayed and elliptical, its edges gnawed away by increasing age and a continual drip feed of alcohol. My short-term memory, which was never terribly good, is pretty much shot to fuck, for presumably similar reasons. The distant past, which I was once sure of, has become a sly and shifting place, a different country in which not only do they do things differently, but they also do things differently as to how you think you remember them doing things, if you get my drift. Now only the generalities remain, along with one or two flashes of total recall – like the toy plane, and the dog bite – so bold that they almost blind, so perfectly brought back that one begins to get a bit suspicious, to doubt their veracity. Sometimes, too, I remember stuff without recalling where it is I remember it from, some strange electrical impulse in the synapses, much like the one that made my old half-breed dog Skipper, when he was especially tired, circle the carpet wearily three or four times and then paw compulsively at the shagpile, as if it were a shallow, dusty depression in the Serengeti surrounded by lethal enemies a million or so years ago, rather than covering the floor of a 1950s-built semi-detached house in Middlesbrough with *The Likely Lads* about to come on the TV and an almost unending supply of Rich Tea biscuits.

It would be easy, given this conveniently acquired vagueness, to be nostalgic about my childhood and – *contra* Sartre – all that remains of it. Given, too, the fact that I was undeniably happy as a kid. But when I look back, nostalgia is not the first emotion which makes its damp and cloying presence felt – although nostalgia is always hovering somewhere in the background, like a flatulent ghost, and I suppose that from time to time it will need to be banished with a big stick. No, the primary emotion I feel, looking back at the years when I was a child, is one of immense guilt: that I do not do things as well as my parents did them; that my basic sense of morality is unhinged and at best equivocal, whereas theirs was, essentially, anchored, and furthermore anchored in decency. No matter how many places I fly to with an agreeably open mind, and with the kids dutifully in tow.

I suppose this seems a strange thing to say, given my parents' views on a whole bunch of stuff, not least the poor old wogs. I don't possess their views about wogs, or at least not all of them. In fairness to my mum and dad, their opinions were not quite as bilious as I may have implied; it was a more nuanced thing, more subtle. My mum, for example, quite liked Caribbean people, because she considered them to be 'cheerful' – and even Malcolm X and Papa Doc didn't serve to disabuse her of this notion. On the other hand, she couldn't abide 'Indians', by which she meant everyone who lived between Aleppo and the Burmese border just east of Cox's Bazar, at which point they promptly became jabbering, slit-eyed, robotic and cruel Chinks. Chinks, then, were quite bad, although not so bad as Japs. Japs were cunning and cruel automatons.

Then there was her mild animus against Jews, which I found utterly inexplicable even when I was very young – but which presumably had its fascistic roots in her East End of London upbringing. I remember well the Yom Kippur War – with my dad and me cheering on the Israelis, whom we admired for their appalling travails, their Western-ness and competence, and my mother howling support for the valiant Arabs, who were nonetheless still wogs, of course, but sort of honest and steadfast wogs, unlike the Jews. A bloody rare thing, honest wogs. That's how we viewed these new TV wars between competing angry wogs, back then: as a sort of Champions League semi-final, take your sides, may the best man win, let's hope it goes to penalties.

My dad, meanwhile, had a vague fondness for 'Indians', a contempt for Americans, a visceral loathing of the French except for General de Gaulle, for whom he expressed qualified admiration, and a sullen disdain for the rest of the world's people, ranging west from Monmouth to Copenhagen. I mean, really, west to east – Monmouth to Copenhagen, via Americas North and South, Asia and Africa. Everywhere, that is, except for New Zealand and Australia, and also – because of that nice Christmas tree they give us every year – Norway. It wasn't racial hatred at all, mind; just disdain and utter contempt.

And yet once, in the year before he died, my dad told me he'd always wanted to visit Valparaiso. As a kid he'd seen it on a map, and heard it spoken about, and it somehow conjured a beguiling exoticism of a place far away where exciting and strange things might happen. Like me, he had a thing about maps, wanting to know where everything was, how all these awful, contemptible places full of dubious people connected up. And so somehow, staring at a map years before, he had got it into his head that exciting things might happen in the Chilean seaport of Valparaiso. It had never occurred to me that he wanted exciting things to happen. He had always rather intimated that he preferred that they wouldn't.

But, all things considered, my parents held a somewhat narrow and rancid view of the world that seems determined to exist beyond our shores, one undoubtedly occasioned by the Second World War – a struggle in which we were opposed by bestial enemies and hindered by cowardly and devious allies, but nonetheless prevailed, as you might expect. And also, one supposes, occasioned by the vestigial tail of our old empire left dangling inside their brains. Whatever the causes, this is all I have on them, my parents – this lofty disdain for billions of people, a disdain shared close to universally among people of their social class and age. Not a raging racism by any means – until the 1980s, my mum and dad voted Labour, and would rather have voted Communist than NF – just a meme rooted somewhere deep inside, and which was usually not articulated at all, just sort of there, and ever-present.

But this is all I have on them; about everything else, they were right. And I, and my generation, seem by contrast feckless and irresponsible, endlessly selfish, whining, avaricious, self-deluding, self-obsessed, spoiled and corrupt and ill. We are the generation that has spent the small but hard-earned inheritance we got from our hard-working parents (mine went on that most irresponsible and selfish of all of our new and expensive freedoms, divorce lawyers), and are now busy spending the money we should be leaving to our kids. And while our own children are temporarily materially indulged, and deprived of that most crucial human right, boredom, they are otherwise neglected, too often considered an encumbrance. My generation is the one which will not wait for anything, because it feels it has the right to have everything now – and this is true not simply in material terms, although that's bad enough.

Again, this isn't nostalgia, a demand for a return to the values of 1964. A friend of mine up in Darlington died of polio in that year; another friend, back down in South London, had rickets. I don't see much benefit in bringing back polio and rickets, still less smallpox, which I remember being terribly scared of back then.* And the various processes which have inculcated in my generation its sense of entitlement and adherence to a sort of endless and witless moral relativism have not all been for the bad, either. It is hard to argue against longer life expectancy, greater affluence, safer workplaces, the freedom to escape from a hopeless marriage, the rights of women to be treated equally, and so on. But a certain moral code has been lost along the way, which has contributed lately to our country becoming close to bankrupt, a nation of broken families clamouring about their entitlements siring ill-educated and undisciplined kids unfamiliar with the concept of right and wrong, where there is an ever-diminishing sense of community and belonging, a perpetual transience, if you fancy a cheap oxymoron.

---

* Actually, having said that, rickets is back. According to the Royal College of Paediatrics and Child Health there was a fourfold increase in this disease of malnourishment (basically, a lack of vitamin D) in the fifteen years leading up to 2010. Also, the *Daily Mail* reported in March 2013 that some bloke in San Diego got a 'smallpox-like disease' as a consequence of doing something jiggy with someone who had been inoculated against smallpox. But that's probably just the *Daily Mail* being deranged.

This kind of complaint is often seen as one of those rather tired why-oh-why right-wing arguments, invariably followed by a finger pointed at those jabbering long-haired liberal bores of the 1960s, with their Marcusian and Gramscian idiocies, who rewrote our education system, demanded the new divorce laws, took over the criminal justice system and so on. And sure enough, there will be some of that in what follows – but it is not even half of the story. At least as many of the most repellent aspects of my generation, of where and how we have become so palpably wayward, so fucking full of ourselves, are the consequence, directly or otherwise, of that singularly grim and vindictive Conservative government of the 1980s. And when those two philosophies come together – they are not so distant as you might think, both concerning themselves, primarily, with self-empowerment – the result is especially toxic; a determination to do away with everything – society, authority – but ourselves.

And then again, there's plenty more that is, on the surface at least, politically neutral. This is why it is so hard to deal with our malaise; because it is the product, in part, of two schools of political thinking which are usually regarded as in opposition to one another – and also of stuff that fits into neither political camp very comfortably. It is a waywardness, then, which muddies all the established paradigms. And, furthermore, all of it contained within a paradox: peace, freedom, affluence, comfort and security are all, you would argue, agreeable entities. But they have caused us a lot of problems, and – as we shall see – they have not made us terribly happy. Peace has made us complacent, freedom has made us irresponsible, affluence has made us acquisitive, comfort has made us neglectful of others, and security has made us – oddly enough – tremblingly insecure. I suppose you could advance the argument that our selfishness has been imposed upon us, much as obesity has been imposed upon the hulking fat tattooed chavmonkey standing in the queue at Burger King for his two supersize cardio-cheeseburgers with bacon, double fries and vat of Coke. That would be a very *now* argument, very 2014; that none of it is our own fault, but it has happened ineluctably, and it could not be otherwise, and perhaps the government should give us some help as a consequence, maybe send us on a course, sort out some counsellors or give us some more money to deal with it. Well, fuck that. We are not totally powerless, not entirely at the mercy of external forces. Our existence precedes our essence, and not the other way around, yes? It is pointless and, I think, cowardly to try to exculpate ourselves on the grounds that we are passive recipients of cultural change which has been imposed upon us, without our connivance. The philosophies we cheerfully embraced came from somewhere; they did not manifest themselves, unbidden, out of the ether. But one way or another, there is something lacking in us; something which previous generations possessed.

Are we as rank as I make out, this generation – the ones born between about 1950 and 1970, the Cold War kids? It is a perverse and narcissistic conceit, that one's own generation is exceptional in some way, usually a bad way. A similar narcissism to that which afflicts the whacko millennialists with their mad pamphlets and their mad fervour, hungry for annihilation, the end-time Christians and the strange people hunkered down in caves awaiting deliverance. And the similarly transfixed end-time ecomonkeys, waving aloft their forlorn polar bears, no less convinced that a more congenially secular annihilation is just around the corner. Every generation thinks that it is in some way the worst, or the best, or the last, or the first, has been singled out in some way – conclusions drawn from imperfect memories of how things once were, and usually addled by a treacly gallon or two of personal guilt and private misgivings. Personal guilt will undoubtedly intrude here, too, because in many ways I am typical of my generation, in my own selfishness: did I mention the divorce, the lawyers, the money, that stuff? The broken family? And this is a book drawn rather more from anecdotal evidence than from science.

It is possible, then, that this selfishness I'm talking about is actually only my own, which through some convenient psychological process I have extended to an entire generation as a long-winded attempt at exculpation. But I don't think so. You've seen our balance of payments, heard about the vast ocean of personal debt, are aware that marriages don't last very long these days, that our schools are not as highly regarded as once they were, that there is much less sense of community in your neighbourhood, a dumbed-down culture blaring out of your idiotbox, a nagging dissatisfaction and acquisitiveness at large, and probably inside your own skull. It comes from us, from me, all that stuff; our generation. You might be inclined to blame the bankers, or the politicians, or the divorce courts, or the teachers, or any one of a number of convenient social groups habitually given a kicking by the red-top press. But it's not them, primarily. It's us.

The next year for Christmas I got a large tinplate garage which had a manually-operated lift to take the toy cars to the top floor, and a ramp down which they exited onto the carpet. That was shit too, now I come to think of it. We never learn.

2

The Tower of Arse

The awful shadow of some unseen Power
Floats though unseen among us

Shelley

If Jesus Christ were to come today, people would not even crucify
him. They would ask him to dinner, and hear what he has to say,
and make fun of it.

Thomas Carlyle

In January 2012 the bald but perfectly formed philosopher Alain de Botton proposed the building of a huge tower somewhere in London to commemorate atheism – or, as he put it, Atheism. This suggestion immediately caused a schism in the new church of atheism – perhaps as momentous as that which rent apart Christianity in the eleventh century, when West and East were divided over stuff like the understanding of the Trinity and how long beards should be. (That particular schism is still in existence, despite centuries of attempts at reconciliation.) For immediately Britain's most senior, gilded atheist cleric, Professor Richard Dawkins, stamped all over Botton's tower idea, saying words to the effect that it was fucking stupid and unnecessary, and in any case 'a contradiction in terms'. The whole spat had a wonderfully Pythonesque whiff to it, these fabulously self-regarding monkeys arguing about the appropriateness of a Tower of Babel which would undoubtedly be situated in someplace achingly secular and similarly self-regarding, like Hoxton or Islington, until God blew it down and smote anyone who had been inside, as you will find detailed in the Sibylline Oracles.

The Tower of Botton would, the philosopher revealed, stand precisely 151 feet tall, and its exterior would be inscribed with a binary code denoting the human DNA. Its height would be demarcated precisely into the various geological periods of the earth, with a 'narrow band of gold' representing the comparatively brief time that creatures almost as brilliant as Alain de Botton, i.e. humans, have been in existence. Gold, you will note; a metal which humans have worshipped on account of its supposed scarcity and irreducibility, although it is rather less scarce than was formerly believed. There are many, many much scarcer elements, including those which mankind has created by itself, in the manner of a flawed and somewhat reckless deity. I would suggest, if Alain is still intent upon building his fucking stupid tower, that he replace the gold band with one made of Einsteinium, a synthetic and extremely rare and short-lived element which was discovered in the cheerfully toxic debris left over from the first ever hydrogen bomb explosion, back in 1952. Something, then, that mankind, in its insuperable genius, made for itself, and of which it can be suitably proud. People visiting the tower would probably be advised to wear NCB gear and get scrubbed down afterwards, almost certainly by low-paid Eastern European babes – but then this would serve only to enhance the overall visitor experience; it would be a positive selling point. And it might also add a subtle counterpoint to the very premise of the tower: not everything we have done has necessarily been wonderful and uplifting. Quite often we're just left with questionable stuff like Einsteinium, which of course was named in honour of a man almost as clever as Alain.

Can you imagine anything more self-regarding than a tower built to worship oneself? Because that's what it is, really – a bit like the marble palace of some Soviet Bloc tyrant beholden to nobody but himself (well, maybe except for the whims of Moscow). An edifice which, even in de Botton's description, celebrates merely an absence of something, i.e. an absence of God – hence Richard Dawkins's correct analysis that it would be self-contradictory. This is what happens when we are freed from the requirement to be humble, to bow down, to accept that we are deeply flawed and are inclined – when liberated from the suspicion that someone powerful and vengeful and probably bad-tempered is watching everything we do – to behave rather badly, and with a consuming arrogance. We build things to praise ourselves, and then, having finally abolished God, we become a God to ourselves. We become gripped by intimations of our own brilliance.

Even before we have built the great Tower of Arse, we get ourselves into practice for the role of deity. We limber up, we do the requisite callisthenics. One such limbering-up exercise, for example, might be to rewrite the Ten Commandments, in our own image – but making sure all the while that we miss out the problematic stuff: the business about not coveting other people's things, and not committing adultery, and how above all we must worship something which is not us, but is beyond and above us, i.e. God. And then replace these commands with vague and transient prescriptions which are so anodyne as to be, in effect, meaningless. Richard Dawkins, though he had no time for the magnificent Tower of Arse, rewrote the Ten Commandments in his book *The God Delusion* as something we could all cling to once we'd killed God. I suppose he did this as a kindness to the rest of us, in the belief that, having despatched God to the waste-paper bin of history, he ought to offer up something to put in His place. For which, thank you, professor. Here are Richard's commandments numbers four and five:

> *Live life with a sense of joy and wonder!*
> *Always seek to be learning something new!*

Isn't that lovely? Isn't that absolutely lovely! That's more fun than 'Thou shall not kill,' isn't it? It is a slight surprise that Richard did not include, perhaps at number eight or nine on his fatuous list of spineless injunctions: 'Always make sure you recycle your rubbish properly, putting the organic material in the green bag and the plastic stuff in the white bag.' And then maybe at number ten: 'Brush your teeth three times a day, and try to floss regularly, although not on public transport.' I once mentioned to Richard – who, incidentally, I like personally, and respect as both a scientist and a propagandist for scientific enquiry – that his commandments seemed to be lacking something. You know: a little rigour, a certain sinew, a sense of permanence. He responded by saying that he thought that you, Rod, of all people, should appreciate that morality is ever-changing, that we do not cleave to the moral code which pertained a thousand or even one hundred years ago. I don't know what he meant by 'you, Rod, of all people'; I think it's better if we let that lie. But his response was a partial evasion. Richard's moral code, unlike the one given to us by Moses, will be defunct next week, it will have a half-life as brief as that of Einsteinium. It is not really a set of 'commandments' at all, but instead a flyer shoved through your letterbox from the local council's Healthy Living subcommittee, or maybe from your nearest NHS provider; it asks nothing of us. Nobody could cavil at any one of its bland imprecations. It is close to meaningless.

Richard Dawkins is not the only person to have rewritten the Ten Commandments, of course – it's been done, by vaulting secularists with the look of destiny in their eyes, plenty of times. The late Christopher Hitchens had a bash too, and his proscriptions were very similar to those of his ally, Dawkins; but at least Hitch included, at number eight: 'Turn off that fucking cellphone.' Yowser, Hitch; how did Moses miss that one?

Belligerent atheism has advanced, these last twenty years or so, partly as a consequence of sexually repressed and educationally subnormal jihadist maniacs blowing themselves up all over the place, which has made us question the attractiveness of religious certitude, and partly through the Wesleyan charisma and intelligence of its most voluble protagonist, Dawkins. We are, in effect, now a secular country, the obeisances paid to even the mild-mannered, clean-shaven and comparatively licentious God of the Church of England diminishing seemingly each week, by statute and by common practice. As J.S. Mill once urged us to do, we have wriggled free of Calvinism and its tiresome constraints; and so we have become dangerously free too of humility and the fear of existential censure. In place of God we cheerfully install ourselves – and immediately begin to draw up plans for building a giant Tower of Arse, a monument to our magnificence, with our own wondrous lives picked out in gold right at the top.

It is no coincidence that this rapid erosion of deference to an omnipotent, unseen other has occurred in tandem with the growth of institutionalised self-obsession, self-pity and public emoting. If there is no unseen other to bow down before, we bow down instead before ourselves; we are all that matters. And it is a short step from this delusion to the following thesis: 'Actually, now I think about it, never mind this WE business – I am all that matters, and my petty vicissitudes, my miseries, will no longer be internalised but shared, at interminable length, with a grateful world.' My parents' generation were infected with none of this stuff, and would have found the current trend for intense introspection – of very boring and stupid people, often celebrities, perpetually 'battling their demons', to use the ubiquitous and carelessly obnoxious phrase – both deeply embarrassing and emetic. Keep it to yourself, your heroin addiction or your anorexia or your alcoholism or your mid-life crisis, you mug; you will answer, one day not too far away, for better or for worse – in the meantime, struggle on with fortitude and reserve.

Not any more. The mantra of our times is this: 'But tell me, how do you FEEL?', and its corollary – that the only thing that matters is how we feel about stuff – has taken on a bizarre, supernatural quality of late. A few years back I turned up at hospital to witness the birth of my daughter Emmeline, and was presented by the nurse with a chart enquiring of me my nationality and race. This was one of those PC bureaucratic procedures, the results of which would be of use to absolutely nobody except deathless bureaucrats, and which would undoubtedly cost a lot of money to process. But anyway, somewhere in the region of eighty races or nationalities were listed across two or three pages. All I had to do was pick one. Then I read a little more closely, and at the top of the page it said that I didn't actually have to put down what race or nationality I really was – that, it seemed, didn't matter. All I had to do was tell them what race or nationality I FELT I was, regardless (it made clear) of my parentage or where I was born. The actuality of who I was had no relevance whatsoever. The facts were of no consequence at all. So I told them I felt Somali. It seemed, in the circumstances, sort of appropriate, even if I was tempted to put 'static traveller' (which is the official description for people who were once travellers but now feel disinclined to move anywhere, so instead remain perfectly still, I'd guess). Still, sometimes I do feel Somali, you know? Fractious and dislocated and, through no fault of my own, unemployable. This enquiry – But what do you FEEL – has invaded every possible discourse. It has become almost the only discourse. It is the main criticism levelled at the people who devise the examinations sat by our children: that no longer are the kids required to actually know stuff, far more important is the emotive or interpretative reaction to stuff.

As if any of it really mattered – how we feel, inside – except to us. What is, is. Is it not?

Equally, the previous old-fashioned deference to an unseen other imposed upon us a responsibility to our fellow human beings: those commandments, the knowledge or suspicion or fear that we were being watched as we went about our nefarious business. We were, after all, equal in the eyes of God, and enjoined to do unto others as we would have them do unto us. It seems likely to me that our gradual rejection, over the last thirty years or so, of a collectivist approach to solving our problems and running our affairs has been at least partly occasioned by the rise of atheism and the slow occlusion of that unseen other. If we are freed from the depredations of a supernatural being, we are, by extension, sort of freed from a responsibility towards one another, too; we become atomised and aloof, we work towards our own ends, beholden to nobody. We succumb to the genetic selfishness which, as Richard Dawkins, in his previous and more palatable incarnation, beautifully depicted; driven onwards, ever onwards to replicate in competition with others, without even being conscious of that competition, altruism existing only as an adaptive trait, the basis of our behaviour largely pre-ordained by a markedly more brutal and callous God, our own genes.

It is undoubtedly true that as orthodox religious belief has retreated, so we have become more nakedly individualistic, more inclined to be immune to the needs and requirements of our fellow men. I suspect there's a correlation. Dawkins, a decent metroliberal *bien pensant* himself, of course, was always at pains to insist that somehow it needn't be this way; that succumbing to the sociopathic and relentless and blind drive of our genes was not inevitable, but could be resisted and overcome. To which I would reply, yes, Richard, and yes again; and either our invention of God, or the actual existence of God – hell, take your pick, science boy – was our most potent means of successfully (more or less) resisting that drive. In place of that, what means of constraining our behaviour do we have? Dawkins's ten commandments? Or Christopher

Hitchens's injunction to turn off that fucking mobile phone? I'm sorry Richard, but it won't wash. Where is the power and the resonance, the force?

My point here isn't to insist from an *a priori* position that God exists; hell, I don't want you to think that I'm a weirdo like my lovely mother-in-law, who keeps averring, with a strange look in her eyes, that we're all drenched in the blood of Christ. In the sense I'm talking about, it doesn't matter if God exists or not. What matters is that our deference to something beyond ourselves, something real or strongly imagined – the feeling within us that we should not be quite so fucking pleased with ourselves, so confident of our decisions and our ideologies – has diminished hugely over the last half-century, and particularly rapidly over the last dozen or so years. Of course, Richard Dawkins, and any decent scientist, would be forced to admit that he could not say for sure whether or not God exists, and so would be left to mumble an embarrassed 'Uh, s'pose it COULD be, but I don't think so, we have no scientific evidence.' But, this being the case, why continue with the frenetic flailing, the adverts on the sides of buses, the polemics? What exactly is it that you are flailing at? 'The irrational, the superstitious,' Dawkins would reply, and point you towards creationist mentalists teaching kids that dinosaurs walked the earth with man on a planet formed 4,500 years ago. Yes, OK, fair enough – I'm with him on the creationists, and I'll sign up cheerfully enough to Charles Darwin for the time being, until science decides that actually he got some of it wrong, which is what of course will happen: all manmade certainties end up being knocked down, as Ptolemy will tell you. But the mentalists promulgating creationism are no more representative of those who believe in God than are Pons and Fleischmann, the proponents of that berserk but alluring notion 'cold fusion', representative of science. If religion is nothing more than a 'meme', an idea which replicates itself 'like a virus', synchronically and diachronically, as Dawkins has suggested, then it still might be a meme worth clinging to, for all that.

Nor do I want to trawl through that futile little argument that hinges upon the damage done to the world through religious ideology versus the damage done to the world as a consequence of atheistic ideologies. The jihadists, with the bombs strapped to their guts, the pogroms, the annihilations, the death camps, the ethnic cleansings, the gulags, the Lubyanka, the inquisitions, the foam-flecked imam urging the destruction of the Jews and the little foam-flecked Austrian Nazi urging the same thing – all that stuff. Was National Socialism an atheistic ideology? Was Stalinism? Stalin seemed to think it was. Marxism? It seems to me, from an admittedly unscientific weighting exercise, that in this argument the scores stand at about one all, with extra time now being played. Maybe I'm wrong.

The more important point is that religion has retreated, and with it deference. I don't mean deference simply towards God, regardless of whether He exists or not. But deference to *something*. Because once you chip away at deference to God, then all deference becomes much easier to do away with. You end up deferring to nothing.

Like the majority of kids growing up in the middle 1960s, I went to Sunday school every week. I did not much enjoy this. On one occasion, when I was about nine years old, I was sent to Sunday school on a morning that my parents were themselves 'too busy' to attend church. This struck me as grotesquely unjust and hypocritical. I was so angry, so fuelled up with resentment, as I made my way to church that morning, that I kicked Gary Lewis's head in halfway there. He had come out of his house to laugh at me dressed up in my Sunday school attire – a ridiculous fucking tweedy jacket with matching tweedy *shorts* set off by a white nylon poloneck jumper. The gobby little child stood on the other side of the road hooting with mirth and shouting insults. I can't remember what, exactly. Something like 'Fucking poof,' I suspect. So I ran across the road and punched him hard in the mouth, something which, as a habitual coward, I would never normally do. Gary was a big, gangling, cheerful kid, if a bit thick – I suppose the sort of person who might now be a presenter on BBC Three. His dad came out to see what the fuss was about, and to his eternal credit shepherded the two of us into their backyard to slug it out properly, while he watched and occasionally commented with admirable neutrality. Reader, I won that fight. It was the anger that did it – not the anger at Gary, but at my mother and father. Gary was just the unfortunate recipient.

Until about 1972 my family went to church every Sunday, almost without fail. I suppose mine was a slightly more religiously inclined household than most at the time, although there probably wasn't much in it. While church attendance in Britain began to dwindle after the Second World War – fairly rapidly in the case of the nonconformist faiths, of which my family were part, less so in the case of Roman Catholics – even by the mid-1960s more than 50 per cent of parents still sent their kids to Sunday school. Whether or not the parents themselves could be arsed to turn up to church and sing absurd and didactic Victorian hymns when they could be digging the garden, they still felt that it was somehow 'right' that their kids should be properly indoctrinated – not so much into a faith, but into a system of mores which were, more or less, shared by the country as a whole. Along with Sunday school came injunctions against criminality – an absolutist, simplistic, Manichean divide between right and wrong – and various other strictures which would today, I suppose, be seen as somewhat right-of-centre and *de trop*: work hard, save money, don't shag around, marry for love and for life, don't get pissed, don't gamble, do as you're fucking told – despite the fact that the church I attended, the Methodists, had long been regarded as left-leaning. Attending Sunday school was also a conscious sacrifice, something one did because it was apparently the right thing to do, and there's an end to it, even if I hated it, most of the time. I'm not so daft as to suggest that if kids still went to Sunday school there'd be no criminality, no private debt, and everyone would love one another. Even by my standards, that would be overstating the case a little. But the decline of religious belief is in the mix, somewhere, as both a cause and a symptom.

Of course, the decline of a sort of semi-conscious adherence to organised religion has not been without its benefits. My point is not that the increasing irrelevance of God has been an unequivocally bad thing. One of the problems we have today is a sort of shrill infantile absolutism, which you will encounter on several occasions within this book. It is largely the construct of the libtard authoritarian left, but, frighteningly, those from beyond that smug and uniquely metropolitan middle-class tradition also succumb to it, often as a consequence of the public opprobrium whipped up by these intolerant and narcissistic monkeys, howling their outrage on the messageboards and the blogs.

Take the example of the decline of religious observance, which we will call 'x'. I am suggesting that certain other stuff, which we might call a, b and c, has occurred as an unintended consequence, or partial consequence, of x, and that we might wish that this had not happened – an overweening narcissism, for example; and the loss of the notion of deferred gratification; the growth of moral relativism; an increase in what, pace Durkheim, we might call anomie; and a society in which the collectivist approach is increasingly rejected in favour of the individualistic, and a concomitant absence of something we might call 'spirituality'. Even here, not all of these unintended consequences have been wholly bad – it is merely that something has been lost along the way, and that it would be better if we still had it, whatever it is. The problem with the liberal faux left is that in this instance – as in many others – it tends to deny that a, b and c have happened at all, despite overwhelming evidence to the contrary. Because, for them, the decline of organised religion is a good thing *per se*, nothing bad can ever come of it, and any suggestion that bad stuff has happened must be denied outright. We will meet more of this witless and totalitarian argument later, especially when dealing with women's rights.

To be clear, there are important caveats. Adherence to organised religion inculcated in the lower orders a mute quiescence and a refusal to ask difficult questions of their economic and political masters. Its strictures on marriage and sexual freedoms made the lives of many people more miserable than anyone, other than a thug, might have wished. There was an anti-intellectual narrowness about its multifarious certainties. And there was other stuff. It meant we couldn't go shopping on a Sunday, or indeed do much else on a Sunday for that matter. (Hell, I wasn't even allowed to play in the garden on a Sunday, which struck me as absurd and vindictive.) And we gathered in cold and musty Victorian buildings, often with corrugated-iron roofs, the smell of mildew and distantly brewed tea and polish from the altar and the pervasive leak of gas from the boiler, to sing stuff at Christmas like my mother's favourite carol:

> Oh little town of Bethlehem, how still we see thee lie,
> Above thy deep and dreamless sleep the silent stars go by.

In 2010 a Church of England vicar decided to ban that particular hymn, incidentally. Why? Because he'd been taken on some sort of exchange visit to the West Bank and the Israeli-occupied territories, and had decided that the words were all wrong. Bethlehem isn't lying still, is it? It bloody well isn't still at all! It's under the jackboot of Israeli oppression! Ban the hymn!

So, to be sure, there are benefits from the decline of religious belief, such as not having to concern ourselves with self-aggrandising narcissistic idiots like the vicar who banned 'Oh Little Town of Bethlehem' (and the one who tried to ban 'I Vow to Thee My Country', for that matter). It's just that there have also been unintended consequences which have been bad for all of us. Some specific, such as the abnegation of deferred gratification and its concomitant, self-sacrifice. And others that are more difficult to define, more ectoplasmic, if you like. But of all of them, the end of deferred gratification is the most important.

3

The Waiting

It's no go, my honey love, it's no go my poppet;
Work your hands from day to day, the winds will blow the profit.
The glass is falling hour by hour, the glass will fall forever.
But if you break the bloody glass, you won't hold up the weather.

Louis MacNeice

Sometimes, although rarely, the speeches Prime Ministers make are interesting and revelatory. More revelatory and fun altogether are the speeches they planned to make but, for one reason or another, didn't. Take the speech that David Cameron planned to deliver on 5 October 2011, his little shiny red face set in a very grim, self-flagellating these-are-hard-times-but-we're-all-in-it-together austerity mode, with the economy mired in recession and a vast public debt that was not reducing at quite the speed he, or anyone else, might have liked. Some well-meaning aide had presumably mentioned to him something like, 'Hey, Dave, never mind the public debt – have you seen the household debt for the UK? Staggering, mate. Gobsmacking. You ought to have a word with the public. Shocking state of affairs, get something done about it.' At the time, Britain's total household debt was a fruity £1.6 trillion, representing 160 per cent of household income, nobody saving anything, the whole thing predicted to rise and continue rising, the entire population living on the never-never like the fat, idle, feckless and spendthrift layabouts they are. Suitably appalled, Cameron planned to say the following stuff, which was duly leaked to the press by his office:

> The only way out of a debt crisis is to pay your debts. Households – all of us – paying off the credit card and the store card bills.

This brief injunction did not immediately reach the ears of the public, however – presumably because someone showed it to the Chancellor, George Osborne. I would imagine that, upon reading it, Osborne will have remarked something along the following lines: 'Christ on a fucking bike! What is this mad bastard thinking of? Get him on the fucking phone right now before he destroys the entire Western economy.' The speech was subsequently rewritten to remove any reference to people being enjoined to pay off their store cards and credit cards. Indeed, if the British public had listened, suitably rapt, to the Prime Minister making the speech he had originally intended, and had thought to themselves, 'Yes, Mr Cameron, you're quite right – I shall pay off the Barclaycard this very moment,' then the country would have been bankrupted by tea-time.

The entire economy is built upon debt. Further, in order to climb out of recession, the government requires us to spend more on stuff – probably useless stuff, but stuff all the same – which means that far from urging us to pay off our bills, the Chancellor would have wished the Prime Minister instead to herd us all down to Argos to buy loads more white ephemeral electronic cockshit, just to get the economy moving. And thus increase our collective household debt, exactly as the oxymoronic Office for Budgetary Responsibility has predicted it will. Hell, read your Keynes, Cameron: you spend out of recession. Or at least, forgetting Keynes, you enjoin the public to spend out of recession, and then charge the gullible bastards a crippling rate of interest to pay it all back, which of course they cannot possibly do. Such as Barclaycard, charging, for example, an advertised initial APR of nearly 30 per cent. And when the mugs have defaulted on that – and, what's that glib little modernist phrase, 'maxed out' their various extortionate store cards – they can 'consolidate' their debts with all manner of Doug and Dinsdale Piranha Loan Shark companies, and lose their houses, or their cars, or their legs. As John Lydon once put it: ever get the feeling you've been cheated?

Credit for the working classes has never come cheap, and their despairing efforts to pay off their debts keep the country afloat. Debt sits on the shoulders of the poorest, and makes their lives a misery. And Britain's gross household debt is now the fourth biggest in the world. In little more than a year after I got the idea in my head to write this book, incidentally, back in early 2011, the amount of unsecured loans and debts owed by the average family in Great Britain increased by a scarcely believable 48 per cent. It now stands at an average of £7,944 per family, or 32 per cent of net annual average income. Tacitly, the government does not wish this state of affairs to end, even if in his more enlightened moments the Prime Minister betrays touching misgivings about the rather beastly workings of modern unrestrained capitalism; it wishes, indeed fervently hopes, that the never-never balloon will keep on rising, that the poorest will keep taking out loans to buy shit things and then bugger themselves senseless trying to pay for them.

The availability of credit – first hire purchase, then credit cards such as 'Access: Your Flexible Friend' (I once had a girlfriend who rejoiced in that nickname) – was heralded as a step forward for the working classes, a sort of democratic capitalistic spirit which would enable them to buy all the useless shit they ever wanted but had previously been unable to afford. The shit they'd gazed at wide-eyed in the shop window. And so, to a limited extent, in the early days it was; as wage rates for the working class rose quite sharply in the late 1950s and early 1960s, a small wedge could be carved off each week for the HP or the savings club in order to acquire a small bunch of hitherto unexpected luxury – a TV or a holiday, say. But, no such thing as a free lunch, etc. etc.; credit, as it exists in its ubiquity today, is a con trick perpetrated upon the poorest and the most vulnerable in society. It doles out an illusory wealth which has, over the decades, disguised the extent to which the incomes of the richest and the incomes of the poorest have become ever more polarised, the trickledown that never really happened and was never really expected to happen, if we're being honest. The poor get their shit stuff, for a while, until it is repossessed along with their oldest daughter, and maybe they forget that they're earning only one two-hundredth of the salary – excluding bonuses – of their chief executive, whereas forty years ago they'd be on about one twentieth as much as the boss.

What follows is certainly not an attempt to condemn the mass of ordinary working Britons for the crisis in personal debt: it is, palpably, not their fault. So relentlessly have they been told to borrow, assured that borrowing's perfectly fine and dandy – the banks do it, the country does it, so why not you? – and so ubiquitous is the availability of credit (as ubiquitous as its crippling rates of interest) that the blame cannot reasonably be laid at their doors.

Indeed, I would go so far as to suggest that credit is an officially sanctioned instrument for ensuring quiescence among the plebs, the worker bees, the lumpen-proles, for making them get on with their arduous work and shut the fuck up because Argos or Currys is only around the corner and you've got that nice loan sorted out from that Russian company, haven't you? Credit has taken over from religion as the opium of the people. Which I suppose is the point. The aim of this chapter is to attempt to explain how and why this happened culturally, rather than economically. We know how it happened economically, and a bit of stringent regulation of the loan sharks and the credit agencies wouldn't come amiss right now, along with an agreeable mass civil-disobedience exercise consisting of a refusal to pay back extortionate interest on loans. Oh, and a much higher minimum wage. And a more equitable distribution of income within private companies, and more, much more which we will come to later in this book. But first, how did we get set up like this? What was the process by which we became ready and willing to spunk our meagre incomes paying back a bunch of avaricious wankers like Wonga.com, or that grasping shitehawk company that used to be advertised by the arsetastic TV *Countdown* kitten, Carol Vorderman? What softened us up to be so easily gulled? And why is it my generation that has succumbed so easily, when my parents and their peers looked on the whole business a little balefully?

By the time I got born in 1960, my parents had risen a little; they were perhaps upper-working class, even teetering on lower-middle. My father was no longer working for the railways, like his brother was still doing and like his father had done before him (they were from Darlington, you understand, a railway town like no other), but now had a job as a clerk working for the Inland Revenue. My mother worked part-time as a secretary in an accountancy firm in Bexleyheath, which was a hell of a step up for her. My dad came from a very respectable, solidly working-class family – chapel, Labour Party, no drinking – in the north-east of England; my mum was from perhaps less obviously reputable stock – orphaned, broken home, evacuated, from Sarf London. But now they were all right, pretty much – now they were doing OK. They had saved for years for the unending pleasures of having me (of which more later), and had moved out of council accommodation and bought their own home, a frowsy 1920s semi-detached house in Bexleyheath. Like 40 per cent of the population in the late 1950s, they had no TV. No telephone either, and no refrigerator, no vacuum cleaner, no car. They did however have a strange, mottled green-and-black washing tub, bought third-hand, which made a noise like Zeus had just seen his VAT bill for the quarter.

But still, they had an inside toilet in a home they owned – both things which my dad's parents, when they were his age, would have regarded as the apogee of bourgeois luxury. My paternal grand-mother, in the early days, had only an outside privy – which I liked, as I hate shitting within earshot of other people, and will some-times go days without attending the toilet if it's near other people, out of the sort of nervousness and self-consciousness which I dare-say Freud would have found revealing.

All that stuff I mentioned above would come in time, my parents knew, when they could afford it – and so it did: vacuum cleaner in 1961, telephone in 1964, TV in 1965, car in 1966, refrigerator in 1968. Despite the encumbrance of having a vile and demanding child, their standard of living improved with graduated ease; these were the days when incomes really did rise, when to whisper the concept of social mobility was not a trigger for immediate hilarity, or bitter anger. Holidays, once a year, to a cheap Methodist guest-house someplace – Hastings, Bournemouth, Llandudno – and then maybe a yearly trip to see my dark-clad northern relatives, and what I still feel is my real home, in Middlesbrough and Darlington and Bishop Auckland. So this was, by the standard of the times, a certain wage-slave comfort, hard fought for, collectively and indi-vidually, grindingly acquired – and for them a merciful release from the post-war years of austerity. We were still, by the measures of the time, poorish, I suppose, but certainly never crushingly so. There was always enough to eat, even if it was stultifyingly dull food; Christ, I can see my grandmother now, dipping bread and butter into the juice of a tinned fruit salad at tea – a weekly treat – at five on a Sunday, before low church Evensong. But I digress.

I would guess that the maroon Ford Anglia, with its pitiful pseudo-Yank grimacing radiator grille and sharply angled back window and light-grey roof, was almost certainly bought on tick, or something like tick; a loan. Its registration number, 123 MKL, and model, dates it between 1959 and 1962, so it was at least four years old when my mother and father bought it in 1966. (I wanted them to buy a racier Triumph Herald, incidentally, but they wouldn't listen. Triumphs, my dad averred, break down too often.) Even so, it would have cost a packet, and money was always tight, so I would guess that some sort of HP deal was involved, although I may be wrong about this. Certainly my parents, and particularly my dad, were very sniffy about HP, about borrowing money in general. It was something done by the impecunious, the rash, the cavalier, the shady. OK, the house was bought on tick, but on a respectable sort of tick, they thought – a thirty-year mortgage with a reputable company (which nonetheless fleeced them). As far as borrowing was concerned, it was sort of OK to pay into a holiday club (we didn't) or a Christmas club (we did), but that was saving for something with your own funds, and not being liable to pay someone back at a rate of interest. Borrowing money was a bit dirty, a bit desperate, and made no economic sense, because you ended forking out so much more. You wanted something, you saved up for it. There was nothing, really, that couldn't wait a while, often a long while, once you had your food and shelter. And this rather stringent view was shared by a majority of the population at the time; HP was used, in the main, very sparingly, and its demands rested much more lightly on the shoulders of the not-so-well-off. Household debt back in those days rose only slightly during the 1960s and 1970s, rarely creeping above 40 per cent of average income; it was in 1979 that it really took off, like an atomic dildo – which is, uncoincidentally, the year in which my generation got its paws on the credit cards. We are the generation that intended to wait for nothing, and could not see the point in so doing.

Something restrained my parents' generation, more than simply the fact that credit was less easily come by, and there were no credit cards as such.* Something more intrinsic stopped them, or limited the extent to which they were prepared to get them-

---

* Well, there was the Diners Club card, introduced in 1962, followed by American Express a year later. Barclaycard started in 1966, Access in 1972. Take-up was slow in those early years.

selves into debt. Look at the slow and painful rate with which those household 'necessities', as they would be deemed today, were acquired by my family, and other families like them. They were married, my mum and dad, in 1954; it took them fourteen years to buy a fridge. They were available, these things, and had been mass marketed since the 1920s (and vacuum cleaners for still longer). Partly it is the case that they were not seen as indispensable, because earlier generations had cheerfully done without them: my grandmother still didn't have a fridge at the time she died, in 1972.

Clearly my parents' generation was defined not merely by the war, and post-war austerity, but by the privations endured long before then. Most of the goods I detailed above would have been unimaginably expensive in the 1930s, and continued to be so into the 1950s. They came down in price in relative terms, but there was still no compulsion to buy them immediately, nor was there the easy means to do so. And debt meant, in the backs of most people's minds, and maybe sometimes at the front, ignominy, bankruptcy and – if your memory was long enough – the workhouse. I mean, my mother wanted a fridge, of course she did (although its only use, at the beginning, was to keep milk chilled in hot weather, and in summer to keep crisp the ingredients of those hideous 1960s 'salads': tomato cut in half, cos lettuce, spring onion, beetroot out of a jar, slice of ham, acrid salad cream), and would occasionally nag my father about the social embarrassment caused by our lack of one. But in truth there was no real social embarrassment. And more crucially, there was no sense in which she felt she had a right to such consumer durables, as if they were something which should automatically accrue, or be immediately available on demand. It was a case, we all understood, of waiting. Saving and waiting. Waiting fourteen years, in the case of the bloody fridge.

This waiting is the thing my generation no longer does, is no longer cool with. It does not wait for anything. It does not see why it should. Life's too short, isn't it? Paradoxically, life was rather shorter back when people did wait – but still they waited.

There's no question that some of the reasons for this refusal of my generation to defer their gratification are bound up in a greater availability of credit, a greater social acceptance of debt, not to mention continual injunctions from TV fuckpigs to take out loans and buy stuff now, this minute, you slavering mugs. We are all of us rather more affluent in absolute terms, even if the gap between rich and poor has widened obscenely; we can, on the whole, afford more stuff. And it is true too that those devices I mentioned – fridge, vacuum, car, telephone – arrived, in a sense, ahead of the burning need for them. We had no ready meals stuffed full of chemical shit which needed to be chilled, standards of hygiene within the home were nowhere near as maniacal as they are today, and there were fewer carpets (these were the days of linoleum) – so a broom would suffice. People did not travel very far in the ordinary scheme of things – the first motorway in Britain opened as late as 1959, and the roads were slow – and in any case there was, until 1964 and that blank-faced vandal Beeching, a comprehensive if somewhat unreliable and laborious rail service. And, of course, what was the use of a telephone until everyone you knew had one? So, desirable these things may have been, but not vital. Of those modern consumer durables I mentioned, the only one for which there was an immediate demand was the television, which is why, by the beginning of the 1960s, more than three quarters of British households owned one. Lucky, lucky, British people.

But there are two or three other reasons, less frequently considered, for this marked difference in the approach between the generations, the willingness to wait and the need to have it all now. The retreat of religion, which I bored you with earlier, is partly implicated, for example. The importance of Max Weber's notion of a Protestant work ethic has maybe been overstated as a reason why Protestant northern Europe soared ahead of its bone-idle Roman

Catholic southern half in the nineteenth century, and had itself a lovely industrial revolution of its own. I have never been hugely convinced that the British working classes, any more than those in Prussia or Denmark, were convinced, in themselves, that religious salvation lay through the path of bloody hard relentless work all of your life, until you died. They may have been told that, but I doubt they believed it. Even the fucking Danes could not be that stupid.

But the other, less familiar, side of Weber's analysis may have some truth to it. Deferred gratification, for example, was a consequence of the non-conformist tradition of self-flagellating denial; the notion that there was something inherently good in not having nice stuff, or not doing nice stuff, that immersing oneself in pleasure, and in the acquisition of things, was a somehow decadent and indecent thing to do. Sacrifice now, reward in heaven. We have no deferred gratification any more; it is as arcane and extinct as the dire wolf and the 78rpm acetate disc and the Empire; it has no force, or resonance, within our land. Children are no longer told that they must 'do without' – unless it is because the piece of tat they are hankering after is beyond their parents' immediate budget; in other words, there is no ideological or moral reason why you shouldn't have everything now, if you can afford it: go ahead, fill your fucking boots, where's the crime, etc. Such indulgence, to my mother and father, seemed obscene. There had to be a modesty of aspiration, a limit to the ambitions of acquisitiveness; it was wrong, horribly wrong, to ask for stuff – if you were diligent, stuff would come to you only after the waiting, after the waiting, after the waiting – after the world had turned a little further on its dumb axis, after the days had traipsed through, with their heads bowed, single file, and when everything was good and ready.

But that's not all, because the other imprecation of non-conformist Christian socialism, and of that work ethic and its injunction to save, was the responsibility each of us had to society, to our fellow men. Saving, for example, was not simply something one did for one's own sake, or for the promise of salvation, but because there was something inherently good for society in it. So too the notion of hard work. Work hard and save, and society will benefit. Somehow. Don't ask me how. Merely that it was deeply ingrained, the self-denial: to splash out on something was to feel guilty. All of those imprecations from the Methodist Church against spending and drinking and gambling were made partly for the benefit of the individual, and partly for the benefit of society. You knew you had a responsibility to society.

I bought my first flat when I was twenty-seven years old, a one-bed in a mock-Georgian block on Peckham Rye, South London. So far as I remember, I'd saved fuck-all – maybe a grand or so in total. Saving seemed a somewhat tiresome thing to do, especially when, that year, I had to pay for the holiday in Bali. My dad gave me a thousand quid, and so I had a 95 per cent mortgage, secured with a £2,200 deposit. My father thought this was an absurd arrangement – to him it was almost beyond belief that anyone would be stupid enough to advance a person of my moral disreputability such an amount of money on such slender evidence. In any case, I was too young to own a property. How old should I be, then? 'Old enough that you've got your finances sorted by yourself,' my father replied with a hint of acid. The money he gave me, though, was just sitting in some account, doing nothing except growing; he spent nothing, on anything. They didn't, that generation. More fool them.

But his misgivings were deeper than that, I knew. Because also, unvoiced, was the suspicion that the owning a flat thing was being entered into for other reasons: I'd met a girl, a lovely girl called Sue, and this was to be our flat. My father had his doubts – not about Sue, whom he liked very much, but about my commitment to this thing, setting up home. It seemed to have been undertaken terribly lightly. He had watched, with some disgust, the joyless procession of the conniving victims of my serial monogamy, in and out of his house for weekend visits; hell, he'd had to wash the sheets. And he needed to alter his Christmas-card list every year, crossing out 'Lucy' and replacing it with 'Sharon', and then with 'Jane', and so on, finding it hard to keep track and not enjoying trying to do so. 'Aren't you with Lucy any more?' he would ask, not having heard her mentioned for some while. 'Sort of yes and no,' I would stammeringly reply, attempting to encapsulate in that phrase the month or two of furious deceit and infidelity which had just taken place. 'It's just that things are a bit complicated at the moment,' I added on one occasion, when his enquiries pressed in more tightly down the phone. 'They're only complicated if you make them so,' he replied.

But no, it seemed to us the right time to buy a place, me and Sue. To buy a place, to get on the ladder. You had to get on the ladder, back in the 1980s – everyone had to get on the fucking ladder, and then cling on for dear life. All of our friends were getting on the ladder – the ones in the south, who had jobs. It was our right to get on the ladder too, then. And not just have the place of our own, but have it furnished immediately: washing machine, fridge, bed, matt-black table, geometric rug. All of that, NOW, please. Fourteen years? We could just about wait fourteen days, and a little grumpily at that. My mum used to tell me that when they first bought that house in Bexleyheath they sat in deckchairs in the living room because they couldn't afford a three-piece suite. I'm not sure if I believed her or not. They bought the three-piece suite just before I was born, and it went in the 'front room' and nobody was allowed to sit on it, except at Christmas for a bit, when the southern rellies came round, and the neighbours, and the vicar. You were allowed to sit on it then. By the day after Boxing Day the room was closed off again. They had that suite – a virulent red wool, ribbed and boxy and probably very chic now – for sixteen years.

My dad would ring from time to time to see how we were getting on in our new flat, now we were on the ladder. He would be preternaturally concerned about stuff like boilers and maintenance charges and double glazing. My replies were always pretty blithe, uninterested, delivered sometimes with the suspicion of impatience. He asked me on one occasion, a couple of weeks after we'd moved in, if we had a sofa yet. I told him we didn't have a sofa – instead we'd bought ourselves a futon.

'What's a futon?' he asked.

'Well, Dad, it's a sort of wooden platform, on top of which you lay a very densely stuffed thin mattress. It's from Japan. Ours is black and white.'

There was a complete silence at the other end of the line. It went on for ages, to the extent that I thought we had been cut off. 'Dad? Dad? ...'

'Rod,' he broke in, sounding incredibly sad, 'why don't you live in the fucking real world?'

4

Move

A house for ninety-seven down,
And once a week for half a crown,
For twenty years.

I watched the homosexual historian David Starkey on the BBC's
Question Time programme a while ago, talking, with great certitude
and conviction, out of his arsehole. He was in the middle of some
long peroration about the bone-idle working class of today, how
they don't know how to work, or won't work, or think work is
beneath them, or can't spell the word work, or don't understand
work in a semantic sense, or something – the usual fucking boring
guff you hear from self-important well-off right-wingers, especially
the heads of industry, but also sometimes from backbench Tory
politicians when they're too far from the Central Office twat-zapper
to be effectively restrained and have begun to froth at the mouth
and gibber and writhe like demonically possessed spastics in front
of the TV cameras or their local constituency association. David
went on to tell us what his old dad did when he was short of work.
Do you know what he did, Mr Starkey Senior? He walked a hundred
miles, or something, in order to find a job. Or it might have been
five hundred miles, or a thousand, or fifty. I can't remember. And
actually, now I come to think of it, he may not have walked – he may
have cycled, or pursued new employment a great distance from
home via the conduit of a pogo-stick, or by swimming the entire

length of every watercourse that hove into view, or by hopping, while beating himself about the body with a birch switch. The exact mode of self-propelled transportation detailed by David now eludes me entirely, for which many apologies; that's bad research, really. Something very fucking arduous, anyway, all in order to find new work, all in order to maintain his pride and provide for his family, to be a man, to be a worker.

That's what he did. He conformed to the Tebbit principle and, metaphorically or otherwise, got on his bike to seek out employment. And the point Mr Starkey Jr was trying to make, the same point made by Lord Tebbit a couple of decades previously, is that the feckless scumbag British worker just doesn't do that any more. He expects work to come to him, he lolls around whining about a lack of work, but he won't go out looking for it. What we need, Mr Starkey Jr implied, is an infinitely flexible workforce.

We already have one, of course. The British worker puts in more hours than any other in Europe, with the exception of the Irish. And look where that's got the poor bastard. Indeed, the least flexible, most regulated and least hard-working people in Europe live in what we once knew as the Hanseatic League – Germany, Norway, the Netherlands; they are also the most affluent countries in the world. Perhaps the British worker should work less hard, then, and be a damn sight less flexible about his working arrangements. Perhaps we'd all be better off that way. But as soon as the unemployment rate creeps up because the government will not invest in anything, and the working classes start getting a bit restive, there's always someone like the otherwise rather wonderful David Starkey to come along and tell them that the reason they can't get a job is that they're not flexible enough, they won't put themselves out – and so that's why the jobs go to the Poles and the Slovaks. Look how flexible and vigorous they are, these broad-faced Slavs! They've hopped all the way from Łódz and Košice, and now Brasov and Plovdiv – and here they are right now, doing the jobs you could have had, you mugs.

Flexible, then, as understood by Mr Starkey, is a synonym – a euphemism, if you like – for 'fucking cheap'. The reason British businesses employ Eastern European labour is that they can pay them three fifths of fuck-all and get away with it; it is nothing to do with a reluctance on the part of the British worker to shift his indolent fat arse and travel a few miles for a job. The Poles and Slovaks have very low overheads here, and a much lower cost of living back home. They don't have families to support in this country, by and large, so they work for less. Have you noticed how minicab fares haven't risen much recently, or have sometimes gone down? You can probably work out why that is when you listen to the driver's accent.

We'll return to the immense joys occasioned to the poorest people of this country by large-scale immigration in a later chapter, and leave the subject for now, after I've told you about the two lads I met outside the Job Centre in Middlesbrough. Skilled labourers, they'd been on the dole for months, and were desperate for work. They took themselves off to the Olympic site down in London, where there was loads of construction going on, but they couldn't get a job, turned away from every site. And, one of them told me, shaking his head, the signs outside the site offices were all in Polish. The Poles had nicked all the jobs.

Yes, yes, I know, you mithering authoritarian *bien pensant*, I can see those hackles rising along your spine, I can see your wet lips forming themselves into the ubiquitous ovine bleat of raaaacistttttt. Of course I know that none of this is the fault of the Poles, I know they are blameless. It is not remotely the fault of the Poles, OK? But once you've said that, where does it leave the lads from Middlesbrough? Or doesn't that matter? Just raise your glass and offer three cheers for the free movement of labour and capital, like any good socialist would. Anyway, we'll come back to this interesting topic. I don't know, incidentally, how those Boro boys got themselves the 260 miles down to London. Maybe they borrowed

David Starkey's dad's pogo-stick. Or maybe they took the fucking coach.

Right now, I'm packing up for a move myself, got the removals people coming round in a week. We're off, sixty or so miles from where we live at the moment, on the edge of London, to near Canterbury (and dangerously close to David Starkey, as it happens). I counted up, and the new house will be the nineteenth different place I've lived since leaving home in 1978, meaning that I've spent an average of one year and nine and a half months in each place. I've lived in the north-east, the south-west, South Wales, London and Kent. I pester my wife on an almost daily basis to move to the north-east of England, but she won't do it because she thinks there are no Starbucks there and she won't be able to buy tampons, batteries or shoes, so it doesn't look like we're going there any time soon.

I think my yearning for the north-east, where I always feel at home, comes from this berserk thirty-four years of rootlessness, a peripatetic existence, a sort of domicile equivalent of fast food. Only during the four years I spent in the small Wiltshire village of Heytesbury did I do that thing you're meant to do – participate in the community – to any extent.

I am hardly alone in this wandering however: the amount of time people spend in any home has reduced enormously over the last thirty or so years; if you're in the private rented sector (where I've been most of the time) the average stay is now little more than a year. Even for home-owners the average duration has fallen and fallen, until it is now just under ten years. We have become every bit as mobile as David Starkey would like us to be; we move hither and thither, packing and unpacking our accretions, for a multiplicity of reasons – not least that we are proud to be participants in a flexible workforce. Like Starkey, the government wishes us to be infinitely flexible workers, to move where the jobs are, to get on our bikes – but the jobs are increasingly short-term contracts with scant possibility of tenure, and so we move on again.

The government, however, also wants us to be participants in something the Prime Minister christened a 'Big Society', a nebulous and ill-defined concept which seems to mean, insofar as it's possible to understand what seems to be a vague aspiration, helping out with stuff in your neighbourhood. But you don't help out in your neighbourhood if you don't know who your neighbours are – and these days one in eight of us do not even know the names of the people living next door. An average of a year spent in a place does not give you the chance to become involved in your neighbourhood; you're basically squatting, looking nervously about you, locking the door tight and pulling back the bolts on the windows. Your involvement with those around you extends only to pushing past them at the bus stop on your way to work. With every year that passes we are leading a more atomised existence, in which the people we meet day to day are of value only for fleeting, instrumental reasons.

My parents, by contrast, moved home a total of three times in fifty-five years. And in each place they settled, they settled. There was attendance (and in my parents' case, involvement) at the local church – a social centre as potent as the local pub. My mother also joined the local amateur dramatics groups in Bexleyheath and Middlesbrough, and was even for a while a member of a Black and White Minstrels troupe – as I have previously mentioned, she had always had a soft spot for African-Caribbean people, whom she thought of as 'cheerful', and I think joining the Black and White Minstrels was her way of paying an appropriate tribute to them. Foremost, though, she was the 'Akela' of a local cub pack, later rising to become a district commissioner, a job that took up all of her spare hours (because during the day she worked). My dad, who was somewhat insular, played a subordinate role in all of these ventures, driving people about, doing the accounts, printing stuff on the Gestetner. In such a way we were connected, as a family, to everyone we lived among; through the cubs and the drama groups and the church. This is not a reworking of Family and Kinship in East London, where the doors were always left open on a terrifying extended family who'd welcome you into their 'omes, gawd bless em, 'ave a banana. It was a 1950s commuter suburb of Middlesbrough, with probably a more transient population than was then the norm. Although, saying that, it was a shock and an upheaval if someone we knew moved – and in the ten years we were there, they didn't do so very often. The place had, despite itself, a sense of permanence and belonging; crime was low, there were no gangs. There was, mind you, a community wanker – the Nunthorpe Wanker – who gained a certain notoriety for a brief while, by wanking at people. I saw him once, in a bush, wanking in a rather leisurely manner. Probably I did not excite him. But the Nunthorpe Wanker aside, we all felt part of a community and looked out for each other. Actually, I suppose the wanker did too, in his own fashion.

In 1975 the Liddle family received 284 Christmas cards – I can remember counting them, slightly in awe and slightly sickened – of which all but forty or so were from the people we lived among, the rest having been despatched by the Liddle diaspora. By way of contrast, last year I got about thirty Christmas cards, and most of those were from fucking PR companies. I realise, incidentally, that this is neither an important nor a scientific gauge of anomie and alienation. I'm just, you know, sayin'.

The exhortation to move to where work exists, endlessly following the job market like a dog chasing its own tail, is only one reason why we have far less of a sense of community today – and probably not the most important, at that. We travel more generally, and do so a lot more lightly, than was the case fifty years back. It is genuinely hard to convey the upheaval, the sense of occasion, the excitement of long-distance travel for people outside the top echelon of society before the late 1960s. My family went by train from London to Darlington once a year, to visit my grandmother and those other assorted ageless northern relatives – and that trip would need to be saved up for, long and hard, for months before we departed. Train travel was, in real terms, ruinously expensive, and laborious. Later we got the car, primarily for the purpose of saving money on train fares – and before such a voyage my father would be out busy tinkering with his vital little instruments, his tyre-pressure gauge and his dipstick and so on, because driving 260 miles was a huge undertaking – anything might happen. We would leave home at 5 a.m., me dozing on the back seat next to the dog, for an unimaginably – it seemed to me at the time – lengthy journey up the A1, which was still, for a substantial part of its route, a simple two-lane road, slow and windy, snarled up with traffic as it made its way through the high streets of dimly remembered outposts of the east Midlands – Long Benington, Retford, Newark. Eight hours later we would arrive in Darlington, the Anglia with an exhausted look on its fly-spattered face, Skipper gasping for water and farting like a wizard. We usually stopped for something very nasty to eat somewhere in Nottinghamshire, and then for something even nastier at the Little Chef near Doncaster.

Travel then was not something which many of us were habituated to, and there was little joy to be gleaned from it. One tended to stay where one was; the psychological impulse to stay in one place was much greater, and by and large people were content to do so; hence they had longevity and tenure in their communities. In the late sixties and early seventies this changed a little; the roads improved rapidly, car ownership hit 75 per cent, and suddenly moving around a bit became a reasonable option, both practically and, more crucially, within the mind. The horizons were opened up; a change of scene gradually became a possibility – especially now that the family and friends you'd be leaving behind were more easily reachable, should you want to reach them, by that newish thing the telephone or via the car. And then – in the south-east particularly – there was immigration, and the resultant white flight. The indigenous working class of London saw their communities change around them and, with ever greater haste, got the hell out – south to Bromley and the Medway towns and Thanet, north to Broxbourne and the increasingly paved-over county of Hertfordshire, east to Hornchurch, Billericay and the new towns of Harlow and Woodham Ferrers, west to Woking and Reading and Basingstoke. They left some behind, of course – usually the older members of their former communities, who were reluctant to up sticks – and, ironically the incomers, Asians from Bangladesh and East Africa, India and Pakistan, began creating the very same tight-knit, mutually dependent communities that their arrival had helped to usurp or replace. I suspect that if the sociologists Young and Willmott returned to parts of the East End they would find people living in a very similar manner to the one they had documented in *Family and Kinship in East London*; only the colour of the skin has changed. And they probably wouldn't be eating pork chops, as the pair lovingly described the white folks doing back in 1957.

But the effects of large-scale immigration were, in this regard at least, comparatively regionalised and minor, certainly compared to the next impulse which gripped hold of us all, first mildly in the mid-1970s, and then with an atavistic fervour in the awful decade that followed. I can think of nothing which has contributed more to the winnowing away of a sense of community than the deliberate implanting of the poisonous notion that a home is not primarily somewhere you live, but a means of collateral to be ever traded upwards.

House prices first began their maniacal upwards spiral in the 1970s, and not, as is popularly believed, in the 1980s. My family moved from South London to Middlesbrough in 1968. We received, by our standards at least, a large cash windfall for having traded a 1920s two-and-a-half-bed semi in Bexleyheath for a 1950s two-and-a-half-bed detached in Middlesbrough. I think the London house was sold for about £3,500 and the new one bought for £2,200, there or thereabouts. Eleven years later, that Middlesbrough house was sold for £19,000, a rise of roughly 750 per cent. But a good proportion of that was down to the Argentinean levels of inflation that pertained throughout Ted Heath's guileless tenure as Prime Minister and the only marginally less inept Wilson/Callaghan regime which followed.

People were moving more than they had done before, for sure, at least in part for the reasons I mentioned above. But the endless, consuming avarice of flogging your property and buying a new one, and then flogging that property, having improved its value by adding a fucking study in the attic and an open-plan kitchen/diner and decking in the garden – that madhouse was all still to come, and largely at the hands of the next generation. Certainly it is true that when my mother and father bought their first property it was not out of a wish to make large amounts of money from it – the house in Woodlands Road, Bexleyheath, was a family home which they would have been happy to stay in forever, were it not for my dad being transferred with his job, and the pull of home, to the north-east.

When I bought my first property, it never occurred to me that this was the place in which I would spend the rest of my life, or even more than a very, very small part of it. I was on the ladder. Everyone was on the ladder. There were countless TV shows about the ladder, and how to get up it and how to screw the vendor out of a few thou, or add a few thou to your own selling price. Everyone was buying houses, and selling them, and then selling the next one, and the next one. Officially sanctioned, institutionalised venality which effectively began with the sale of council houses, the 'right to buy', which has left us with almost no council stock at all, save for the residuals – the piss-stained skagheaded shitholes nobody in their right mind would want. Of course you only bought your council property in order to sell it: that was the point, to cash in just like everyone else was cashing in. Flogging your house became an obsession which, regardless of the predictable property slumps, has still not yet abated.

I don't think this madness ever really commended itself to my parents' generation; they found this new way of viewing where you lived as an absurdity and the economics upon which it was founded a chimera, a bubble that was sure to burst one day soon. Which of course it did, several times. But it remains a singularly British obsession – no other country in the world has this rapacious and desperate housing market, and we are making ourselves extremely unpopular by exporting the greed to France and Germany and Spain, purchasing second homes, buy to lets, timeshares, apartments and hideous villas abroad, raising the prices of property on the Continent with every year that passes so local people can't afford to buy. And back at home moving, always moving; having an investment only in the baldest sense of the word, in the mortgage. Having no investment in the community you live in, or in the people who live around you, because you're always ready to move on again, to buy bigger and better, and thus trouser more almost wholly imaginary money. And as a consequence, the poorest of us – an ever-growing proportion – are forced into private-sector lettings, because there are no council houses left.

Our infatuation with house prices is perhaps second only to the credit card as having had the most deeply corrosive effect upon what we – although obviously not Mrs Thatcher – might call society. And, much as with the credit card, you wonder how come my generation was so easily gulled, so taken in, and so mindless of the effect upon others. The rather sneering quotation at the beginning of this chapter is from John Betjeman, of course, bemoaning the fact that the lower-middle classes, the *hoi polloi*, the bald young clerks and their suburban wives, who do not know/the birdsong from the radio – were buying houses at all, ghastly little people that they were. This is pure snobbery, of course and we should not pay it much mind. But not all objections to the social calamities of the housing market should be so easily dismissed, even if that's the familiar monetarist charge levelled against those who cavil: you are standing in the way of democracy's perfect expression, the democracy of the free market; what right do you have to stop someone making money and, uh, bettering themselves? Ah, well, you've got me – none, in the end. I have no right, and so it will go on: even a catastrophic slump in the market dulls the appetite only briefly. My argument is simply that the fervid acquisitiveness has not made this country a better place in which to live; we are more estranged, physically and metaphorically, from one another than ever before.

Other stuff has also made us move around, here, there and everywhere. You might reasonably chuck into the mix the rather greater alacrity with which we got divorced, a number which has risen almost exponentially since the late 1960s. Divorce usually means someone moves out, unless you're really weird, and often away from the area inhabited by their embittered or merely awkward former spouse. We also, since the 1970s, began to choose to live by ourselves at a younger and younger age (a process which may now be in reverse), and to demand more floor space for ourselves, because, hell, we deserve it. It is a fact not often remarked upon by the Green lobby that every single advance since 1970 in making houses more environmentally friendly – and there have been many such advances – has been entirely negated by the fact that we no longer wish to live with other people; that we want instead to curl ourselves in isolation, and fester. I don't know why the Greens don't make more of that; I suppose because it would require them to make non-pc judgments about how people live their lives, and we couldn't have that.

★

There's a new word the sociologists use to describe communities that recover quickly in the aftermath of catastrophe, economic or otherwise: they use the word 'resilience'. I don't know why, but this annoys me. It sounds like something they've just thought up, in a committee meeting, someone called Roz and someone called Hugo, delving around in their brains for some new concept to give to the world: *resilience*. Too often when they talk about resilience they mean nothing more than affluence: it will come as no surprise to you to learn that in a recent study by the Institute for Public Policy Research, Guildford emerged as more 'resilient' than Tower Hamlets. Well, fuck me sideways, etc. But I would bet that communities where the simple turnover in residencies is low tend to be more *resilient* than those in which the turnover is high, even once you have factored out differential income levels. I don't know that for a fact, it's just a guess. And I would guess too that there is some correlation with the crime rate.

I envy my mother and father the deep sense they had of always belonging to a community, the importance they put upon investing their time and effort in stuff like drama clubs and cub scouts. It is something I have largely neglected to do; I've never really been around anywhere long enough – it's the sort of thing that requires commitment and longevity. There are still cub scout packs, of course, but many fewer than thirty or forty years ago. There are still amateur dramatic societies – but, again, fewer. The churches and the pubs have been closing down too.

So how do we occupy our increased leisure time now? After watching TV, the next most popular leisure activity is buying shit in shops. We like nothing more than wheeling a trolley around a huge shop and filling it up with shit. Retail outlets, malls, hypermarkets – you name it, we'll spend a weekend buying shit in it. And the other thing we do these days, a growth industry almost on a par with buying bits of shit in shops – we go to the gym. We've replaced the communal with the solipsistic, the acquisitive and the narcissistic.

5

The Culture of Narcissism

> For death remembered should be like a mirror,
> Who tells us life's but breath, to trust it error.
>
> William Shakespeare

> Butterflies are always following me, everywhere I go.
>
> Mariah Carey

The last thing I remember my mother ever saying to me was, 'Rod, I'm frightened.' She had terminal cancer, and what she was afraid of, reasonably enough, was dying imminently. She knew she was close to death, and so did I, and so did my dad and so did the doctors and nurses who attended to her in this harrowing room in the hospital in Cardiff. The room knew too. There was something about the room: its scrubbed beige implacability, its suffocating warmth, its watchfulness – somehow, in a way I can't explain, its connivance, a connivance in the unending procession of death which it witnessed, the room from which nobody leaves alive, and with its terrible and pointless clinical appurtenances. She said this thing to me while I was sat at her bedside holding her hand, just 'Rod, I'm frightened,' and, emaciated and frequently delirious though she was, whacked out on the morphine and eaten away by the cancer, this brief and entirely rational admission seemed shocking, staggering even.

It was the first time it had been said aloud, the first time the death thing, the possibility of the death thing, had been admitted in the five years since the cancer – once supposedly eradicated – had made its inevitable triumphant return. The cancer she had first noticed on that pleasant afternoon in Wales, as we walked along the footpath, twelve years before. For the final three years of her life there was absolutely no doubt whatsoever about what the outcome would be, my father and I were assured; there would be no remission, there was nothing anyone could do, no drugs, no surgery: that, I'm afraid, they all said, sadly, shaking their heads, is that, sorry. Three years of quite explicitly terminal illness, but never admitted between us in the presence of my mum, even though of course she had been told the same thing by the surgeons. Never admitted, as if it were some kind of dirty secret, something shameful and pornographic. So when she said this thing about being frightened, I didn't know what to do, how to respond. It was a sentence of ghostly clarity, it had a kind of supernatural force, as if it came from beyond her, and it left me speechless. The mantra had been the same for the last three years – Mum, you're going to be fine.

That's what we said. We chivvied her along, we patted and reassured and cheered and lied. And she lied back. We knew and she knew she was going to die soon – but the pretence was nonetheless kept up, all the way through; it was a kind of agreement. And so that's what I said to her then, at the bedside, or words to that effect. 'You're going to be fine. Mum, don't worry, you'll get over this.' You know the sort of thing? The sort of thing you say? Such a vapid and evasive lie when she wanted something better.

Only a few weeks before, she had collapsed at home and lay on the kitchen floor, paralysed. The doctor was called, along with an ambulance. 'How are you feeling today, Margaret?' the doctor enquired as she was being hoisted by three blokes onto a stretcher. 'Lovely, thank you, doctor,' she replied. 'Lovely.' There was no intended irony. *Lovely. Top of the world. Never been better.*

I remember plenty of times with my mum and dad when such reflexive or habitual stoicism seemed surreal, or idiotic. The refusal to admit to pain or distress in such extreme circumstances does not strike me as commendable – or, for that matter, useful. It is self-abnegation to the point of lunacy, isn't it? But the last thing you wanted to do if you were my mother, or my father, or a good proportion of that generation which spent its golden years of youth cowering in a tube station from the V2s or on a boat somewhere, trying to kill Krauts, was to make a fuss. The notion that your palpable distress was of significance to anyone else, or even noticed by anyone else, was anathema, and indeed rather embarrassing. You soldiered on, you didn't moan, you made the best of things, put a smile on your face – all that stiff-upper-lip bollocks you hear about from the Second World War: the corner shop with its sign saying 'Still open for business!' despite the fact that, consequent to the previous night's air raid, the shop no longer existed; the milkman delivering his wares to a non-existent street; the searing fires, the rubble, the dust, the dead bodies and the vision of your own imminent death fizzing away, just beyond the edge of your eyesight. Against such a daily backdrop your own concerns, your upheavals, your petty miseries, your hardships, counted for less than nothing. There is something almost fascistic, as well as wholly glorious, in the extent to which personal concerns were put aside – there's a war to be won, others are suffering more than me, and so on. Oh, for sure, it was not entirely like that during the war years – there were strikes, there was looting, there was an anger that the rich had it much easier and still thronged in the Café Royal of an evening getting pissed and eating rather nicer food than everyone else. But rancour was not the dominant state of mind, or does not seem to have been; mostly, people really did just get on with stuff and kept the complaints to a minimum. There was an awareness that the thing they were in, this war, was bigger than any individual.

Hell, you know all about the Second World War: your TV channels are full of it, there is a seemingly insatiable public desire to squeeze every last detail out of its now desiccated entrails. Turn on your TV on any night of the week and I'll wager that Hitler will be making an appearance somewhere, shouting at lots of people or making his famous camp little salute, or doing that jaunty dance he did when he was really happy. Adolf is by some margin Great Britain's favourite character from history, for his madness, his comedy value, his dire threat, his convenient embodiment of untrammelled, Continental, evil.

Other countries, and especially the poor Germans, are puzzled by our perpetual gloating, our revelling in the immense, hideous tragedy of World War II, sixty-nine years after it ended. Indeed, after sixty-nine years of unremitting national decline, they would quietly point out. They suspect that we are so interested, so avid for stories of heroism, because we won. And that's partly correct; but it's much more than that. I think we look back on the war with fondness, and even envy, because the British people then are thought to have behaved, by and large, in an exemplary manner; there was selflessness, sacrifice, resilience and, of course, a berserk sort of stoicism. I think we enjoy thinking of ourselves behaving in an exemplary manner. It matters little as to whether that exemplary behaviour, back in those grim days, was sort of the only option available. Whatever, that modest predisposition somehow stuck with the generation that endured it all.

They did not speak much of the war, my mother and father, but its deprivations undoubtedly shaped them. I heard a little from my mother about being evacuated, and how her family's house in Bermondsey was flattened and they were resettled in the rather more pleasant East Dulwich – something which, my mother said, ensured that her own father retained forever a soft spot for Hermann Goering and his brave pilots. From my father there was very little, although he once told me how he and most of the crew on his MTB much preferred Germans to Belgians, and Belgians to the ghastly French – as I mentioned back at the start of this book.

But the war lies deep within the minds of all those who lived through it; in the case of my mother and father, as in many others of that generation, it manifested itself as a refusal to make a fuss, to become upset or inflamed, to complain, to whine – not least because since the war there has not been so very much to whine about, all things considered. Perhaps it made them too quiescent and undemanding of others, but that's a pleasant contrast to how we are now, the generation that followed them. I mean, with the best will in the world, you wouldn't call us 'stoic', would you? You wouldn't accuse us of being slow to complain, of being resilient, of subordinating our own inconveniences for the greater benefit of others, would you? These are generalisations, of course; I'm sure it is true that my parents' generation had its percentage of whining halfwits, just as today some of us may show a little reserve, and dignity, and fortitude. What I mean is that these are not the things that immediately come to mind when you think of how we are now. Something different comes to mind.

Take one of our big concerns these days, now that we no longer have the V2s raining down, or the shadow of the Bomb hovering above us: obesity. Being very, very, fat. That is what gets us worked up today.

You may remember the newspapers being full of a story about a girl in South Wales who had to have the front of her house knocked down because she was too fat to get downstairs, or indeed shift her enormous arse out of bed. They had pictures of this poor lass, and she was indeed fucking gargantuan, like a crude cartoon of a very fat person, an enormous sallow mound of blubber and e-numbers and carbohydrates and compacted shit. The earliest reports put her weight at sixty-three stone, although this was later revised down to a svelte fifty-five stone. Obviously one felt sorry for her, lying there as the demolition men and the paramedics went about their work – but the thing that grated was the constant insistence from her friends and from herself that she wouldn't have got this fat *if she had been helped.*

Helped? Helped not to eat? Why would you need to be helped not to eat? Imagine the utter mystification this plaint would have engendered in my parents' generation. And yet today it is the constant refrain from some people who are so obese that they need help, and the corollary that somehow, through some form of transference, their weight isn't their fault, and other people should take responsibility for it. I heard one chap on the radio who had just come out of hospital because his heart had blown up, exploded or something, as a consequence of eating way, way too much. And despite having received the appropriate life-saving medical treatment, he was angry – angry that he wasn't being given further help to stop him eating more stuff. Remarkable. And you hear the same thing from those other victims of disabilities which have been cruelly imposed upon them by some vindictive and mysterious third party – alcoholics and drug addicts. My argument, incidentally, isn't that we should refuse to help these people, because it's all their own fault; I think we should help them while letting them know, in a perfectly pleasant manner, that it is indeed their own fault – because time and time again this notion does not seem to have struck them. It does not seem to have occurred. Instead, they seem to suffer from a reversal of the sort of stoicism manifested in the previous generation: instead of refusing to encumber others with one's own misfortunes, we shriek that unnamed others, society, is to blame, and that we deserve some form of redress.

Some, from the political right, will say that this is a consequence of the welfare state, which has inculcated a sense of dependence in all of us, the debilitating idea that it is always there to pick us up when we fall, that it is therefore responsible for us. I don't think so. It may be a consequence of the way in which the welfare state has developed, mind, with the gradual dissolution of the notion of a deserving poor and, by extension, an undeserving poor; the erosion of the distinction between people who are in the shit through no fault of their own, and those who have made their own beds very badly indeed. We are, as Richard Hoggart put it in *The Way We Live Now*, riding a wave of relativism – 'the obsessive avoidance of judgments of quality, or moral judgment'; there is no blame to be attached to anything anyone does; we should not judge, we should not blame. And so, of course, as a consequence, people come to expect not to be judged and not to be blamed. People who cannot work because they are 'disabled' by, say, alcoholism or obesity, but who nonetheless have several children to support, do not remotely blame themselves for giving their kids an awful life – they blame you, and me, and society. And they will demand, as a right, a larger house, and therefore a larger bill for you and me to pay, because the notion that they should look out for themselves a little bit either has not occurred to them, or has occurred to them but appals them in its apparent callousness.

Such stories, of which there are several every day, are the stock in trade of the *Daily Mail*, and so, by a simple process of opposing everything the *Daily Mail* stands for, the left has come to support the rights of people who are, in all honesty, simply feckless and, in the end, anti-social. This is, I think, a grave mistake. It is not so much the doling out of money that worries me particularly – all in all, it's a hell of a lot less than is lost to the country by the affluent avoiding paying the appropriate amounts of income tax, or the money siphoned off abroad by multinational companies, a point Dacre's rag rarely makes – it's the refusal to judge, to apportion blame when blame clearly should be apportioned. And this chronic evasion means that people begin to externalise their self-made problems; they start to believe that the troubles they have are the most ghastly iniquities which have been imposed upon them, and which someone else ought to sort out. Further to this, and more recently still, their problems have become officially medicalised: they are no longer fat gannets, then, who like pizza and cake too much, but people 'with' obesity, a purely medical condition, just like toxic shock syndrome or bowel cancer. Likewise with alcoholics; they are no longer just pissheads who can't stop drinking, they have been ennobled by an illness, stricken low by something which has been placed upon them; they suffer from a 'condition' that can be 'treated'. Again, I have no objection to their receiving help; that isn't really the point. The point is the refusal to allow them to take responsibility.

This perpetual whining is just one aspect of what has been called the 'victim culture', although it might be more accurate to call it a narcissistic culture. It is the elevation of the self to a level of unparalleled importance, a delusion which is at its worst sociopathic and at its best simply irritating. You can see it in the speed with which we complain, incessantly, that our rights have been infracted; we have become bizarrely fractious and intolerant when we believe we are being transgressed upon, when someone has made an observation which nips a little at our sensibilities. Our reaction is not simply to disagree, but to howl with outrage – as if we had some existential right to live a life free from ever encountering offence, our lives cocooned forever away from the possibly hurtful observations of other people. We are not thick-skinned these days; we have skins as fragile and tenuous as the surface tension of blood. And our propensity to take offence at these slights has been rewarded by rafts of legislation which make it a criminal offence to make such slights in the first place. Amendments to the Public Order Act (1986), or the Race and Religious Hatred Act (2006), certainly impinged upon the freedom of speech; but more importantly, more dangerously, reinforced the epic, narcissistic delusion that we should all be immune to judgment, to criticism, to observation. And that if this immunity is compromised, then the filth should get involved, pronto.

My favourite example of this came when the government decided to enact legislation to make it a crime, effectively, to disrespect the religion of Islam. This decision was taken to placate the narcissistic sentiments of some Muslim 'community leaders' who wanted special protection for their tribe above and beyond that which was already in place under the perfectly adequate Public Order Act. The previous year, though, the government had enacted legislation to protect Britain's homosexuals from unpleasant aspersions and slights – and so you might begin to guess what happened next. The boss of the Muslim Council of Britain at the time, Iqbal Sacranie, appeared on the BBC PM programme and delivered himself of some mildly hostile comments about homosexuality, entirely in accordance with his (and my, for that matter) understanding of what Islam has to say on the subject. No sooner had he finished speaking than the police got involved. Old Iqbal was questioned at some length about what was regarded as a 'hate crime' – i.e. stating a point of view which was held not only by the majority of Muslims, but also by a fairly large proportion of Christians, Hindus, Sikhs, Baha'i believers and indeed some atheists. And so we had the wonderful scenario of a state making it illegal to disrespect Islam, or discriminate against people who subscribe to the Islamic faith, subsequently sending the police round to the house of a devout Muslim who had simply expressed what he believed to be a tenet of his faith. Why didn't someone send the police round to investigate the police, for disrespecting Islam? I have a dislike of Islam, on account of its bigotry and homophobia; I do not, as the government wishes me to do, have a huge respect for it as an ideology. But nor do I think that Muslims should be arrested for stating what they believe is a fundamental tenet of their religion. What a delightful madness it all was, two delusions clashing together, the state left hapless in the middle. No charges were brought against Iqbal in the end.

It is there too, this narcissism, in the self-aggrandising and self-importance of the social networking sites – the nonentity celebrity tweeting that he has just eaten a fucking sandwich, or the non-celebrity tweeting that he has just seen a nonentity celebrity eating a fucking sandwich and is therefore about to eat a fucking sand-wich himself; an endless demand to look at me, take me seriously, I am important, I AM. And of course it is present too in the very nature of modern slebdom, where the only purpose is to be famous – not for what one has achieved or created, but simply because one IS. The reality shows comprised of witless, emoting exhibitionists; the supposed talent contests on which there is almost no talent on show, just needy people who desperately wish to be well known; the hyperbolic shrieking of the audiences, demanding to be heard, whipped up into a state of narcissistic fervour. And in oh, so many other things: the mutton-headed breast-beating 'respec'' culture, whereby an individual has the right to be respected regardless of whether or not he is, in all honesty, a fucking idiot and a thug to boot – and if you disrespec' him in some way you might well get a knife in your throat.

This street culture is only an extreme example of the way the rest of us have become, a sort of hideous exaggeration of the narcis-sism that is now protected under the law. You might even say that obesity itself is a form of narcissism, a narcissistic reaction to a narcissistic society, as R.D. Laing might have put it, if he wasn't dead. Go on, keep feeding yourself, keep feeding yourself, fatso, cram it all down – indulge. It's your right. Let nobody tell you it isn't. Let nobody tell you it isn't. You are eating because that's all there is to do: acquire, consume, eat, feed yourself until you fuck-ing burst.

There is a brilliant essay by Slavoj Žižek on our current narcis-sism, in which he invokes both Freud and the entertaining, if some-times difficult, French psychoanalyst and philosopher Jacques Lacan. This is Žižek on the narcissism of the computer-game player

– the games console being the almost perfect expression of modern, solipsistic, shop-soiled narcissistic rage:

> Consider the interactive computer games some of us play compulsively, games which enable a neurotic weakling to adopt the screen persona of a macho aggressor, beating up other men and violently enjoying women. It's all too easy to assume that this weakling takes refuge in cyberspace in order to escape from a dull, impotent reality. But perhaps the games are more telling than that. What if, in playing them, I articulate the perverse core of my personality which, because of ethico-social constraints, I am not able to act out in real life? Isn't my virtual persona in a way 'more real than reality'? Isn't it precisely because I am aware that this is 'just a game' that in it I can do what I would never be able to in the real world?

Žižek is probably right; but only up to a point. For the problem is that those palpably useful ethico-social constraints are being weakened, by the hour. The neurotic weakling, suffused with a heightened sense of himself, is no longer content to confine his virtual persona to the screen; it is the perverse core of the personality, with its vaulting braggadocio and now ingrained insularity, which increasingly makes itself evident in the real world. We are becoming our own avatars.

It may be that our epic and touching self-love had its roots in the pathological narcissism of the 1960s counterculture, which morphed, almost intangibly, into the self-growth and self-awareness post-hippy shite of the 1970s. This, with some caveats, is the theory behind Christopher Lasch's The Culture of Narcissism, a clever book which annoyed many people on both the political right and the left in that vile decade, the 1980s. I am always resistant, however, to theories which place the blame on the immediately preceding decade and its odd peccadilloes. My suspicion is that this has been a more gradual process, which began at the end of the Second World War; that where once – as the tiny evacuees waited patiently, clutching their tatty brown suitcases, at King's Cross station for their ominous trains to unknown places far away, my mother among them – there was the pressing requirement to sublimate the personal, the selfish and the individualistic for the good of society, this constraint has gradually dissolved over the intervening decades of comparative peace and prosperity and gentle national dissolution. Now there is no sublimating at all: it is all out there, in the open. And this moronic fugue, this howling – that I have been transgressed, or I am a victim, or I demand redress, or simply and exultantly LOOK! I AM! – is the conscious expression of a society which, underneath, is fractured into a million different parts and no longer has any sense of itself as a cohesive whole, and therefore with a concomitant moral responsibility to others. What we have instead is an infinitely atomised morass of acquisitiveness and complaint and insularity and braggadocio.

Bring back the war, then. There is nothing new in suggesting that during wartime a population shows greater togetherness and – that new word – resilience, as the sociologist Émile Durkheim would attest from well beyond the grave. But the point here is that those admirable qualities of humility and resilience persisted long after the Potsdam Conference, long after rationing had been abolished, and long after the welfare state had been brought into being. The suspicion is that the germs of it existed before the war, too, and that the lack of such a mentality today is a consequence more of the post-1950s cultural mindset. A very different mindset, inculcated by the subsequent baby-boomer generation in both the mid-1960s and the early 1980s. From the sixties we acquired the insistence upon self-expression and the overthrowing of a conservative social agenda in favour of one in which, after a fashion, anything went and was beyond all reproof. A reaction, of course, against the buttoned-up, constrained and often absurd stoicism of the preceding generation. And as those free-living and endlessly expressive baby-boomers got older and wealthier, so their individualistic demands shoved them to the political right. From the 1980s we received the human right to be endlessly, pointlessly acquisitive, to look after our own interests and fuck the needs of the rest, to deny – à la the Prime Minister of the time – that such a thing as society even existed. The free market (insofar as such a thing exists at all) became the only arbiter of personal morality. I will return to this theme in a bit more detail later, this confluence of two toxic philosophies.

My mother hung on for a month or so after telling me that she was frightened, although she never spoke rationally again. Dad and I would attend at her bedside as she lay there, thinner by the day, tanned orange somehow by the drugs, occasionally spouting fantastically absurd stuff into which we would try to read meaning. She asked me on one of those occasions if I had managed to successfully escape the clutches of the evil black pirates – as if continually playing in her head was this strange and frightening interactive video game, before interactive video games had been invented. I told her that I had indeed escaped, and that the pirates were now totally fucked and out of the picture, nothing to worry about; there's nothing to worry about. She died twenty-eight years ago to the day I am writing this, 31 May, and was one year older than I am now. My father continued with a sort of life.

6

Married With Kids

> Ah, love, let us be true
> To one another! For the world, which seems
> To lie before us like a land of dreams,
> So various, so beautiful, so new,
> Hath really neither joy, nor love, nor light,
> Nor certitude, nor peace, nor help for pain

Matthew Arnold

When I was ten years old I thought it would be a funny thing to call my mum a 'lice-ridden whore'. It was funny, I thought, because it was sort of surreal, a bit over the top, coming from a ten-year-old kid, especially as profanities of any kind were a capital offence in our house. Only a couple of years previously I had been smacked and sent to bed for having said 'hell', and before that given a proper beating for having stood at the top of the stairs with a sheet over my head going, 'Whoooooo, whoooo, I'm the Holy Ghost.'

Anyway, I knew, as I chuckled to myself about the possibility of calling Mum a lice-ridden whore, that it wouldn't be funny at all if I was, say, sixteen, whereas it would have been much funnier if I had said it to her when I was five, or better still a baby, perhaps as my very first words – and I privately reproached my younger self for not having done so. And then, having conceived of this act, I found it impossible to desist from carrying it out. This is a problem I still have today. Something occurs in my mind which strikes me as absurd, or ludicrous, or simply funny, and I cannot resist saying it, or writing it down. I forget that a lot of other people will certainly not find it funny, and may indeed be offended. Sometimes, too, I don't spend long enough considering the feelings of the intended subject of whatever it is that has jumped unbidden into my mind. I blithely assume they'll get the joke. Or maybe that they won't get the joke but it won't matter because it's still a joke and I know it's a joke and that's that. I can't remember who it was who said that jokes are the last refuge of the bourgeoisie – some grim and over-valued post-Marxist like Gramsci, probably, or maybe Adorno. I understand that point, but I do not agree with it. I think the prole-tariat should be allowed jokes too. We all need a refuge. But I do not think for long enough sometimes, that is true.

So, having chosen the appropriate moment, I called my mum a lice-ridden whore and she beat the shit out of me with a stick. Fair enough. I have no great objection to that, and had none even as I was lying on the carpet trying to fend off the blows of the cane, with Skipper capering around and barking and yelping in alarm and attempting to position himself between me and Mum, ever the principled conscientious objector. Ah well, she didn't get the joke, I thought to myself – it was always going to be a close call, that one, the lice-ridden whore thing. But better to murder an infant in the cradle than nurse an unacted desire, or something. Actually, William Blake meant the opposite of that when he wrote it, but I have chosen to interpret his line in a very literal and self-serving sense.

The canes were kept in a corner of the kitchen, by the fridge. I think they had previously been used for supporting broad beans. You bind them into a kind of pyramid and the beans wrap them-selves around, all the way up to the top if you do it right. I'm trying to grow some now, so we shall see. Anyway, I broke all the canes in half one time when my parents were out, a sort of soft-left juvenile storming of the Bastille or burning of the Winter Palace – but this was a mistake, as the blows were far more injurious when administered with a shorter shaft of wood, the energy from my mum's arm less dissipated, I suppose. More direct.

It was always my mum who administered the beatings, and they were very few and far between, probably a lot less frequent than I really deserved. All my friends were smacked or beaten by their parents; it was the norm, for better or for worse. I was unusual in that my dad never got involved, or at least did so only once. My mother was quick to rise to temper and easily goaded, whilst my dad was placid and imperturbable. But I think there was probably also an ideological difference between the two of them as well over this issue, at least by the 1970s when people were beginning to question the morality and indeed the efficacy of corporal punishment.

As I mentioned, my dad hit me only once. It was when I was about fourteen. I had been involved in some row with my mother, almost certainly my fault, maybe goading her and giving her lip, while my dad sat there in the armchair trying to watch the *Nine O'Clock News* with Kenneth Kendall on the BBC. Eventually she started screaming at him, 'Why don't you do something, Ned? Why don't you impose some discipline upon this boy? You just sit there and do absolutely nothing.' 'What do you want me to do?' he asked, and my mother screamed back, utterly exasperated, 'HIT HIM!' And so he got up slowly from his chair with a grim expression and smacked me in the mouth with the back of his hand. My mother, still infuriated, stormed out of the house, shouting about how useless he was. I put my hand to my lips and found blood, and a tooth partly dislodged; suffused with shock and appalled self-righteousness, I gaped at my dad and said to him, 'You've knocked one of my teeth out! How could you do that?' And before he could reply I stormed out of the house too, crying. I hung out at the shops, smoked a couple of cigarettes I'd ponced off one of the kids down there – those awful menthol-flavoured Consulate things which were all the rage amongst us under-sixteens, until the cool kids discovered the utterly ridiculous More© brand – and then, not much later, made my way home. My dad was still in his chair, but he stood up when I came in glaring at him with the bitter rectitude of the victim. He looked forlorn and beaten and distraught. He said, 'I'm sorry. I'm sorry. But what am I to do, Rod? I can't win either way.' He wasn't used to hitting me, he didn't know how hard to hit, or where, so it wouldn't cause too much damage. That's why he'd knocked one of my teeth out, I realised. I said, 'That's OK,' and sat down to watch TV with him, waggling the dislodged tooth every so often in a rather theatrical manner. My mum came home later, still wrapped up in her fury. God knows where she'd been.

I was the cause of most of the discord in our home, I would reckon. When there were rows – or at least those rows to which I was privy – it was usually about something I'd been up to. But there were not many rows, all things considered, and not much in the way of discord. I remember some non-Rod row once when my dad stayed sitting in his armchair, reading the Evening Gazette, refusing to rise to the bait, my mum barking away at him and hurling contumely and insults and imprecations until she suddenly left the living room and disappeared into the kitchen. She emerged a few moments later bearing a washing-up bowl full of water, which she threw over my father's head as he sat there in his chair. He didn't shift an inch, he just shook the paper a couple of times and went right on reading the Gazette. I was actually ROFL, before ROFL had been invented: rolling on the floor with laughter. It was the funniest thing I had ever seen, it was better than Cleese pretending to be Hitler in front of those German guests. The incident had no seriousness or import buried within it, so far as I could tell, despite my mother's genuine anger.

Were there other, more private, rows? Was the washing-up-bowl thing an expression of deeply suppressed rage and dissatisfaction? Were there divisions between their respective aspirations, nagging doubts about their relationship, their marriage? Were there infidelities, or even the distant prospect of infidelities, or just yearnings to get the fuck away? Was the word 'divorce' ever mentioned, perhaps in the heat of an argument? I don't think so. I don't know for sure, but I don't think so. My mum was a confiding sort, so I think I'd have found out from her if she was terribly unhappy, or even a little bit unhappy. But no – they rubbed along, as they say. They seemed to love one another, and were satisfied with what they had. In eighteen years I remember not a single argument about the division of household labour; it was shared, more or less equitably. There seemed to be no sexual jealousy, either, or at least none was shown in front of me. There did not seem to be much of a romance going on, I'll admit, and this – when I was older – disquieted me a little, the apparent lack of passion, the quiescence, the detumescence. As an adolescent I felt that this was settling for less than they were worth. But they seemed instead satisfied and content. Not resigned, mind you, just settled, mutually supportive – an efficient and happy unit.

I may be wrong, of course, and beneath the surface awful stuff may have been bubbling away which they skilfully shielded from me – but I don't think so. It was what they had, for better or for worse, and they settled for it. Was this because the alternative, separation, was still socially unacceptable? Or economically not viable? Perhaps they were not of the temperament for affairs; or maybe the whole business was unthinkable, for all the reasons quoted above and more besides, just something quite beyond the pale, something that was simply *de facto* wrong. I don't think the thought of it ever occurred, and if it did, they took it to the grave with them.

On the whole, that generation did not get divorced. I mean, obviously, some did. I remember calling round at my best friend Tim's house in Guisborough sometime in '76 and there being this weird atmosphere in the place, Tim looking strange and being evasive and uncommunicative, something shadowy taking place off-camera, the air in the rooms stretched out and gravid, and me bouncing around incongruously in my usual Tiggerish manner, sort of like Zebedee at a funeral. Eventually – a trained observer, remember – I sensed something was up, and asked Tim what it was. 'Mum and Dad are getting a divorce,' he said quietly. I cannot tell you how shocking that sounded, as if he had announced a death. Which in a way he had, I suppose. This divorce, the strangeness of it, the upheaval, the mutual acrimony, became a large part of my life for the next couple of years, not least because of my anxieties about how to behave towards the estranged couple, both of whom I saw regularly and adored. I knew too, of course, even in my adolescent solipsism, that the experience was rather more impinging for Tim than it was for me: it was scarring for him. He does not look back on mid-adolescence with indulgent fondness, with misted nostalgia, with happiness, as I do. He would rather not talk about the time. He would rather it had not happened. And back there in that familiar front room of his house in Church Square he had about him a reticence I had not seen before. It wasn't simply that this was an awful time for him, with his parents splitting up. There was something about it that was desperately shaming, too. He was embarrassed, as well as strung out on the misery of the business.

But Tim's parents were the only people I knew at that time who got divorced, and by and large divorcees were regarded with grave suspicion, and especially women divorcees. In fact, if you look at the divorce stats for the UK, Tim's mum and dad were, as ever, being terribly *au courant*; they were just slightly ahead of the game. The figures show a gradual and at times almost indiscernible rise across the last 150 years, with a sharp spike in the immediate post-war years (following a loosening of the laws allowing divorce in 1937) and then a huge increase in the mid-seventies, following the 1971 Divorce Reform Act and subsequent amendments. In 1970 fewer than 60,000 people divorced; by 1981 the figure had risen to

150,000, and it kept on rising until about 1986. It kept on rising even as the numbers of people getting married reduced year after year. Just recently it has begun to rise again, after a brief and gradual downturn. The divorce rate today is about 42 per cent of all marriages, which suggests that it is still, rather wonderfully, in the minority; however, fewer couples marry today than at any time since 1862. The institution is squeezed from both ends, in other words. People do not seem to have so much faith in it any more. The divorce rate has risen 170-fold over the last hundred years, and fewer of us are marrying. In 2010, the last figures I could find, almost half of all children born in the UK were born out of wedlock. And, as we know, non-married relationships do not last as long, on average, as married relationships (for which the average, since you asked, is just under twelve years).

This is a huge shift, and little discussed. The Roman Catholic right bangs on about it every so often, when the mood takes them, but nobody pays very much attention, because it is just the left-footers inflicting God on us, interceding in our beholden right to do what the hell we want. The political mainstream these days is very clear: no stigma should attach to divorce or to those who have been divorced – after all, we have 'no fault' divorces, in which it is OK for both sides simply to agree that they've given up the ghost. Or just one side, for that matter, regardless of what the other spouse might think. And certainly we are all clear that there is no difference in status between a family in which the two adults are married and one in which they have decided just to live together, m'kay, don't see the point of marriage, just a piece of paper isn't it, in the end, etc. But we kid ourselves a little, because these latter relationships do not last as long, and when there are children involved, the little bastards, that's a problem, isn't it?

It certainly *seems* to be a problem, when you talk to the people involved, especially the poorest people. I spent a couple of days standing outside the Job Centre in Middlesbrough, interviewing everyone who came out for a piece on unemployment I was writing for the *Sunday Times* magazine. The stories were all the same – shit jobs or no jobs, agency jobs paying fuck-all, or just sign on the dole. Casual work, short-term contracts paying the minimum wage or less than the minimum wage for a two-day week, a fugue of hopelessness. But there was one other thing that stood out – the most remarkable fact of all in a way, even though it was theoretically nothing to do with the article I was writing. I suppose I must have interviewed a hundred people, and every one, EVERY SINGLE ONE, was either the product of a 'broken home' – i.e. their parents had split up – or had kids but was separated from their original partner. Every one!

I realise that this is not a scientific analysis. I know that it was not a carefully weighted sample, just whoever I could get to speak to me (and some people, of course, told me to fuck off back to London). But this experience had not made them happy; it had made them very unhappy, in most cases – and in almost all cases it had either financially crippled them or made it virtually impossible for them to look further afield for work. One way or another, as a consequence of their living arrangements, they were fucked. Emotionally, financially. The younger ones talked about the problems they'd had as a consequence of their parents being split up, and the succession of strange men, or women, hanging around the house whom they now had to try to get along with, and in general did not like terribly much. And the older ones – I mean sort of around twenty-one and over – talked about how they couldn't get regular work because they had to look after their child (the women), or how they couldn't afford maintenance for their kids, who they hardly ever saw (the men). None of them said, 'I had a child with my girlfriend when we were both seventeen and now we've split up. Let me tell you, it's absolutely terrific. I'm really delighted both with the lifestyle choices we made and the ease with which society allowed us both to have a kid and then to leave it in the fucking lurch.' None of them said that, if my shorthand is to be believed. In every case that I came across, they either regretted their situation – but, of course, regretted it as if it had been imposed on them by an outside agency and was really nothing to do with them (just like the other big problem, the drinking) – or, if they were the offspring of a broken home, they blamed one or the other of their parents. Incidentally, the majority of people I spoke to scored double top: came from a broken home and were also themselves responsible for a subsequent broken home. Yowser.

Why did they do it, then? Why have the kids in the first place? And having done so, why split up? What was the point of all that? Was it simply ineluctable, just something that you did, because everybody else did it? Have some kids right now, can't feed them, but never mind; in any case I'll clear off after a year or two. Something to which they gave not a moment's thought? Or just something they were into for a while and then, mysteriously, suddenly were not? Did the women have kids young because they could think of nothing better to do, and the men connived in it because, hell, that's what you do, give 'em the kids if it makes 'em happy? Was it – as the right insists – the benefits that are on offer once you've dropped a bairn? I don't think so – or at least, I don't think that this is the crucial point, even if it helps facilitate what is, in the end, a bad decision. In a way it is more just a case of how things are: having a kid at a young age is OK even if you can't support it – we've got a right to have kids come what may, everyone's agreed on that. And breaking up after a year is OK too, because everyone's agreed it's usually for the best. If the two of you aren't getting along, just make a fresh start, the kid'll be OK – everyone's agreed that everything will work out fine. Except when you're poor, it doesn't work out fine. It doesn't usually work out fine if you're not poor, either. But it definitely doesn't work out fine when you're down at the bottom. Certainly not for the kids – of which more later. But not for the parents either, in the end.

I did not put those questions I asked in that last paragraph directly to the out-of-work Middlesbrough people and their bastard offspring, so I have no way of knowing the answers. But I am divorced too. I deserted my children for my own personal happiness: it is as simple as that, regardless if I sometimes reassure myself with caveats, with a rationale which I have constructed for myself out of cardboard or tinplate over the years.

I do not feel much better about the business knowing that because maybe 80 per cent of their friends are from broken families too, or because their entire extended family is shot through with divorces, they at least don't need to feel abnormal. I think that what I did was selfish, no matter how happy I am now, or how much I love my wife, with whom I've been for ten years and who has been wonderful with my two sons. It was rough on my ex-wife, obviously – who would point out, with some justification, that it is harder for a woman in her forties (and with kids), as she then was, to find a new and lasting relationship than it is for a man. Beyond that, though, it was a betrayal of my boys. Having made the decision to have children, I should have stuck with it. But I didn't; my personal happiness seemed to count for more than anything else.

And when it came to making that decision, everything said go, it's your right, fill your boots. Society had no real opprobrium to expend, although, in fairness, the Daily Mail managed to find some. But in general, I could explain that I wasn't entirely happy in my relationship, that she had her faults too, y'know, m'kay, that it was time to get the hell out. And so it became another no-fault divorce.

And, once the lawyers had gotten involved, wrong on an epic number of levels. The first thing that went was the house I had bought; that went to my ex, rightly enough. Then there was the money from my dad's house, the one he lived in until he died, the last house my mum and dad lived in together, their poshest house:

£180,000, virtually all swallowed up on legal fees. What a staggering and immoral waste of money. It would have been better, it would have been more worthwhile, if I had spent the entire £180k on crack cocaine. I mean, fuck – it would at least have gone up in a sort of smoke that was momentarily pleasurable. Instead it was frittered away on that most fantastically repulsive of modern luxuries – divorce lawyers. Oh, those lucky lawyers. You think of what it cost my mum and dad to build up to having a house like that, the countless years of scrimping and saving and slogging away. All gone, in virtually a moment, tossed off as if it were nothing. And it is not the money, *per se*, that I am grieving about here: it is what that money represented to my mother and father. When my father died, I took possession of the old wooden attaché case in which he kept his personal effects. These included my parents' savings books, dating back to 1953, money they were putting by so they could give their son a good wallop of cash when they died, fifty years of scrupulous and painstaking accounting. Well, that's what I did with it. Cheers, Mum, Dad.

And it's become a familiar story, despite those online offers of a quickie divorce for £37. We may have got rid of our manufacturing industry over the last three decades, but the gleeful parasitism of the lawyers, fuelled by our own stupidity, has taken up the slack; the number of solicitors has risen tenfold in the last twenty years, and divorce has been one of their most lucrative sidelines.

And there's another point. The loosening of the divorce laws, and the swift removal of stigma from those who have been divorced, came from the top down. It was designed to enable the more affluent in society to continue to pursue that most compulsive of post-1960 pastimes, serial monogamy. Presented as a great blow for modernity against the vicissitudes of the Church, bringing in a new era of freedom and self-determination, the 1971 Divorce Reform Act was in truth enabling only to those who could afford to divorce – which is why, in the early years, its effects were largely confined to the middle classes. If you are affluent enough, you can split up the family home and make sure the kids still have the sort of material lifestyle they enjoyed when the family was together: the money stretches. Sure, there is still, often enough, the emotional disruption, the acrimony, and the kids not really understanding what the fuck is going on – but at least they are provided for financially. There is no such provision for those further down the social scale: the children are almost always immediately subjected to financial privation, no matter how assiduously the CSA badgers the departed father for his twenty-quid-a-week maintenance. The mother is immediately worse off, and is usually sent scuttling back into the kitchen, unable to afford the cost of childcare, which would enable her to work. Like so much socially liberal legislation presented to the electorate as a wonderful means of acquiring those most liberal of things, freedom and equality, divorce reform benefited only the well-off, by and large. The working class bought into it, and ended up broke. In truth, it was legislation designed to enable the affluent to fuck around with impunity (no fault, remember!), and hang the rest.

Hang the kids. Children from broken homes make up 80 per cent of the population of Britain's psychiatric units. Various studies, from mainland Europe and here in the UK, suggest that children with only one parent suffer twice the incidence of psychiatric illness, suicide attempts and alcohol abuse. They also suffer lower self-esteem, are more likely to engage in sexual activity at a younger age, and are far more likely to use illegal drugs. They are also more likely to be sexually abused, they score significantly lower on intelligence tests, are more disruptive at school and show higher levels of aggression. They are also more likely to end up unemployed or in less well-paid jobs. Whoever the 1971 Divorce Reform Act was brought in to 'enable', it was certainly not the children. It was not the children, and it was not the poor. And with the exception of those women who were able at last to get the hell out of physically

abusive relationships – far and away the most beneficial consequence of the Act – it was not the vulnerable.

Where's the glamour, though, in staying married? Where's the
glamour in resisting temptation? From the early 1960s onwards,
high-end culture extolled the virtues of sexual transgression – adultery, divorce – as being synonymous with freedom. John Updike's
novel Couples, published in that most fractious and infantile of
years, 1968, was perhaps the first to explore the ramifications of the
post-Pill paradise, all these zingy new freedoms, through the adul-
teries of ten fairly-well-to-do Massachusetts married couples, and
in particular the short but well-hung serial adulterer Piet Hanema.
Hanema: anima. The man is life itself, avidly fucking his way
through the female population of the fictional town of Tarbox. His
only transgression, in the eyes of the other couples, is to make his
adultery, and subsequent divorce, public. Unconfined sex has
become a sort of church, in Couples, at which the youngish middle
classes each week kneel and pray. An agreeable replacement for the
real church, which in the novel burns to the ground. Conflicted and
prescient, Updike was himself a gently wavering Episcopalian and
student of theology who nonetheless was not averse to a bit of side-
line shagging, here and there. There is something extremely attractive in the decadent lifestyles of the affluent white-collar monkeys
in Couples, their beautiful and spacious timber-framed New England
homes and uproarious parties, the kids parked with childminders
or just left to their own devices.

Couples certainly had its impact upon me when I was sixteen. But
from Updike, via Roth and Barth and Amis and Bradbury and virtually every serious novelist, and playwrights like Ayckbourn, you get
the message: this is where life is, in these transgressions, in this
clamorous excitement. This is what we are here for. And in the
background the fugue of idiocy, the moronic inferno, of celebrity
fuckstories, who they are fucking and for how long they are fucking
before moving on and fucking someone else. 'Why do they do it?'

the late columnist Simon Hoggart once asked rhetorically, of the sleb marriages which last three days and the endless, indefatigable, gruesomely detailed infidelities. 'Because they can.' And so, because this is a meritocratic world, can the rest of us; because we're worth it.

The alternative, I suppose, is to be caught sitting in your armchair watching Kenneth Kendall on the TV and having a washing-up bowl of water poured over your head by your wife, who is no longer the minxy life model from Camberwell Art College you met in those still-austere days of 1952. Where's the glamour in that, etc.

Should they have divorced, my mother and father? Not because they were unhappy, or the relationship was abusive in any way; simply because, hell, there's a world out there, and it's surely time to move on. So many things to see, so many people to do. But that new, burgeoning culture did not speak to them the way it speaks to us now. They were still marooned in that boring time of responsibility and propriety. Thank Christ.

The counter-argument is smooth and difficult to assail. Why deny people the right to escape from marriages in which they were unhappy? Sure, why would you, without dragging poor God into the question, and those vows you made to what is widely perceived by our masters to be a wholly fictional being and of irrelevance. But even allowing this, it rather depends upon your definition of unhappy: whether it is a grinding, unrelieved misery which harms you and everyone around you, or just the sort of existential dissatisfaction you feel when you watch an advert on TV and compare it favourably with your own life. Or you have met someone else and really quite fancy her, if you're honest. Phew, what a scorcher.

And then, the argument goes, onwards and slightly deeper – that the single-unit, monogamous nuclear family was an economic construct designed to facilitate the Industrial Revolution, and that it may have outgrown its usefulness, now we no longer have any industry and women are not expected to confine themselves to the home. Well, maybe. Maybe that's right. In which case, design some sort of system which might reasonably replace the nuclear family, for the benefit of all rather than just the affluent. For the benefit of the children.

The notion of romantic love was a construct of balladeers in thirteenth-century France, much as it is still the mind-numbing staple of balladeers today. Beyond that, sexual relations were a thing of pragmatism and organisation, a sort of historic, tripartite compromise between what our respective genes told us to do, and what society, or God, wanted us to do, and what made economic sense. That self-fulfilment stuff was well down the agenda. But there was a happiness in this arrangement, I suspect. Today, marriage is entered into too lightly, and cast off too easily.

My dad sort of dissolved when my mum died. He had passed out in the consultancy room at Middlesbrough General Hospital, just slumped to the floor, when she was first diagnosed back in '74 – and then eleven years later, when she died, did the sort of strung-out and medium-term equivalent. He took little pleasure in stuff, he existed, he went from day to day. He was there, for a while. He said to me once, shortly after Mum had died, that at night, when he went to bed, he would settle down and then suddenly be awoken by the feeling of the bed going down on the other side, this distinct shifting – he felt the weight of my mum getting into bed with him. He felt it utterly, unarguably. It happened. It was real. He said this to me just this one time, looking for an explanation, hoping that I might be able to explain it away somehow. What is it that's happening up there at night? Is it her? How can it be? He was the least superstitious and sentimental of men, the least credulous. When he died I found photographs of my mum in his otherwise empty bedside drawer; smiling standing by some roses; another on a boat in Scotland with him, their hair blown askew by the wind from the loch; and then a third, standing in her smartest stuff, surrounded by snow, outside the front door of our house in Middlesbrough, Christmas Day 1976.

Maybe they were just lucky, to have had that. And then again, maybe longevity tends to make that happen.

7

Grand Theft Auto versus Boredom

From the moment they get up in the morning to the evening, when they are passed around by their parents from one activity to another, literally they have no free time to be children and to relax. The idea that we live in a world where children have incredible choices, and where parents are laid back, chilled out and 'just get on with it', is a myth. It bears no relationship with reality.

Frank Furedi

Got to tell you, I'm feeling a bit nonced out right now. We are in the middle of noncegate as I write, the country rocked by revelations that the late BBC disc jockey Jimmy Savile almost certainly nonced every child in the land, from Wick to Truro. It is sometimes said that albino people have enormous reserves of energy; clearly that was the case with Jimmy. Hundreds have come forward with nonce scars, some of them allegedly inflicted by the ghastly man almost fifty years ago. But it's not just Jimmy: literally dozens of other famous dead people are alleged to have been nonces, and some live ones too. There are a bunch of Nonce Inquiries taking place, Nonce Trials resulting in painfully few convictions; the whole nation has gone nonce mad. It is a nonce jamboree. Incredibly, it seems that there are also nonces afoot who are not famous at all: Muslim Asian gang nonces, for example, noncing their way around the decrepit old mill towns of the north-west of England, preying on decent, upstanding white Christian girls.

We will return to the Asian noncegate business later, directly and indirectly. But at the moment there is a self-righteous fury stalking the land. Why weren't the children listened to when they first made their allegations? They must be listened to now, and by extension, as a form of restitution, believed, without query. I am not so sure about this. But either way, it's the only story in town.

Well, it's one of two. We are also tearing ourselves up about race again. These are our current twin obsessions: race and paedophilia. To be called a racist, or a nonce, is about the worst thing that could possibly happen to someone, even if the allegation is not true. This says something about us, something complicated and a little scary. It has the whiff of Salem about it. And as far as the noncing goes, it requires a certain doublethink. As others have pointed out, we all thought the Alan Bennett play *The History Boys* terrifically funny and revelatory and progressive. It was about a teacher noncing his pupils, basically. The noncing was rather approved of, in the play. Nobody has yet daubed graffiti on Alan's house, or set fire to him; we would rather put our enjoyment of his play, and our progressive attitude towards it, out of our minds for a while. Maybe we just tell ourselves that it was progressive, liberal noncing. And then we remember with fondness the novel, and the rather more recent film, *Lolita*, which was about an older man called Humbert noncing a schoolgirl. How can we hold these thoughts in our heads co-terminously, while we are on our nonce rampage?

And then again, regarding the Savile case, many of the allegations of sexual abuse date back to the years between 1971 and 1975. This was the first time popular music was directed straight at fourteen-year-olds, and especially fourteen-year-old girls. 'Do You Wanna Touch Me?' sang Gary Glitter. What bit of him did you think he was referring to? Are we surprised that this overtly sexual 'teenybopper' music – from T Rex through Gary Glitter and The Sweet to David Bowie – had certain, you know, ramifications? You could, if you were minded to, and determined to continue with your nonce rampage, call that entire era of music a sort of mass grooming exercise, to use the fashionable term. And at gigs the girls (and boys) met the bands. And the glitzy and famous promoters and DJs and producers. And stuff happened. And the fact that 99.9 per cent of it was entirely consensual – I would guess – should be discounted? If someone had given me the chance to have sex with Suzi Quatro when I was fourteen, I don't think that I would have debated the ethics of the issue for very long. Sadly, nobody ever did. They never did. And now I come to think of it, I still don't know what 'Can the Can' means. I could have asked Suzi, afterwards, in that warm glow. But it never happened. But I did lose my virginity at the age of twelve. Things were different then. It is certainly true that paedophilia has gained iconic status as a crime in the last fifteen to twenty years; it has a cachet now that it never had, a sick glamour, a direct route to the country's viscera. People did not think it was OK, back in the 1970s, as such – although it is true that there were considered to be gradations, differences between the various transgressions, which the shrill absolutism of now will not allow. Now, with its nonce registers and nonce checks and nonce alerts and vigilantes righteously beating up loners and daubing graffiti on the houses of paediatricians.

More pertinent for me, in this chapter, is why we have this clamorous obsession. I don't wish to get too psychological on you all of a sudden, but it does seem to me that there is a bit of over-compensation at work. I think that collectively we feel a certain guilt at how our children are, and how we are with them, the lives they lead. Far more children this year will succumb to one of those weird eating diseases, anorexia or bulimia, than will be subjected to a noncing of some kind or another. More than double the number of kids who are implicated as victims in child-sex-abuse convictions in the UK will be admitted to hospital because they tried to kill themselves. That puts the problem into some sort of perspective – even if the vast array of child-sex-abuse charities and pressure groups insist that the crime is grossly under-reported, as you might expect them to do. Where did all this stuff come from, the gorging and puking and starving, and the lacerated wrists and the empty pill bottle?

We have let them down, the children – and the nonces, for once, are not guilty. Not let them down materially, because even the poorest child in the country today has more, far more, in material terms, than did the poorest child forty years ago. In real terms, the income his guardians, whoever the fuck they are, receive is much greater than would have been the case in 1965, say (when his guardians would have been referred to, more or less accurately, as 'parents'). Children today have more food, more clothes, more stuff. Much more stuff; maybe in some cases more stuff than they know what to do with. They may experience relative poverty more – indeed, they unquestionably do, seeing that the richest and the poorest of us are now separated by a gulf so wide it appears unbridgeable. But they experience absolute poverty to far less an extent.

Ironically, you might think, one of the problems facing kids these days – one of the things we all bang on about – is at least partly caused by a greater absolute affluence: obesity. I was in Sunderland not so long ago, working on another feature for the *Sunday Times*, and was obliged to visit a few junior schools. Fuck me, the kids were fat. Two thirds of them were what you might call overweight, while a good third were really morbidly obese, puffy-faced, narrow-eyed, flabby, panting Mackems, running around on their little trotters after a ball in the gym, bless them all. All of them harbouring a sugar 'n' salt jones which came from a diet of fast, brown food – sometimes given to them by the school, occasionally prepared for them at home, but more often than not bought from some high-street franchise: burger and fries, nuggets and fries, pizza. We know all this, it is well documented, and various commendable do-gooding sorts, such as Jamie Oliver, have tried to address it, without much success. And it's boring to go on about. When I was a kid there was a strict proportion of one fat kid per class, and he was usually fat for glandular reasons and was bullied relentlessly. I am not suggesting that this was a good thing.

As a short digression, some people – absolutists – get angry when you suggest that obesity is partly a function of affluence. It suggests that somehow the parents are to blame, rather than society. And yet it is patently clear: prepared convenience foods are, in general, more expensive than uncooked and unprepared vegetables and many kinds of meat. Crisps and burgers are not especially cheap. I was allowed crisps as a kid about once a fortnight, as a treat – not because they were bad for me, but because they were costly; they were surplus to the family budget. Ditto, of course, sweets and fizzy drinks. Like William Hague, I remember the 'fizzy pop' man doing his rounds when I was a very young kid in South London. It was a Corona lorry, and the bloke would knock at the door to be told almost always that we didn't require anything, thank you. And even when we did buy something, on vanishingly rare occasions, it was bloody lemonade rather than what I wanted, Cream Soda. I had tasted Cream Soda once, and could not believe that anything could be so wonderful. I'd been bought it from some sort of stall, in Crayford.

It is also patently clear that prepared fast food, the cooked stuff on which that idiot Osborne was determined to impose VAT, is much more expensive than food you prepare yourself. There are one or two exceptions – the McDonald's cheeseburger at £0.99 seems to me very good value indeed, and it does a reasonable job of filling you up. But as a rule, prepared fast food consisting of decent ingredients is much dearer than the stuff you would make at home. There are many, many more food outlets on our high streets than was the case when I was a kid (or even a young adult), which suggests that an awfully high percentage of us are prepared to fork out, that we have the money to spend.

This was certainly not true thirty or forty years ago. As a kid I remember eating out perhaps seven or eight times in total between the ages of five and fifteen, and this was usually in cheapo cafés, no licence. When I was about fourteen, and we were on a day trip to York, I pestered and pestered my parents to let me try a Chinese meal for lunch. I had never had any kind of foreign food, not even Italian, unless you count Heinz spaghetti hoops. Like many of their generation, my parents thought all foreign food was evil. But, remarkably, my father – looking worried – consented to this suggestion, and rather nervously we went inside a Chinese restaurant in that bastion of oriental cuisine, York. My mother waited outside on a seat. The waiter brought the menu, and my father and I looked at it long and hard and wondered what the hell it was all about, and then we both ordered steak-and-kidney pie and chips. Still, I had some lychees for dessert. That was my first Chinese meal, and my father's first and last.

At least half a dozen, maybe more, years earlier, my father, with much greater enthusiasm, took me into a Wimpy burger bar which had just opened in the Broadway, Bexleyheath, and he had a burger with some chips and I had some sort of frankfurter, I think. Again, my mother waited outside on a seat. I can remember four other meals I had out with my parents back in those days, but I think I might begin to bore you. But it was a very big deal indeed, eating out back then, even at really cheap places. Even on holiday, when meals were prepared by the side of a very busy road on the Primus stove, or consisted of shockingly dull salads, which I hated. People didn't eat out, except for special occasions. By 'people' I don't mean Cameron and Osborne's families, or those people who *have had their struggles too*, I mean the bulk of the population, the rest of us. But now the pizza restaurants, the burger bars, are crammed full every hour of the day. It seems, to me, pointless to deny that one of the causes of obesity in the young is that fast food and ready meals are more easily available today than they were half a century back, and that people can more easily afford them.

There are, of course, plenty of other reasons why people eat this awful gut-racking shit. We have less time these days; the kids get fed the stuff at school and develop an addiction to it; we wish to spend more of our time on leisure pursuits – watching TV, masturbating to pornography on the internet, getting drunk – than preparing meals. And women go out to work, whereas once they stayed at home and cooked. (Listen, absolutists; I am not saying they SHOULD stay at home and cook, or anything like that. I am just saying that it is probably a contributory cause of kids having bad diets. Not the main cause, or even in the top five. Just one of them. It doesn't mean I think women should stay at home and cook. Do you understand that point?)

I remember too the early convenience foods: the crispy pancakes filled with a sort of cheesy ejaculate, the pizzas with spongy bases and a dried-up gobbet of sugary tomato sauce on the top, the boil-in-the-bag blocks of fish in livid uranium sauce, the dried reconstituted bits of beef which, when you added water, magically became 'stroganoff'. We went for that stuff, a bit, in the early to mid-1970s. We had a little more money then, we were better off. My father even started brewing his own wine, which was left to ferment, or something, upstairs in the airing cupboard. Jesus fucking Christ. I wish you could have tried my dad's 'Sauterne', a sort of acrid soup with a faint aftertaste of rotting eggs. Thinking about it makes me gag, reflexively, and also miss him even more. But the brewing of wine was a hint that things were looking up, I suppose. Later, he stopped brewing wine and started buying the stuff, in bottles, from shops. We drank, on average, half a bottle a week, with Sunday dinner. Liebfraumilch and Entre-Deux-Mers. I was pushing sixteen by that point.

So, the kids are fat. Never mind. There are worse things kids can be, such as nonced or dead. But the obesity problem is interesting because, indirectly, it points us towards two of the areas where I think we have let the kids down, where we have compromised their lives.

I remember the headmaster of some comp talking about the effect Jamie Oliver had wrought on his pupils. It was one of those schools that the chef had visited with the television cameras, to show that nutritious meals that were attractive to the kids could be provided cheaply; it needn't all be pizza and burgers. It might even have been that school in Rotherham where furious *Untermensch* harridans were seen pushing pies through the school railings to their saturated-fats-deprived offspring. I forget. But anyway, this educationalist said he thought that what Jamie had done was all very good and laudable, and it was nice to see the kids tucking into penne with courgettes or what have you, and this stuff was still available on the school menu – but that now Jamie had gone, the kids much preferred to choose pizza for their lunches. Which, he said, was disappointing. We are back with that obese Welsh girl from the earlier chapter, the one who was the size of a fucking planet and whose house had to be demolished to get her to hospital. Her parents did not wish to regulate the amount of food she had too rigorously, because it somehow seemed an intrusion. But children are not, in general, capable of making sensible decisions which impact upon their future. They make decisions based upon the here and now. They are not old enough to take the long-term view. And the appropriate response to that 'disappointed' head teacher is this: don't offer them fucking pizza, then, you halfwit. That will assuage your disappointment immediately. Or at least that particular disappointment. You may have others, of course, which I cannot at this moment in time help you with.

Or take this example, from forty-odd years ago – roughly when it all began, this business. The headmaster of my junior school in Middlesbrough was taking a bunch of us older kids for a walk, a couple of miles to Stewart Park, with its lolloping wallabies and rather forbidding lake. It was a warm day in July 1970, not long before the end of the school year. It might even have been the last day of term. The next school year we would be attending a brand-new junior school that we had watched, with some excitement, being built adjacent to our own. The old school would be taken over by the under-eights. Every day we saw this smart new edifice growing before our eyes, and heard rumours about a cool sports hall and lots of light and air. On the walk, one of us asked the head, Mr Watson, what the classrooms in the new building were like.

'Oh, there aren't any classrooms, as such,' he said. We took this in, slowly.

'Well, where will we have lessons, then?'

Mr Watson smiled. 'There will be no formal lessons, as such,' he said. 'There will be an informal maths area, and an English area, and a crafts area, and so on. And the idea is that you will go to these areas when you feel you need to learn some maths, or English, or what have you.'

'When we FEEL we need to learn some maths?'

'Yes, that's right. There will be no set times for any subjects. You will be able to choose.'

I thought he was taking the piss. But he seemed perfectly serious. I remember asking him something like the following: 'What if we never feel the need to learn some maths? What if we instead feel the need simply to play football all day, every day?'

He smiled down at me. 'Oh,' he said, 'well if that's the case, you'll play football every day. But I don't think that will happen.'

Beginning in September, I played football pretty much all day, every day, for a school year. I even got in the district or county team, I got so good at it. I can still keep a ball up in the air indefinitely, even now. All my friends did the same. I did no maths whatsoever for ten months. I just, y'know, never felt the need. And nor did anyone else.

Actually, I say I did no maths at all – that is not quite right. I took the 11-plus in spring 1971, and passed, which supposedly meant I would be going to a grammar school (in fact, it changed to a comp the day I arrived, I think). Anyway, one morning one of the teachers, a chap called Mr Duncan, corralled a bunch of us who had passed the 11-plus and told us he was going to teach us some of the maths we would have to know when we got to our serious new school. 'Nah, we're playing football,' we told him, but to no avail. 'You're coming with me,' he said, 'like it or not.' He took us not to the open-plan maths area – which you could drift away from whenever you got bored – but to the school's only closed-off room with a proper door, the music room. And he shut the door firmly and taught us maths all morning. It was, like, so unjust and so boring. One maths lesson in ten months. I was shit at maths all the way through secondary school. But well done, Duncan.

We are back with Richard Hoggart and that 'obsessive avoidance of judgments of quality', I guess. Except that if this is injurious for society as a whole, and redolent of a sort of existential confusion, it is doubly, triply, so when applied to children. And yet it has been the dominant paradigm in education – and, to a lesser extent, the home – for the last fifty years. 'Children,' as the very counter-cultural novelist Heinrich Böll put it, 'are civilians too.' Well, sure. But shifting the burden of responsibility onto children to know, at every stage, what is best for themselves is an absurdity and unjust, as well as being a cop-out. We may not mourn those long days of kids pinioned to desks learning everything by rote, and regurgitating that knowledge in arid and stressful exams; but there must be some middle way. Examinations, as has already been mentioned, have shifted from being based on knowledge acquired to the juvenile interpretation of phenomena, with the consequence that the children may not know much about anything, but they know what they think. Factual stuff, such as grammar and spelling, is no longer considered especially important – indeed, to correct a child's spelling might lower his or her self-esteem in some way, which of course is the worst of all possible scenarios. Facts are less important than how the child feels. And as this paradigm has persisted, so the country has slipped lower and lower down the education tables, from having been among the best in the world, to slipping out of the top twenty. I do not really care about that, although it is a useful indicator of something or other. It is the rest of the stuff, the attendant consequences, which bother me more. Such as these:

- Children leaving school know less stuff. Both potential employers and university clearing houses bemoan the illiteracy and innumeracy of school-leavers. Their basic lack of knowledge, their ignorance. Employers use this, sometimes, as an excuse for taking on foreign workers, especially from what we used to call Eastern Europe.
- The stock and status of teachers has fallen. From being figures of authority, who must be respected, and who inculcated knowledge in their charges, they have too often become classroom entertainers, clowns, and, at worst, 'mates' with their students. It is often remarked upon – usually by teachers – that parents these days tend always to take their child's side in disputes with the school. The status of teachers must have receded, then, because it was not ever thus. When I was at school, my parents were implacable in supporting the school whenever I might have had a gripe or a moan. Indeed, I rarely griped or moaned about being caned, or held in detention, because it would be assumed without question that I had got all I deserved, and I would probably face some subsequent sanction at home for having blabbed about it. But if the teachers are no longer figures of authority, in the old-fashioned sense, why should the parents take any notice of them? If the teachers treat the kids as equals, then in disputes

the parents are bound to pay little heed to what the teachers say. It is their word against that of their offspring, and their word has no more force than that of a child. The teachers we most respected as kids, incidentally, engendered a certain fear among us, a foreboding. I suppose you could call it the juvenile equivalent of 'respect'. I do not think that teachers are encouraged to develop that sort of persona any more. All of this has been exacerbated by the constraints placed upon teachers who need to discipline children: today, the vaguest graze of an arm across a child's shoulder can provoke a charge of assault. The recourses left to teachers to deal with problem kids are now gossamer thin, and transgression sees them kicked out of a job and possibly prosecuted. They are, then, terrified of their charges. But in any case, who are they, these 'mates', these clowns, these factotums, to even contemplate disciplining a child?

- The children – the students – emerge, as a consequence, with a highly developed, perhaps unreal, sense of entitlement. They have not been corrected; they have instead been indulged. The world, later, will come as a shock to them, I think.

- If their teachers are not qualified to tell them stuff, to correct them, to let them know in uncertain times what is right and wrong, then surely their parents are even less qualified? Why take any notice of them? The winnowing away of authority from teachers subtly subverts all attempts by adults to correct, admonish, inculcate, direct.

- The removal of any element of competition from academic study – i.e., those class lists which show how shit you are at, for example, maths, because you came twenty-seventh out of thirty-two – suggests to pupils that the world beyond school is an amenable consensus where your lack of ability will not matter one bit, it will be gently and invisibly assuaged, it will not count against you. This is a delusion, and it is demotivating. It is even more demotivating for the least able kids; they are consoled in their uselessness and not encouraged to improve.

- Learning stuff, lots of stuff, can be very boring. But the very act of doing so also inculcates the notion of discipline, and the realisation that sometimes it is a very good thing to suffer boredom for a while in order to benefit later. In other words, it reinforces the notion of deferred gratification, and sacrifice for future good.

- It is the poorest kids who suffer most from this modernist approach to education. Middle-class children have the amenities, the infrastructure, at home to compensate. The poorest kids depend upon school as their sole conduit of learning. A policy, or ideology, designed to improve the chances of the least well-off has had the result of penalising them still further. This is probably the most important of all the objections I have raised.

OK, I overstate the case a little. But it is still a strong case, for all that. An ideology introduced, partly via the various educational reforms of the 1960s, has conveniently transferred the burden that we, as adults, bear towards our children, and placed it on the shoulders of the children themselves. It was a consequence, one supposes, of an often laudable anti-authoritarian sentiment which permeated much of society and which found those old qualities of obedience and discipline and deference and hierarchy ludicrous and eminently disposable. And a similar fracturing of our apparent ability to discern between right or wrong – these derogations merging, for a while imperceptibly. A possible consequence, as I have mentioned before, of the gradual erosion from the memory of the great rights and wrongs of the Second World War, replaced by the subtler distinctions of the Cold War. And the philosophies which were attendant upon that change, the unchallenged rise of the subjective, the suspicion that everything was a refraction of a refraction of reality, and of the truth, insofar as such a thing exists at all.

What has happened in the education system has happened, too, across society; we have been propelled in a direction which, at first, may have been the right direction – but has long since ceased to be so. It has gone too far.

As a democratic society (and as even in some undemocratic societies) we are at the mercies of ideologies which suddenly achieve ascendancy and then grab us by the throat and will not leave us alone, dragging us ever further towards the outer reaches of their respective programmes, making a fetish out of an idea, imbuing the institutions of society with an implacable absolutism and the requirement to effect wholesale change or revolution – when all that was needed, really, was a gentle tap on the tiller. Right-wing ideologies (privatisation, monetarism, the glory of acquisitiveness, deregulation) every bit as much as left-wing ideologies. Give the man credit, Marx – or Hegel – was right in this regard: society really does progress through that unholy trinity of thesis, antithesis, synthesis, even if it is not to a final dénouement which Marx would have envisaged, let alone approved of. But we wait so long for that blessed synthesis. We wait so long for the intellectual fury to be spent, to be doused by the mental blather of its own extremes, and to be gently absorbed. There is no end to ideologies, Mr Fukuyama. They will keep on coming.

Or perhaps all of that is rubbish, the stuff about ideology – the bits where I intended to look for a deeper meaning to this bestowal, upon our kids, of the burden of actually bringing themselves up, of deciding everything for themselves when they are palpably ill-equipped to do so. Perhaps it is just more evidence of a sort of epic laziness on our part, and a general diminishing of our collective involvement in their lives. After all, as I've mentioned before, some of us (including me) now consider it perfectly reasonable to absent ourselves mostly, or almost entirely, from their lives, as a consequence of divorce or just that thing, 'break-up'. Something, we tell ourselves, which was quite beyond our control and will not necessarily impinge upon the kids – although it does, it does. Of course it does.

But something else is going wrong, alongside the stuff with the teachers, something attitudinal, about how we see them, the kids. A short while ago UNICEF carried out a survey of well-developed Western countries in an effort to see how happy the kids were. A total of twenty-one countries were ranked according to the happiness levels of their children, and the UK came twenty-first. The problem, it seemed, was the material well-being of our children, something I mentioned earlier. Somehow the British kids had acquired from us British adults that desperate ambition to acquire and consume, and were sickened and distraught when they were not enabled to do so. As UNICEF put it, the UK parents felt under 'permanent pressure' to ply their offspring with attractive consumer durables – Wiis and Xboxes and the like – way beyond that which was expected in even more affluent countries than ours, such as the Netherlands (where, incidentally, the children were happiest) and Denmark. British kids, then, are squeezed by ideologies from the left and the right. From the left: you are your own masters, sort out right from wrong and take no shit from supposed figures of authority. From the right: live, consume, die.

In other ways too, the kids are fobbed off. They are assuaged and coddled by corporations, in lieu of a parent. Expensive, pre-packaged entertainment too often takes the place of low-tech interaction, i.e. what we might call human beings talking to one another without the intercession of a mouse. The children these days burrow right down in their dank, smeggy pits with Grand Theft Auto and blast away with their guns at those whores, blam blam blam. They may not know what whores are, whether or not whores are, on balance, a good thing; they just know that to blast the fuck out of them gives them extra points, so blam blam blam they go on their little consoles, finger jabbing away like billy-o, the points totting up on the scorecard.

And on a related point, one which has not been the subject of a UNICEF report, so far as I am aware, there is that other thing we have withheld from our children these last forty years or so, kept back from them, terrified of what it might do to them: boredom. It is a grossly underrated thing, boredom. The act of being bored imposes upon the bored person the requirement to think for himself. Or herself. Almost always as a child I was left in a situation where boredom was a distinct possibility, if not a certainty. There were no computer games, or mobile phones. Nor did my parents have the money to buy them for me even if they had been available. Children's TV began at ten to five on a weekday and ended, perversely, at twenty to six with five minutes of sub-toddler fare – *The Magic Roundabout* or *Hector's House*. You remember Hector, a floppy-eared lugubrious dog whom I always hated, forever taunted by some hugely irritating French cat. The rest of the day was a lacuna; if not filled by school, then a sea, a sea of potential boredom. For the under-tens there was nothing at all to fill the time – they were left to their own devices. And that was good. Leaving kids to their own devices like that is beneficial, stimulatory, even exciting. The stuff you make up, when left alone for long enough! The games you create, the worlds you inhabit! But we run in fear from this now, the idea that the kids might suddenly announce, in that singularly irritating monotone whine, 'I'm bored!' Instead we arrange stuff for them, their timetables are crammed with scheduled things, we franchise out their imaginations, we wrench from them the possibility of independent discovery. And of course we do this partly because we fear for them. We do not wish for them to be bored, of course, and we think that we can buy boredom from them with consumer durables, corporate entertainment and early-evening courses in taekwondo.

Also we worry that if they are bored, they will wander off, they will be at risk. Somewhere just beyond the hedge at the bottom of the garden, Jimmy Savile is waiting with a bag of sweeties or the drooled promise of puppies. Or maybe just a non-nonce car, driven too fast by a pissed imbecile, maybe it is that which frightens the parents. Either way, we excise from them the terrible, minuscule, possibility of risk – and so 10 per cent of them start puking up their dinners in the toilet, another four thousand a year try to kill themselves, and two thirds of the rest just pig out, farting, on the sofa in front of *The Simpsons* – cocooned and torpid. You cannot excise those twin terrors, risk and boredom, from their lives, and it is a very bad thing to try to do so. We have got it the wrong way around. At school they should learn the value of discipline and schedule, at home they should be allowed to run loose a little. And if the parents worry, then so be it.

8

And All Women Agree With Me About This

K – 'What does today's woman want? That's the big one.'

E – 'I agree. It's the big one all right. It's the what-do-you-call ...'

K – 'Or put another way, what do today's women think they want versus what do they really deep down want.'

E – 'Or what do they think they're supposed to want.'

David Foster Wallace,
Brief Interviews with Hideous Men

I have been racking my brains, trying to think of a way to outdo Kenneth Clarke MP, the one-time Justice Secretary. It has not been easy. I wanted a title for this chapter that would annoy more women than Ken's statement, made on BBC Radio Four's *Woman's Hour*, that 'most women agree with me about this'. He had been addressing the subject of rape, and having delivered himself of a number of statements with which quite possibly not a single woman in the country agreed, he said that thing: 'And most women agree with me about this.' It struck me then that even if they had agreed with him about rape, and how there are different kinds of rape – sort of nice rape and nasty rape – they would have immediately changed their minds as soon as he said, 'And most women agree with me about this.' Even if he had said it about something pretty anodyne, such as cheese, as in 'Cheddar is the tastiest kind of British cheese, and most women agree with me about this,' I suspect it would have put women's backs up. I don't want to generalise, but they really hate that kind of presumption, women, in my experience. And when it refers to something which women believe is their exclusive domain, such as rape, say, or shoes, it really gets their fucking goat. Anyway, I thought about this for a long while, and the only thing I could come up with that was better than Ken's comment was to replace the word 'most' with 'all'. It's not hugely inventive, is it?

It was a strategic thing, a tactical thing. I thought that if I gave the chapter a title that would immediately piss women off, then if they read on they might slowly be won over by my argument, and think at the end, well actually I do agree with him, a bit, despite that chapter heading – it wasn't quite as bad as I expected. I'm still of the opinion that on the whole it's for the best if men do not involve themselves too deeply in women's issues, on the grounds that we may well not know what the fuck we are talking about. It seems, again, a bit presumptuous. A bit patrician. So I thought, well, I'm on a hiding to nothing here anyway, so let me try something strategic and tactical. Who knows, it might work. Hit them with a sort of double bluff. I've tried this before, writing about women's issues, and it didn't work, and I had to make an apology and stuff. I don't suppose it will work this time.

Because there is a lot of absolutism about here, which makes rational and objective discussion a little tricksy. And to tell you the truth, I wasn't even aiming for rational and objective. In fact, let's ban the words 'rational' and 'objective' from this discussion, because I'm never convinced that they exist anyway, as free-standing independent entities. They are rarely free-standing entities; they are contingent, and more like, say, a conservatory than a shed. Or a lean-to. On this subject, I am quite a modernist.

Nor is my own family much help in this conundrum. Typical of their age and class in so many ways, on gender stuff they were slightly different. To be sure, my mother gave up her job – she was an accounts clerk – for eight years to look after me, while my dad went on working. That, so far, is typical. And she had been ill-educated, a consequence of the war, her gender, her class and so on. She put herself through night school with my dad's encouragement, doing a bunch of O-levels and then A-levels; sometimes I used to go with her and sit at the back of the class writing poems and stories which the poor bastard of a teacher felt duty-bound to mark. I was six or seven at the time, a precocious and bumptious little brat. But self-improvement was a big thing with my mother, along with the grinding annoyance that women did not get a fair crack of the whip and that there were a lot of spastically useless men around, running things. My father, unusually for those days, agreed entirely, despite the fact that his own northern, Methodist background was wholly and exclusively patriarchal. He was an insular and shy man, reserved and rather placid, and I think he found himself bowled over, swept away, by my mum's exuberance and passion, and was inclined therefore simply to concur with her. I don't think that ideology played much of a part in my father's unusually supportive role, despite his (early) adherence to the Labour Party. Love and a desire for quietude, maybe, and also pragmatism. For the household chores were shared equally, or pretty close to equally: my father did a good 70 per cent of the cooking, half of the ironing, half of the laundry, and at least half of the childcare. He never dusted, though. I never once saw him with a duster.

But then again, maybe it was ideological after all, because I remember my father being enraged, infuriated – and he was very difficult to rouse to anger – when the Midland Bank rang him up to tell him that his wife had tried to withdraw £30 from their joint account, and was this OK with him? They rang him at work. Those were the days, huh. But even then, I think it was probably more that he just felt for my mother in her abject humiliation, standing before the little shit of a teller in the Middlesbrough Midland branch, keeping her standing there waiting with the murmuring queue growing behind while he rang her husband to check that she should be allowed to withdraw money from her own fucking account. She had cried when she got home; she had been mortified, and felt like a criminal. I remember that evening. I remember thinking, 'That is how the world is with me, a child. The world must think women are children too.' My dad gave the teller a ferocious mouthful, and the next day they switched their custom to the National Westminster Bank – *Venceremos!* Direct action! I'm sure the Nat West was a much more enlightened institution. They should have gone with the Co-op, of course.

But that was how it was then – as women of a certain age will tell you, as my mum would tell you, were she still alive to do so. Women were, as the gobbier of them rightly put it, second-class citizens, their views considered hilarious or inconsequential, utterly absent from any and all decision-making processes, regarded as suspicious if they were seen alone in public, valued solely for their child-rearing abilities and deprived, in most homes, of financial independence or even jurisdiction. Those who worked – and only a minority worked until that great shift in the middle of the 1970s – constituted a secondary or auxiliary labour force characterised by low skill, low pay and low aspiration. They waited longer than men for promotion, if they were promoted at all. They were paid much less than men for doing precisely the same jobs (an odd quirk which continues, in some areas, to this day), and were discriminated against relentlessly and institutionally.

At school they lagged behind boys. Teachers still devoted the majority of their attention to boys, despite a plethora of studies showing that they were ignoring the girls. There was no career map for them: shop work, factory work or housework – that's your lot. In my own school, a decent comprehensive with a Labour councillor, Joe Morgan, as headmaster, kids for the first three years had two hours a week of metalwork, if you were a boy, or domestic science if you were a girl. No choice in the matter. I would much rather have done domestic science – i.e. cooking – but there we are. Nor were girls allowed to study what was then called Technical Drawing, but which morphed into Design and Technology. It was very clear: if you were a boy, you were almost certainly headed for either Blackett & Hutton's steel mill in town, or British Steel at Redcar three or four miles away. If you were a girl, you were going to be a housewife. No argument. And that was still the case in the late 1970s – even after Blackett & Hutton had pretty much closed down.

You know this – or you know most of it, leastways. If you had to make a list of stuff that changed for the better between 1950 and 2000 – and there are a lot of things on that list – then the changed status of women in society would probably come top. Which is not to say that things are right now; they are not. All of this needs to be said, and then said again, and then sort of shouted in a weird strangulated yelp, because whatever caveats there are, they are no more than caveats. Good stuff happens, but sometimes as a consequence of good stuff happening, bad stuff happens too. Or questionable stuff. Such is the purblind absolutism of our times – and especially with regard to this issue, much as it is with anything connected to race – that the law of unintended consequences is usually swatted away, and anyone who suggests that bad stuff might have happened, by accident, unhappily by chance, is simply dismissed as reactionary (which may sometimes be true) and more usually just wrong. The bad stuff DIDN'T happen at all, we are enjoined to believe – it didn't, it didn't, it DIDN'T.

But it did, like it or not.

The 1970 Equal Pay Act eased women's workplace struggles a little, although far from entirely – there were still, you know, loopholes. Greater ease of divorce enabled women to have a little more of a sense of independence: they were not tied, ineluctably, to some perpetually farting and abusive halfwit, as they had been in times gone by. There was the intimation, then, of freedom, of a kind – legalistic, social, cultural and financial. The march of women into the workforce had begun. In 1971, only 40 per cent of women worked; today the figure is more than 75 per cent. This is an enormous change in society, almost beyond imagining – and it happened largely over twenty years, up to about 1993, when the whole thing slowed and sort of plateaued. And this was good for women, and therefore, by extension, good for society, both morally and financially – there is no argument from this quarter on that particular score. But it is inconceivable that such a momentous change could happen without there being a downside, without there being losers, without society – or parts of it – suffering in one way or another.

The most obvious losers, initially, were men, or some men. If a vast number of women are going to join a workforce, then unless the economy expands at the same rate, a whole bunch of men are going to be put out of a job. And, of course, that's what happened: male employment declined from 93 per cent in 1971 to 75 per cent in 1993. Who cares? A small price to pay for the partial emancipation of half of our nation's people. Yes, I'm with you, I agree. But, just for a moment, who were the men who were put out of work? Were they the clever, well-educated, high-earning men? No, of course not. Women were still largely barred from those jobs, anyway, because of hidden or not so hidden discriminations. Instead they were the men down at the bottom of the employment ladder, those who had been earning the lowest wages and were now earning no wages at all. And so you began to see an – at first – subtle distancing between the comparatively well-off and the really not very well-off at all, the really fucked-up poor. Still, we are all agreed, small price to pay, etc.

In some cases women took up the slack for their families: there was only one wage earner, and, for the first time, it was the woman. But in the majority of cases that is not what happened. Women who were employed tended to marry men who were employed too. This is something called assortative mating, of a kind, and it is also very much down to the law of unintended consequences. It is not what we expected, or hoped, would happen, and we had not given much of a thought to it. The result then was an even greater financial division between the haves – even if they did not have that much, in the great scheme of things – and the have-nots. Suddenly there were lots of families bringing in two incomes, and lots of other families bringing in no income at all. Still, nobody is arguing that this migration from the home to the workplace was a Bad Thing overall. It wasn't, it's just that there were – you know – caveats attending the glory. None of them the fault of women.

And it is true that women were – and still are – concentrated in the lowest-paid of occupations – at first, briefly, in the manufacturing and secretarial sectors; only later did they begin their slow and tentative march into the professional and managerial classes. Still largely a secondary labour force, as they had been during the war, mindlessly fitting those fuses to bombs in terrifying subterranean plants rife with the whiff of sulphur and cordite and heavy metals and oestrogen.

As an example of these unintended consequences, we already have a greater disparity between the moderately well-off and the really poor, a deeper division within society, a problem that will itself one day need to be addressed. And then there were the kids.

Who looks after the kids, then, if Mum and Dad are both at work? Someone does, probably; someone else. Previously, in working-class communities, the extended family. But not any more. Families became isolated, as people moved to where the work was. They employed independent childcare, nannies and so on, at substantial cost. Eventually nannies would come to cost more than one or both parents could possibly hope to afford. The middle classes, meanwhile, called them au pairs, and paid them fuck-all, cash in hand. Some girl, latterly called Svetlana, and probably quite fit. But I digress – what happened to the children?

On the whole, the kids did not do so well at all. According to one study published recently by the leftish Joseph Rowntree Foundation, and carried out by the leftish Institute for Social and Economic Research, they were unhappy and underachieving. The children born in 1970 to working mothers were much more likely to fail educationally, more likely to be unemployed, more likely to suffer psychiatric problems or mental stress than those born to mums who stayed at home and looked after their children. Irritatingly, the amount of time a dad was at home with the kids mattered not one jot. It was the mother who was important. There may well be some explanation as to why the father was less important as a – what is it called? – care-giver. Perhaps he was not pulling his weight, dad – any of the dads among all those people (more than 1,200) who were studied. You can't tell with dads, you can't trust them. Maybe even though he was at home he just lay on the sofa watching golf or repeats of *Top Gear* and let the kids run riot. I don't know. The people who did the survey didn't include stuff like that. Incidentally, I have not cherrypicked this survey: the overwhelming majority of longitudinal studies and surveys on the subject suggest that kids whose mums went out to work perform more poorly at school and end up in worse jobs and are sometimes a bit doolally, you know, in the head. I haven't seen one longitudinal study which would suggest otherwise. I have seen a few pieces which, devoid of evidence, suggest that this needn't be so, mind.

More unintended consequences, then. But these are still just caveats. This is not an argument for women to stop working. It is just caveats.

Trouble is, it's hard to get away with saying them. An awful lot of people on the liberal faux left take the view that women's rights are not nearly advanced enough now (which may well be right), and that there have been simply no negative consequences, ever, to have come from those rights which have been already won. They do not shrug their shoulders and say, 'Yes, well that may be so, and it's a problem we should probably address one of these fine days, but it does not remotely suggest that it was wrong for women to make that advancement into the workplace.' That would be the sort of sensible answer – and all women agree with me about that. But they do not say it. They will fight tooth and nail to deny all and any reports which suggest, even for a second, that there may have been negative consequences to an otherwise wholly laudable social development. I suppose you could call it a post-Leninist stance, although that does a disservice to the late Vladimir Ilyich, who was many things but certainly not a fucking moron. Children are no worse off as a consequence of women going out to work, and there's an end to it. There has been no increased disparity in wealth in society as a consequence of women going out to work, and there's an end to it. I have even heard liberals assert, with great and righteous conviction, that the huge increase in the number of women going to work did not remotely mean that there were fewer jobs around for men. Which is sort of like arguing that two plus two equals three. But no, no, that would be a reactionary observation. How dare you, etc. This sort of mental, purblind absolutism is one of the curses of our age, and it is far more a fault that one associates with the metro faux left than with any other shade of political opinion.

Thing is, they will stick to this line – that these negative consequences simply have not occurred – even as they are arguing (rightly) for better childcare for mums and families. Because one of the possible answers to this increasing problem is proper, structured, regular, affordable childcare available to all. I can see that. It would be expensive, but not impossible, even if the right is at this moment trying to chew away at the notion of paid maternity leave and nursery care at all. But why would you argue for better health care if everything at home is tickety-boo and the kids are all right? Why would you need it?

More unintended consequences. It was noticed that women

who had children suffered in their careers, or lost them altogether. They went off, they had a kid, they came back – if at all – very slowly, taking baby steps, losing all that credit and experience they had built up with their companies. Employers were frequently unsympathetic to them having children at all, so the women left their jobs, or were sacked. New Labour, in a commendable attempt to address this particular problem, introduced a raft of changes which guaranteed women statutory maternity leave and the guarantee of their jobs back at the end of it. The maternity leave that was on offer still lagged behind the sort of deal that was available in some of the Scandinavian countries and Germany, but it was a step forward. A bunch of weeks on 90 per cent of full pay and then a bunch more on a thinnish rate – all the way up to fifty-two weeks, in the end. But mothers only. No paternity pay for dads. The dads could take a couple of weeks, at most, and a lot of employers looked a little darkly even at that. At the time this obvious, sexist, discrepancy was pointed out: you want dads to be better involved in childcare, to take their share of the burden – yet you ignore their role entirely. They get nothing. It is women who bear the burden, came the reply, and it is women therefore who must be properly compensated.

You can guess exactly what happened. Don't forget that, as we have seen, a high proportion of women who are in work have male partners who also work. If you are old enough you will remember the rise of the DINKIES, the double-income no-kids couples. Imagine that you are the man in a double-income partnership and your wife or girlfriend becomes pregnant. And you are not just a man, but a very, very new man who wants to take at least 50 per cent of the childcare burden upon himself, preferably more, although not breastfeeding just yet. Even so, you are impeccably liberal and supportive and open. What's more, your wife is doing much better in her job than you are in yours. She is in a more senior position, and she earns more money. You sit down to discuss, in a democratic and consensual manner, who should take time off work to look after the new baby – Oliver, or Olivia, whatever it might be – during that first year. All the evidence so far suggests that it should be you – the wages stuff, her seniority, your own political disposition, which means that you understand, in a very real sense, the sacrifices that women have made in the name of childbearing throughout history, the deaths, the confinements, the strangled careers, and you are determined that this will not happen following the advent of this particular child, given your willingness to subvert the tide of reactionary history. So there is no real argument. And indeed, as it transpires, there is no argument: when you place the facts upon the table, the two of you, she gets nearly a year off, some of it at her full salary (or close to it) and most of the rest of it at about £130 a week, whereas you get bugger-all. So the decision is made for you. A policy designed to improve the position of women in the workplace actually reinforces all those old notions about childcare which any self-respecting feminist believe should be challenged. And all women agree with me about this.

As a consequence of this obvious anomaly, the right has weighed in, demanding that maternity leave be scrapped. Sheila Lawlor, from the rightish thinktank Politeia, has argued for this under the hugely convincing pretext that it does not help women terribly much – but really, one suspects, because the business community does not like to fork out for maternity leave. The real answer would be absolutely equal leave for both father and mother, a policy which we are at last groping towards, very slowly. But some form of bone-headed and simplistic absolutism dictated the original policy. Incidentally, the countries with the highest standards of living in the world and the highest levels of that thing 'happiness' – your Scandies, largely – have equal leave for men and women. The more equal a society is, the fairer it is – on any number of issues – the more successful it is. Or maybe it's the other way around, and the success came first, before the fairness.

Are women happier now than they were thirty or forty years

ago? You would expect so. Yet the problems are not simply caused by the fact that women feel they have not attained full equality – although that is undoubtedly a factor – but also by not knowing what they should do with their lives, an uncertainty as to where their priorities lie. We will come back to this.

There has also been a hilarious reductivist feminism at work which seeks not merely equality of opportunity, but equality of outcome, everywhere, in everything, now. Every job should have an equal number of men and women doing it, from the bottom to the top. Some would argue that without this frantic bean-counting, it is impossible to provide true equality of opportunity. But it may run counter to what women themselves actually want; it may also fail to account for differences of aspiration between men and women, differences which may be learned or hard-wired. By bean-counting I mean the sort of reports which suggest that there are '6,000 women missing from top jobs' (Equalities Commission, 2007) and those which claim that thousands of women are missing from senior or boardroom jobs in the City of London – figures calculated simply by measuring the disparity in the number of men and the number of women holding such jobs. I have no doubt that, in some cases, maybe in many cases, women are still discriminated against. But isn't it possible that there are more men than women working in the City of London because, on average, a higher proportion of men than women have the inclination or the aptitude to work in the City of London? Perhaps most of those women are missing not because they have been prevented from taking up those jobs as a consequence of sexist practices, or a sexist society, but because they simply do not wish to do them? Which is not to deny that some may be put off by what they perceive, probably rightly, as a macho and sexist attitude among those insufferably bumptious little monkeys – it is simply to acknowledge that there may be other stuff in the equation too. Observations such as this are often seen as deeply reactionary; they come up against the fabulous absolutism that rules this entire discourse. It is true, I suppose, that three hundred years ago women were cautioned against getting themselves too much education, in case their brains exploded. And I can see why my argument, then, would seem to some to be scarcely more advanced, logically, than that. Yet is it not merely possible, but likely, that the sexes do differ, in what they want and what they're good at? Isn't it as clear as the differences that exist between them physically? Some of it, perhaps even much of it, may be down to conditioning, i.e. it may be imposed upon women. But isn't it likely – or if you're a feminist of the particularly reductivist variety, isn't it even possible – that some of those differences are inbuilt and immutable?

I don't want to get too enmired in the nurture vs. nature debate, although I suppose I already am, a bit. Thing is, it gets boring almost to the extent of being pointless, with the same stats flying hither and thither. We know that boys and girls differ hugely in the way they react to stuff, the different things they like and dislike, from the first few days after birth regardless if they are brought up for those first few days in a gender-neutral environment, where no assumptions are made either way, a bit as if the babies were in a Guardian editorial meeting. (Imagine spending your first few days on earth in a Guardian editorial meeting. Later, I suspect, a long way down the line, you would end up crouched in your local high street with a machine gun, picking off the shoppers, filled with an incoherent rage.) But either way those seem to be clear and simple genetic differences, hard-wired. The universality of this kind of gender division throughout every single known and documented society, from the smug pastry-stuffed Danes to not terribly 'progressive' people with poison blowdarts and a lifespan of about, oh I don't know, twenty-five, in Papua New Guinea, suggests this even more strongly. One or two evolutionary psychologists, approaching the matter from an avowedly feminist point of view, have tried to suggest that these differences are epigenetic rather than genetic. In other words, something environmental is needed to trigger this gene which begins to separate us along the lines of gender. Hell, maybe. But even if it's epigenetic, that gene needs to be there in the first place. But enough already.

Let's look instead at where we are now. Look at the way in which even in those institutions which are pretty much free of discrimination, men and women gravitate towards very different jobs. In general. Not exclusively, just on average. Take the National Health Service, which is about as pristine in this regard as it is possible to get. Indeed, more than 55 per cent of people studying for some sort of degree in medicine in Britain right now are women, and the proportion has been around or over the 50 per cent mark for a good decade. But how many of them end up being consultant surgeons? Almost 92 per cent of consultant surgeons are male, and this figure is not significantly shifting, or at least has not done so yet, despite enormous efforts to get women involved. But that's not all, because even within that narrow band of occupations – consultant surgeons – there is great variation. Women make up quite a healthy proportion of general surgeons – although of course nowhere near half – but a much smaller proportion of neurosurgeons; we are in the very low single figures here. This sort of disparity is reflected across a whole bunch of occupations: the more specific and constrained and singular a skill, the more likely it is that very few women will take it up. The more general or diffuse the talents required, the more likely that they will. Perhaps a problem here is that these specific skills take a very long time to train for? Maybe. Maybe that is part of it, but it is certainly not the whole of it. One very rare specimen, a female neurosurgeon, a woman called Helen Hernandes, was interviewed recently, and suggested that institutional sexism was not remotely a problem, and most certainly did not hold women back in her vocation; she suggested that this was an 'excuse'. That's a bit harsh; maybe it's less an excuse than simply a lack of inclination on the part of women. Maybe when you boil down the abilities, men in general are more likely to possess the requirements for being a neurosurgeon. Which is not to say that all men would be better neurosurgeons than all women – I would rather be treated, if my brain exploded, by Helen Hernandes than by, say, John Prescott. Merely that a greater proportion of men will show such a proclivity than will women.

Women, meanwhile, are making great inroads into what is arguably the most important part of the NHS: general practice. Right now some two thirds of GP trainees are women (which, perversely, is worrying the GMC, because they fear these women may flit off sometime soon to drop a sprog and we will be left with a dearth of family doctors). But again; it is the general versus the specific.

And not just that, but women may also be better at occupations which rely upon communications skills (such as, uh, listening). For example, an enormous proportion of speech therapists are women – in the US it is something like 92 per cent, and not much less over here. Why should women be drawn to speech therapy in such numbers rather than, say, thoracic surgery or radiology?

Or look at the subjects which the women of the future are choosing to take at school today. There have been hundreds and hundreds of studies, dating back at least thirty years, agonising over why so few women wish to become economists. Money has been ploughed into this problem, and at every level girls have been exhorted to take an interest in economics. It has not worked – and frankly I'm with the women on this one. An arid and abstruse and arrogant pseudo-science which is about as much use to mankind as astrology or phrenology, in my view, and I speak as someone who got an A-level in the fatuous subject – largely by quoting reams of *Das Kapital*, which I'd studied in private, as a preparatory measure for taking over the world. Still women show not the remotest interest. Only 30 per cent of A-level economics students are girls, and an uncannily high proportion of them drop out in the second year. The percentage of economics doctorates awarded to women – after all the decades of handwringing and articles in the press and pressure on schools and universities – 8 per cent. Exactly what it is for consultant surgeons, although I have not proven much of a correlation here. But that's after all those studies, all those recommendations, all that action to raise the number. Eight per cent.

And physics? Pretty much the same. Again, there has been enormous work over the decades to get girls more interested in science, and especially hard science such as maths and physics, as opposed to girly science like biology. Roughly 30 per cent of A-levels in physics are awarded to girls. Incidentally, 'girly science' is a technical term, and all women agree with me about this, as do all physicists.

There is something else going on here which makes one suspect that some of the various disparities, or maybe some of the causes of some of the various disparities, are not entirely a consequence of discrimination, overt or subconscious. You can begin to group together the stuff which women are, in general, good at, and the stuff which, in general, they are not. The key here being the words 'in general'. There are clear demarcations; it seems unlikely to me that they are all exclusively driven by conditioning or sexism.

But let's leave this tendentious issue aside; we will know the answers only when there is true equal opportunity for all, and we don't have that at the moment. More pertinent to me is this: are they happy, the women? Are they full of joy as a consequence of these relatively recently acquired freedoms and rights? They do not seem to be. Even more than the men, they are caught these days, strung out between two poles, unsure which way to turn. Job or kids? Am I betraying my kids by devoting myself to my career, or am I betraying myself and my gender by sacrificing my career to look after the kids? Is it enough to be at home, without earning, without making a mark? There is something narcissistic about the very question, a whiff of that self-actualisation stuff of the 1970s, the suggestion that it is never right to subordinate yourself; you must be a fully realised person.

Why must you be? Part of the problem is, once again, doubt and insecurity. Even if women were constrained, discriminated against and demonstrably second-class citizens in the 1960s and 1970s, they at least knew where their place was. They knew what was expected of them, and what they might expect for their own lives. That their place was subjugated is not remotely in question, nor, again – just to stress – would I suggest that the rights that have been afforded women over the last forty years were anything but entirely right and justified; in fact they do not go far enough. But as a species we thrive on certainty, on knowing where we are and what we are meant to do, on having clear lines of demarcation. For women, these easy, if terribly confining, certainties have gone. It is good that they have gone. I repeat, in case the point did not register: it is good that they have gone. But there are always unintended consequences.

9

Class

*I was not the one to invent lies: they were created in a society
divided by class and each of us inherited lies when we were born. It
is not by refusing to lie that we will abolish lies.*

Jean-Paul Sartre

The newish Archbishop of Canterbury is a man called Justin. This
is a hopeful sign, isn't it? If it's Justin today, it could well be Dustin
tomorrow, or Darren or Kaylon or Dappy. There is something
non-u about the name Justin, I reckon. Although, having said that,
the only other Justin I know went to public school – that's Justin
Webb, the TV and radio journalist and a sort of friend and colleague
of mine from way back when. And actually it transpires that this
first Justin I mentioned, Justin Welby, the new Archbishop of
Canterbury, went to a public school as well – Eton, as it happens.
Hell, who'd a thunk it!

Names can be deceiving. The great, if strange, French decon-
structionist Jacques Derrida once wrote a book about the defining
qualities of the names we are given, or those which are imposed
upon us. I think Jacques would have agreed with me that 'Justin', as
an Archbishop of Canterbury, is an anomaly, a quirk, a signifier of
something or other, something which should be deterministic but
somehow with Justin Welby turned out – in the end – not to be.
Because nonetheless, Justin went to Eton, not a comp in Rochdale.
The person most people expected to become Archbishop, when the

previous incumbent Rowan Williams announced his departure, was called 'John' and received his early education at a plain and simple village school near the rather awful Ugandan capital city of Kampala. In Kampala, giant marabou storks gather like hideous feral giant hoodies on the street corners, flapping with cumbersome menace around the steaming, foetid rubbish tips, the sort of birds you can imagine taking over when the world, or at least humanity, comes to an end. Those obsidian eyes filled with stupidity, and those sharp dangerous beaks. That's pretty much all I know, first hand, of Kampala. I was not there for long.

But in the end John didn't get the job, and Justin from Eton is now installed in Lambeth Palace. It didn't come as much of a shock to me – nor, I suppose, to most other people in the country, insofar as they gave a toss one way or the other as to who is the boss of this desiccated and fissiparous communion. Justin seemed, at first, at pains to play down his privileged background, insisting that he was comparatively 'thick' for a bishop, as if people might have imagined that there was a one-to-one relationship between gilded provenance and intellectual ability; but we already knew there isn't, because we have George Osborne as Chancellor of the Exchequer. The right-wing writer Charles Moore put it better, in the *Spectator*, suggesting, wittily and I suspect approvingly, that the Church of England was merely keeping in step with modern Britain, which at this time seemed to wish for Old Etonians to run all of its major institutions; or if not an Old Etonian then someone from a decent English public school – one of the good ones, not one of those rather *nouveau* cheap ones filled with too many earnest slitty-eyed East Asian kids and rife with drug abuse. This has been a very good decade so far for those who, like Moore, think it just and fitting that we be run by Old Etonians and Old Harrovians and Old Wellingtonians and Old – oh, fuck, I don't know, whatever the little gremlins who went to Repton are known as. Old Reptilians? They are back, running the show, hurrah.

So John didn't get the job, and he went off to write a column for the *Sun* instead. That's more like it, you might think – not so many public-school boys doing that sort of thing, are there? He is in a more amenable *milieu*, and it will be better for him in the end, he'll be in his element. Oh, but you'd be wrong, so wrong. Almost 70 per cent of top national newspaper columnists went to fee-paying schools, whereas this gilded elite, the expensively educated, comprise just 7 per cent of the population. Their hegemony within this industry is every bit as marked as it is within the Church of England. In fact, anywhere there is power, or dosh, the sons and daughters of the wealthy predominate. Columnist for a newspaper, Archbishop of Canterbury – both much, much, more likely if you went to private school.

I wish Justin well; it will not be an easy job. I do not hold against him his expensive education. It would be unChristian to do so, for a start, and I am still a Christian. Also, when dealing with individuals, with living and breathing human beings, this is what we are all enjoined to agree out of basic compassion and empathy: that it is wrong to hold their background against them; it is not their fault. And so we don't, as a rule – although we may have the odd snigger now and again when *samizdat* pictures of them as Oxbridge students cavorting in their fucking penguin suits emerge. (This hasn't happened with Justin. Yet.) But in general we are warned not to concentrate our annoyance, if there is annoyance, on the particular – save it for the broader point, we are told, the general principle of the need to improve social mobility; leave the individuals out of it. It's not Justin's fault that he went to Eton, is it? And so, as I say, we don't castigate him for it.

For fifty years or more we have conceded that it is not right to judge an individual by his background, that it is that lifeless and inanimate thing, the structure, the social system, which is to blame, not the individual – and by and large we have gone along with this fair-minded and decent injunction. Usually, of course, it is the privately educated but terribly, terribly liberal masters of ours who most fervently enjoin us to embrace this state of mind, not to be petty and bitter and cruel. And I'm sure they are right. So we don't blame the individual, we do as we are told and blame the system and hope something might be done about it, one day. We even sort of go along with them when they tell us that despite having attended a school which demands in excess of £30k per year in fees, from which they elided directly to Oxbridge, from which they elided to a job either facilitated directly by their parents, or indirectly via their provenance, and from which they elided to a position where they run the entire fucking country, that we should leave complaints of our own comparative poverty aside, because let me tell you, whatever you may think – *they have had their struggles too*. These individuals have also had to fight. Are they not human? Do they not bleed when you kick them in the head, or maybe the balls? Yes, they bleed, they hurt. We all struggle, we all have stuff to overcome. The truth is, we're all in it together, you see. That phrase ring a bell with you? We're all in it together.

You will see these special people who *have had their struggles too* on *Question Time* and *Newsnight*, and read them in your daily newspapers, shaking their heads sadly and saying it is quite wrong that such an enormous percentage of the top jobs in the country go to people like them who *have had their struggles too*. And something must be done about it, some mechanism must be put in place to ensure that people who have just – no italics – had their struggles are able to compete on an equal basis with people who *have had their struggles too*. And yes, of course, the person speaking is one of those who went to private school and is now head of the C of E or the BBC or Coopers & Lybrand or the Bar Council or the Tate or the Royal Opera House or Ofcom or Christ help us, whatever institution you care to mention – or, I forgot this, is perhaps the Prime Minister or the Chancellor or a member of the Cabinet – and while he feels that it is important that something should be done, right now, RIGHT

NOW, to level the playing field, so to speak, because social mobility is a Good Thing and the class system is a Bad Thing – he does not feel, on balance, that his own powerful sinecure is the direct consequence of an immensely privileged background. Nope, give the man credit – he's thought about it long and hard, and nothing could be further from the truth. He is one of those people who *have had their struggles too*, you see. He is there, in his position, because frankly *he is worth it*. He is the exception. He is not to be found in the statistics. His own elision to an important position was simply the consequence of, well, I suppose one would have to say individual brilliance, nothing more and nothing less. The statistics are shocking, of course, and oh dear God we need to improve social mobility – but those stats do not remotely implicate HIM. He is above and beyond them.

Everyone who is part of that small tranche of the population – 7 per cent, remember – who *have had their struggles too*, rather than, you know, actually struggled, thinks similarly, of course. All of them. If they didn't maintain that fiction, then they could hardly carry on, psychologically, with whatever it is they are doing – running the Bank of England, or the Arts Council, or what have you. So they all wish to do something about social mobility, but none of them thinks that their wealth and success is a consequence of privilege. This fiction is vital to stop them from being eaten up with guilt and self-doubt and madness, I suppose, no matter how useless they might be at their jobs. Or, for that matter, how good.

If you, reading this, are one of those people who *have had their struggles too*, try to understand that the thing that really annoys the rest of us is that you insist that you are one of those people who *have had their struggles too*. Just shut the fuck up about the struggle bit, please. It may be discombobulating, a bit of a let-down, it may grate on the palate, when a Sancerre is insufficiently chilled, but it is not what the rest of us, with respect, would categorise as 'a struggle'. Obviously, I'm sorry you had to put up with it, and I'm glad that you recovered in order to attain your current position in life – we're all very pleased about that, and we've booked a band and put out the bunting. But please, when it comes to struggle, you do not know the meaning. You may know the meaning of everything else, but you do not know THAT meaning. So on the struggle thing, just, y'know, *do* be quiet.

And let's be absolutely clear regarding the facts. As I say, people from fee-paying schools – the clearest and simplest indication of privilege that we have in this country – comprise about 7 per cent of the population. And in 2012 they also comprised 62 per cent of the diplomatic service, some 58 per cent of those working in the law – rising to 80 per cent when you get to High Court judges and the very top barristers – and 55 per cent of senior civil servants. They also make up more than 60 per cent of the top echelon of those in the City of London, some 70 per cent of surgeons and consultants, and 55 per cent of journalists, rising to more than 70 per cent for national newspaper columnists and editors – the top echelons of every single institution we have, bar none. This is even more pronounced when you examine the top echelons within the top echelons, the elite within the elite. The *Daily Mail*, which is not necessarily in the vanguard of the glorious proletarian revolution, reported that 80 per cent of the very top jobs in society are held by people who went to private school (although presumably these were also people who *have had their struggles too*). Eighty per cent.

So when they tell you that 'We're all middle-class now,' or 'We're all in it together,' just remember that such a statement is, if I can put it like this, a downright lie. And it is more of a lie now than it has been for a good thirty or forty years. But we still mustn't take it out on the individuals. Hell, they've had their struggles too.

Does this stuff matter, except as ammunition for chippy little monkeys like me, a bit of point-scoring and a welcome chance to indulge in resentment? Only in that we in this country like to think of ourselves as a meritocracy, yet we are very far from being one, and this grates a little, and makes us feel, you know, cheated. It means society is less cohesive, more distrustful. Beyond that, it matters too because the more meritocratic a society, the better it tends to fare, both economically and in terms of those multifarious other indicators like life expectancy, standard of living and so on: the more equal a country is, the more successful, by and large. And of course it matters morally, I might add as a sort of afterthought. We lag way, way, behind the rest of Europe for social mobility, and especially the north-western European countries (from Scandinavia down to Germany) with which we share a common cultural heritage. We are on a par in this regard with another country with which we share a certain cultural heritage, the USA: both of us are down at the bottom for social mobility. Maybe it's the case that the more stridently a country proclaims its commitment to equality of opportunity, and meritocracy, the less equal it actually is.

For Britain, this was not always so. When, in 2010, the Old Etonian Prime Minister David Cameron announced to the Conservative Party conference that 'We're all in this together,' it was met with frank incredulity and gales of laughter, and the fatuous fucking statement has rightly come back to haunt him on an almost daily basis. Earlier Prime Ministers – even Tory Prime Ministers – could get away with saying much the same thing, and if the population didn't exactly fervently concur, at least it wasn't falling off its chair with grim mirth either.

From the end of the Second World War through to the close of the 1970s, Britain either experienced rapid and energising levels of social mobility, or somehow, through some pleasant collective narcosis, thought that it was experiencing this. There is some dispute about the real extent to which vast swathes of the population, the majority, were enabled – i.e., given a bit of a chance. Sometimes though, a feeling is enough to hold a country together, even if the reality isn't quite there. Either way, it kept us going, both the reality and after a while the illusion. Certainly post-war Britain experienced rapid and sustained prosperity, without a major recession, until 1973. The average wage more than doubled between 1960 and 1971, and the state pension reached its height at 24.8 per cent of average earnings at the end of the 1970s, before it began its inexorable decline to almost complete worthlessness. Home ownership increased. More pertinently, the 1944 Education Act – introduced of course by a Tory, Rab Butler – raised the school-leaving age to fifteen (and later sixteen) while introducing a free tripartite education system (grammar school, secondary school, comp), meaning that everybody got to go to school. As you might have expected, this massively increased the demand for university places, and so by the end of the 1950s only some 15 per cent of applicants were getting in. So more universities were built, and existing technical colleges transformed into universities, expanding the number of places available from 110,000 in 1962 to 150,000 by 1967, and then 390,000 by 1973. The main beneficiaries of this were women and the working class. And so, taking all this stuff into account, it was possible to believe that we really were all in this together, that the wealth was being spread around a bit, even if the gap between the really rich and the really poor was rather wide (although nothing like so wide as it is today).

Justin, the new Archbishop of Canterbury, used to work in the oil industry, for the firm Elf Aquitaine. He had been a bishop for slightly more than one year when the C of E gave him the top job.

John, the man who most people expected to become Archbishop of Canterbury, has been a cleric all of his adult life. In his early years he got his head kicked in fairly frequently by Idi Amin's thugs in his native Uganda, for saying things with which the pig-ignorant and half-witted dictator vigorously disagreed. John had been a bishop in the Church of England for a little over sixteen years when he was passed over for the job of Archbishop.

Listen, I don't have it in for Justin. He seems like a very kindly chap, and in his first year in the job he has made a series of thoughtful, humble and decent observations about society, and even about Christianity. I like the man. And I'm sure that he has had his struggles too. I'm not saying that John should have got the job, or that Justin isn't up to it, or even that John didn't get it because – as Charles Moore suggested – the synod decided to keep in step with modern England by appointing someone who had been to Eton. Who knows what went on in those discussions? There could be loads of reasons why Justin was preferred to John. Maybe they didn't like John because he's a darkie. That would be shocking, wouldn't it? I'm absolutely certain that it is not the case. I'm absolutely certain that John's skin colour did not come into the argument. I'm fairly certain, too, that Justin's provenance was not mentioned during any of those discussions; I'm fairly sure nobody stood up and said, 'We've got to have Justin, he was a bloody good fag at Eton.' I'm fairly sure that nobody made reference to Eton at all. It doesn't work like that.

Coincidentally, Justin is the great-nephew of Rab Butler, the Conservative politician who introduced the 1944 Education Act. Small world, huh? Anyway, that's enough about Justin. Or enough about Justin Welby.

The secondary school I attended was a comprehensive called the Laurence Jackson School, in the market (and, at the time, steel) town of Guisborough, about ten miles south of Middlesbrough, in North Yorkshire. It was a very big school, with something like 1,850 pupils in the year I left. Insofar as it was possible to tell, I was probably one of the posher kids there; my dad by this time had a white-collar job, and our house was owned by the building society rather than by the local council. I think also, by this time, my mum and dad had stopped thinking of themselves as working-class, although they never quite considered themselves middle-class. Their fathers' occupations were both solidly working-class – train driver on my dad's side, postman on my mum's. But I think they thought that they had bust loose a little, left those old shackles behind them; hell, we had a car, and a Labrador. Or at least a Labrador-cross.

But the difference in income between my family and the families of the very poorest kids at the LJS would have been so small as to be almost unmeasurable, and none of us had any accumulated wealth. If my mum and dad ever seriously considered themselves middle-class, they were fucking kidding themselves, as I quickly discovered when I returned, years later, to London. We simply had a few of the trappings of comparative affluence: the mortgage, the insurance policies and what have you.

When I joined the BBC *Today* programme at the end of the 1980s, I noticed very quickly that almost everybody else who worked on it had been privately educated. Not all of them, but most of them. I also found that there were no fewer than five people, out of a staff of about forty people, who had been to Eton. This probably does not surprise you. In fact, if I'd asked you to guess how many of them had been to Eton you might even have hazarded at around about that number; that's how used to this sort of stuff we have become. But can you imagine how astonishing it would have been if I had found five members of staff had been to the similar-sized Laurence Jackson Comprehensive School in Guisborough? What would be the chances of that? A billion to one? Probably less. In my first week on the programme a friendly soul took me upstairs to the canteen for lunch, and almost before we had sat down I recounted my chippy observation to him. He smiled and said, 'Ah yes, Rod, but just think how proud your poor old mum and dad would be to know that you're now mixing with people like us. They'd be SO thrilled.' I thought that was very funny; humour, the last refuge of the bourgeoisie. That was Justin Webb.

By this time, the end of the 1980s, social mobility was well into retreat, even if the Conservative government of the day was considered to be of lower-middle mercantile stock, rather than properly high-born. The egalitarian tendencies of Margaret Thatcher's government, and its perceived mistrust of old money and privilege, of the old Tory establishment, have been serially overstated, but it is nonetheless true that it was less obviously, less visibly a government of the old ruling class than the one we have now. And that sort of visibility matters, as Cameron is finding out.

The point being that class, as an issue, is back with us. In a way, 2012, the year in which I began this book, was the year of class. This is the government that wanted to put VAT on pasties but not on *foie gras* or oysters, a decision which would have been less controversial had it not been perceived by the public, by the commentators, and even by some of the Conservative Party's own backbenchers, to have been an act typical of the sort of people who did not even know what a pasty was, let alone eat them with any regularity. It was the rather scary, bleached-blonde Scouser backbench Tory Nadine Dorries who stated (twice – just in case it got missed the first time) that the Prime Minister and his Chancellor were a couple of 'arrogant posh boys' who did not know the price of a pint of milk.

Thereafter, the Labour leader Ed Miliband was able to play on this theme explicitly, in a way which previously had been considered inadvisable. In a speech to the Labour conference, Ed – who is about as working-class in sensibility as a bowl of wasabi peas – was able to point to the fact that he had attended a state school; not Eton, not Rugby, not even one of the shit fee-paying schools where everyone's on drugs. It helped, of course, that his father Ralph was a Marxist, and thus ideologically opposed to private education (although, of course, the middle-class liberal left does not always refuse to put its money where its mouth is in such a manner). And Ed's background was still fairly wealthy.

But anyway, during 2012, class seethed and bubbled away beneath the surface, it registered with the public in a way that had not been seen for a good fifty or sixty years. The centrepiece of 2012 was the London Olympic Games – and again, class reared its head. The unexpectedly magnificent opening ceremony, choreographed by Danny Boyle, showed the working classes of England sweat-soaked and ragged, hammering away at their huge, infernal machines, a reminder of just who built the country during the Industrial Revolution, in case we had possibly forgotten. And as Britain's athletes loped or pedalled or jumped their way to glory, it was pointed out that an unfeasible number of them had been educated at fee-paying schools. Just think how brilliant we might be, as a sporting nation, if such facilities were open to all of Britain's children. And toff boy Osborne, the Chancellor, was roundly booed when he appeared before a vast crowd of spectators to present some medals at the Paralympics. It appears that 2012 was the year we became rather more class conscious – as well we might.

It may seem an odd thing to say only four years after the country (partly) elected a Conservative government, but my suspicion is that the mood of the nation has swung a little towards the left these last few years. Not towards middle-class liberalism or faux leftism, of which more later, but towards the traditional ideas of the left. That this has not been reflected in people's voting intentions is, I think, a consequence of a disastrous last Labour administration, and also an absence among the mainstream parties of a realisation of what the traditional left stood for. Within the Labour Party, the Blue Labour tendency has at least grasped this, and there is evidence that its thinking is beginning to have an effect upon the party's leadership.

For example, for a quarter of a century or more, nationalisation was a filthy term. We were all seemingly agreed that the days of the taxpayer bailing out British Steel and British Leyland were over; let the market rule, and let the devil take the hindmost. From 1987 onwards the Labour Party dared not mention nationalisation. An aspiration to control the commanding heights of the economy? You must be fucking joking. The concept was doomed. And then came the collapse of the banks and their effective nationalisation – a process begun, of course, by the most right-wing President of the USA for eighty years, George W. Bush. Suddenly the notion that it might be a good idea if the public, or the government, had some sort of control over important parts of the economy, those bits that have a resonance beyond their immediate spheres, became popular once again. If we can bail out RBS, why not the Corus steel plant on Teesside, seeing that it is crucial to the well-being of the area? Nationalisation, and direct government intervention, has been at least partially rehabilitated in the minds of the public. It is no longer an idea that is completely off-limits, attractive only to Trots and mentals. This is only a guess, but I suspect that if a vote were held now, the country would gladly decide to take the utilities – gas, water, electricity – back into public ownership, so that they were run for the benefit of the nation rather than for short-term profit. High energy prices and a lack of investment in infrastructure, along with the fact that a majority of our energy and water companies are foreign-owned and therefore owe no allegiance, nor show any commitment, to the people of Britain, would, I think, persuade the electorate to vote in favour of public ownership. I think it would be a pretty close call with the railways, too – which would certainly cheer up my father, and his father, and his father before him, all of whom worked on the railways. The tide is turning.

Likewise, the disparities of wealth in society. There seems to be a consensus that the salaries and bonuses earned by bankers are an obscenity; and would still be an obscenity even if they were any good at what they do. Even the right-wing commentator Ferdinand Mount has bemoaned the growing disparity between the wealthiest and the poorest in our society, and in particular the vast and widening chasm within companies between the pay of executives and those who toil at the lowest level. The elegant and thoughtful Ferdy – the former political editor of the *Spectator*, so scarcely a rabid left-winger – has proposed limits for executive pay. Limits to top people's pay! From a Tory! There are even signs, here and there, that the trades unions are being rehabilitated, that 'giving the workers a shout' is back in vogue. Those union-led marches against cuts to the public services seemed to have a fair amount of public support, despite the usual hostility from most of the press.

You begin to think: what would have happened to Tony Blair if, in the run-up to the 1997 general election, he had advocated nationalising the banks and the utilities and maybe the railways, putting a limit on the amount executives could earn, banning six-figure bonuses for bankers and restoring to the trades unions some of the rights that had been stripped from them by the previous Conservative administrations. I do not think he would have won his landslide. I think he would have got about as much support as did Michael Foot in 1983 – who stood on what was regarded as an extremist manifesto, which nonetheless did not quite go so far as to advocate all of the above. The Tories, back in 1983, destroyed Labour with a clever advert which placed the two manifestos, Labour and Communist, together and showed scarcely a hair's breadth between them. 'Like your manifesto, comrade …' was the slogan. All a bit different now that the likes of Ferdinand Mount and George W. Bush are signed up to various disparate parts of it. It is largely the 'credit crunch', or the recession, or the banking crisis – call it what you will, that has made stuff like nationalisation palatable once again.

And then, there's class. Having been pretty much absent from serious political discourse for the best part of fifty years, it now has resonance again. People are aware that we are still ruled by the sons (and, to a lesser extent, the daughters) of the wealthy, and that this is neither fair nor practical. They are more aware of it now because it is so obvious, so clear, so in your face. When we look back at the 1960s it is the egalitarianism we miss, the social mobility, the idea that for those who were not high-born it was now at last possible to achieve, to enjoy a decent and comfortable life, based on your abilities. This was at least part of the reason why my mother and father, and millions like them, felt that they had a sort of stake in society; that at least it wasn't actively militated against them, as had previously been the case. They felt they were sharing in the increased prosperity of Britain, and therefore did not feel sullen and dispossessed, alienated and averse. It was, by and large, the 1980s which did that to people, under the guise of a meritocracy.

Fortunately, the mask has slipped a little this decade, and the public is a little less quiescent. I think the tolerance we afforded to people *who have had their struggles too* has worn a little thin, and a good thing too. My own maxim is never to trust someone who has been to a public school, even if they are terribly nice – perhaps especially if they are terribly nice. Always keep your eyes open and your hand on your wallet. There is a class war, and they are the enemy. This statement seems too stark – it seems histrionic, it seems adolescent, it seems unfair, doesn't it? That is because we have been gulled for too long, and are being gulled now more than ever before.

IO

Deference

My parents used to do their shopping in Middlesbrough on a Saturday morning, but later began to avoid the town centre in case they ran into me selling copies of the *Socialist Worker* outside the Cleveland Centre. Or at least trying to sell copies of the *Socialist Worker*, without, usually, very much success. 'Sssssooooocialist *Worker* – neither Washington nor Moscow but international socialism,' I would bellow, keeping an eye on the trade being conducted nearby by our loathed recidivist rivals, the Workers Revolutionary Party and the International Marxist Group. Only rarely did I sell a paper, and then it was usually to friends. The most frequent comments I received were 'Get back to bloody Moscow,' and 'Socialist Worker? You've never done a day's work in your life!' and 'Fuck off, you silly little cunt.' All of which held a certain truth, I suppose, except maybe the Moscow bit. If I remember rightly, we hated Moscow every bit as much as we hated the capitalist West: 'state capitalist' was how we referred to the USSR. But then, we hated everything – we were millennialist in our fury and absolutism.

There were some kindly, decent people in the Middlesbrough branch of the SWP, and at the meetings held above a pub on a Thursday night I enjoyed being part of this close-knit, minuscule and fabulously earnest cabal, planning to hand out weapons to the ICI workers down at the Wilton works when the great day came. Downstairs it was just a typical working-class Middlesbrough pub with very hard-drinking, tough-looking men downing their dark pints in seconds. I usually slunk out unobtrusively in case one of them glassed me. But on one occasion a regular – not a party member, just one of the hard drinkers, a huge bloke with a Boro tattoo and a cap-sleeve shirt – offered to buy me a pint. He clapped me on the shoulder and said through his beer, 'I fuckin' respect what you're doing up there every week, lad. Someone's got to do it. Government's let us down, and the opposition are no better.'

Nervously elated, I said thank you very much – and suggested maybe he come and join one of our meetings sometime. This would have been a great coup for me, as we didn't really have any proper working-class people in our branch, just social workers, students and civil servants.

'I might do that, lad. I just might. Ought to put me money where me mouth is. We've got to find some way of kicking the fucking niggers and the Pakis out.'

I've never drunk a pint quicker, before or since, nor dissembled in such a cowardly manner. I don't think the SWP Central Committee, or indeed Martin Luther King, would have been terribly proud of my equivocations that night.

Being a member of the SWP was an act of confected, exhibition-ist faux rebellion, which may or may not have been forgivable in a sixteen-year-old. Even then, at sixteen, I had profound doubts about the desirability of violently overthrowing the state – and especially the idea of handing out weapons to the sort of chap who bought me a pint that night in the pub and who hadn't really, if we're honest, quite grasped the nature of our political programme. My SWP membership was really a pose, a case of showing off, and of lack of responsibility – a case of infantile leftism, as Vladimir Lenin would have put it, or radical chic, as Tom Wolfe would have put it.

There was a lot of that sort of stuff around, at the time – lots of extremists demanding the unattainable or the unworkable, bitterly fervent in their fatuous certitude. This was a febrile political time, when the ultimate narcissism of direct action was very fashionable; if the IRA didn't blow you up, the PLO might well do, or the Red Brigades or the Red Army Faction or, in the USA, the fabulous Symbionese Liberation Army, led by the usual sort of messianic narcissistic headcase, a man called Donald DeFreeze who, in 1974, made one of his few decent decisions in life by shooting himself in the middle of his skull. One of his few entirely successful actions, too, mercifully: one wondered why he hadn't done it earlier. Every time you watched the news in the mid-1970s dinky little terrorist bombs would be popping off somewhere or other, murdering or maiming people who were not, in the eyes of the terrorists, innocent – nobody is, you see; if you're not part of the solution you're part of the problem, etc. You are tacitly complicit. They've quietened down, most of them, since then, but the same shrill absolutism and certitude can be heard in the hysterical denunciations from the metropolitan liberal left today, the world over (but especially in London); a grim insistence that everything they say is beyond possible contradiction and that those who dare to contradict them should be punished somehow; they may not have the guns any more, having loaned them to the jihadis, but Gramsci's heirs still have that good ol' 'revolutionary' authoritarian mindset. It is that thing, narcissism, once again. Problem now is, they run much of the country, without a mandate. They sort of won in the end.

In the early to mid-1970s, domestic and to a degree much of European politics was mired in a torpid consensus, a Butskellite/ Christian Democrat/Social Democrat alliance wedded to welfare capitalism and a mixed economy which allowed room for considerable amounts of state ownership. I suppose shocking amounts of state ownership in Britain, if you're not keen on that sort of thing (I am keen on it, as it happens – but we'll come back to that). It wasn't only the public utilities and the railways and heavy industry that were owned by the state, but your friendly local travel agent too –

Thomas Cook, for example was a nationalised company. It's hard to imagine now, but some 60 per cent of our economy was state-owned – in that sense at least we were not so far behind, say, Yugoslavia or Hungary in the Eastern Bloc. This is presumably why most of the foreign relations experts at the time agreed that the most likely outcome of the Cold War was something called convergence, where the two economic systems came to resemble one another so closely that to all purposes they were the same thing, an argument that would have commended itself to my colleagues in the SWP, I suppose. As ever with a consensus of experts, this was a wrong analysis based upon an inability to foresee sudden political change. Soviet Communism was to collapse, *pace* Marx, under the weight of its own inherent contradictions, exacerbated by a newly hawkish West led by Ronald Reagan and Margaret Thatcher, who forced the benighted, sclerotic empire to throw unfeasible amounts of money at its lumbering defence industry. As we now know, it went bust.

In much the same way as World War II defined my parents' generation, so the Cold War defined my own; not privation and fortitude and the actual presence of death on a daily basis, then – but an interminable gibbering paranoia, a state of being perpetually frit and thus querulous and antagonistic towards our own leaders. A state of mind described perfectly in that old hippy Jeff Nuttall's work *Bomb Culture* (1968). For my generation this stand-off between West and East seemed – wrongly, I would reckon now – less Manichean than that which had galvanised the generation before, the moral imperatives on either side less clearly defined. We watched proxy civil wars being fought between more or less identically vicious Third World tyrants from the left and right in unimaginably humid Third World shitholes – Vietnam, Angola, Mozambique, the Congo, Chile – and were at best unsure where lay the rectitude. Allende or Pinochet? Old 'No-go' Diem or Ho Chi Minh? Way too close to call, way too close.

And, forever fizzing away in the middle distance, the prospect of an automated annihilation that would allow no room for individual heroism or stoicism, just a sudden extinction that would leave behind, briefly, invisible traces of stuff like Einsteinium. I was intermittently terrified, when I thought about it. I had a recurring dream, somewhere round about 1981, that both the Russkies and the Yankees were chasing me personally with a nuclear weapon. I'd keep running, trying to outpace the missiles, diving into culverts and cellars, but the bastards knew where I was, and cowering behind a boarded-up door I'd see out of the corner of my eye the shiny tip of a rocket heading my way in shimmering slo-mo and I waited hysterically for that famous scintillating flash, the heat of a thousand suns. Which never actually came – either in that typically solipsistic dream of mine, or in reality.

Meanwhile, more prosaically, in Britain we had that post-war consensus, two parties within which the mainstreams differed, ideologically, very little at all. The first general election of 1974 seemed to be contested on the single point as to whether the government should give in to the miners' pay demands before they took strike action, or maybe wait until after. The result was, pretty much, a dead heat. And yet, however inept and paralysed those 1970s governments of Heath, Wilson and Callaghan may have been, my parents' generation had not quite given up on them. They were not preternaturally disaffected, as we were and now are. There was still a respect for, if not a deference to, the ruling political class, and a certain faith in the democratic process. Voter turnout had declined gradually since the high point of the 1950 general election, when 83.9 per cent of the population voted, returning the Labour government to office by a whisker. Support for the two major parties remained high throughout the quarter of a century that followed the war, almost 97 per cent of those who voted in 1951 choosing either Labour or Conservative. The Liberals, under the appalling Jeremy Thorpe, made a breakthrough in May 1974, but still the election results suggested a satisfaction with mainstream party politics, both through turnout (79 per cent) and support for the three main parties (97 per cent). Compare that to 2001, when the turnout had slipped to 59.4 per cent, or even the more crucial 2010 election, where turnout was up to 65 per cent – but a full 11 per cent were no longer voting for the Conservatives, Labour or the Lib Dems, but for a myriad of others: the Greens, UKIP, the BNP, lunatics, single-issue obsessives. The story of the last twenty-five years has been one of increasing public disenchantment with mainstream politics, a cynicism towards both the politicians and the machinations of the main three parties, a suspicion that no matter who you vote for, the bastards will still win in the end, and they will not make anything any better. Our two main parties have lost millions of voters since 1987. Why? Is it the politicians, or is it us?

Both, one supposes. Certainly, my parents' generation did not hold the polity in the sort of corrosive contempt in which it is held today. There were scandals from time to time, and the public was for a while suitably scandalised; but these scandals did not arrive week after week, with a sort of crushing inevitability, one piled relentlessly on top of the other. Partly this was the consequence of a more compliant and respectful media – it is perhaps the case that just as many scandals were taking place back in the 1950s and 1960s, but we simply didn't know about them. But the result's the same, whatever way you slice it.

And there were other, probably more telling, differences between the politicians of then and now. They were then less constrained in what they were able to say – freer from the shackles of party orthodoxy and, more importantly, from the hastily confected hyperbolic outrage from single-issue pressure groups, or media columnists, or bloggers, or tweeters. As a consequence they tended to speak in a language which was both immediately intelligible and connected to the public, rather than in anodyne and often meaningless clichés stapled together and designed primarily not to remotely offend anyone. By and large, political heads do not, these days, poke above the parapet, and if they do they are soon picked off. Our sensibilities are so tender that almost anything stated in plain and unequivocal English is liable to grotesquely offend someone, somewhere – and they will assuredly have their revenge. The howl-round, these days, from those determined to feel transgressed is so immediate and vituperous that it makes it pointless to, for example, advance an original idea or challenge an orthodoxy, or even express the simple, unvarnished truth as one sees it. Either your career will be over, or you will be forced by the party apparatus to make one of those familiar cringing apologies, suggesting shamefacedly that your words have been taken out of context and you didn't really mean it and you're really, really sorry if you gave offence and you pray to Christ that all this enervating prostrating will be enough to keep the hounds off your fucking trail for a few weeks, that you might keep your job.

The consequence of all this is that politicians now speak a different language from the rest of us – a strange and vapid discourse, utterly disconnected from the way in which ordinary people speak. Look through the manifestos of all three parties for the 2010 general election: there is almost nothing that any sane person could disagree with, and almost nothing that means anything at all. It is all designed not to offend. For a perfect example of meaningless dissembling, incidentally, try to get hold of one of Gordon Brown's interviews back when he was Chancellor of the Exchequer, and invited quite regularly (why, I now ask myself, why?) onto the BBC Today programme. Brown would refuse to answer any question directly, and would instead simply chunter endlessly about nothing, as if he were a contestant on a surreal version of Just a Minute – all the way up until the pips went.

And then there are the politicians themselves; they are also no longer 'one of us'. The Labour Party my dad voted for, with jubilance and hope, in 1945 put forward candidates who were former miners, railwaymen, steelworkers, soldiers, teachers, journalists; the number of them who had elided gracefully from public school, via PPE at Oxford and a political research job to a safe seat in some blue-collar north-of-England bastion was vanishingly small. Now, the reverse is true: few of our politicians have a hinterland consisting of a previous life in the real world; they are an abstraction, remote and aloof. Their politics are not formed through experience, but are instead happily bestowed or acquired. From the 1940s to the late 1970s my parents felt as if they were governed by people who *represented* them, at an intrinsic level; they were of the same stock, these politicians, *ergo* they might just understand. Would you feel that now if you were a Labour voter in Stoke-on-Trent, and represented in Parliament by the handsome historian Tristram Hunt? Or in Hartlepool, if you had been represented by Peter Mandelson? Or in Sedgefield, formerly represented by the famous Newcastle United supporter Tony Blair? I do not mean this as an attack upon the individual MPs, least of all poor Tristram Hunt. It is of course a good thing, a hugely commendable thing, that someone as clever and likeable and able as Hunt should wish to earn probably less than he could in civvy street and dedicate his life to public service. I am glad he is in Parliament; if he stood in my constituency I would vote for him – partly because I respect and like the chap and even, despite being heterosexual, slightly fancy him – and partly because I'm a Labour Party member, and thus compelled to vote for the official party candidate. If this were a perfect world, though, Tris would be representing Hampstead and Highgate, rather than Stoke-on-Trent. But one of our most gilded luvvies, Glenda Jackson, is already there, just about (with a majority of forty-two), and you can't really get more Hampstead than her, not even Tristram Hunt.

Too often, in the case of both parties, although especially Labour, gleaming and usually public-school-educated monkeys with not the remotest connection to the area or knowledge of what life is like there are parachuted into safe seats because they are attractive, media-savvy, wanky London metro-liberal *bien pensants* by disposition, and happy to toe the party line. The constituency associations carp and cavil and sometimes even succeed in putting one over their London masters. Such was the local anger in Blaenau Gwent (effectively Nye Bevan's old seat of Ebbw Vale*) at the imposition, via an all-woman shortlist, of a candidate they didn't want that the local party rebelled, and their original choice was elected instead. Such defiance is all too rare, though.

So that's one way in which politics has become removed, by one nimble step, from the people. Another is the diminishing importance both of the individual MP and the grassroots party member. I still remember when party conferences, on both sides of the House, were febrile and tumultuous occasions, where party policy could be changed on a vote from the conference floor – in fairness, perhaps changed to something really, truly, fucking stupid, which would give the following day's press a good laugh and an enjoyable chance to stick the boot in. But still, they were occasions which possessed the faintest intimation of democracy, and into which the real world, with its absurd conceits, flawed and daft, regularly intruded – to the intense discomfort of the horrible party managers. That is no longer allowed to happen, of course. The conferences these days are as micro-managed and choreographed as an Olympic synchronised-swimming routine, tied up neatly for the bone-idle TV crews and the following morning's unquestioning headlines. The only thing that really matters is the timbre and tone of the leader's speech and the length of the subsequent ovation, which the pol corrs dutifully measure on their BlackBerrys. A voice of dissent from the floor is, these days, dealt with peremptorily – and even brutally, as pensioner Walter Wolfgang discovered at the

---

* The constituency of Blaenau Gwent didn't come into existence until 1983, long after Bevan's death.

Labour conference in Brighton in 2005, when he had the temerity to suggest that Foreign Secretary Jack Straw was spewing half a million cubic litres of disingenuous warm liquid shit over the audience on the subject of the Iraq War. Wolfgang was manhandled out of the conference hall by two bullet-headed security thugs, and became for a while a *cause célèbre*, a symbol of the emasculation of party conferences and the reflexive Stalinism of the party managers. Something must be done, everyone agreed, as Wolfgang made his slightly incredulous but dignified protestations to the delighted TV crews waiting outside the conference centre. And indeed something was done: Wolfgang got a profuse apology from the party, and the party managers quietly resolved, one assumes, never to let mad old bastards like that inside the conference hall in the first place. Job done, then.

Wolfgang, incidentally, was absolutely right about the Iraq War. If ever there was an example of a political elite dispensing with even the trappings of democracy, of believing everyone but their own tiny cabal to be thick or wrong or simply misguided and thus to be ignored – then the decision to invade Iraq is it. The Cabinet bypassed and kept in the dark, its mild protests dismissed or ignored, or its supine members suborned into a sort of cowardly agreement; select committees and the House of Commons – and the general public – serially misled; the security services co-opted into an arm of government propaganda; and the BBC, when it accurately reported what the scientists and security services were really saying about Iraq's supposed weapons of mass destruction, eviscerated in a campaign which ultimately led to the enforced resignation of its Director General and Chairman. The sort of government behaviour you might have expected in, say, Uzbekistan or Venezuela.

Twenty-five years before all this took place, I got seriously interested in journalism on account of the book *All the President's Men*, wherein two *Washington Post* journalists succeeded, brilliantly, in uncovering the corruption and authoritarianism at the very heart of President Richard Nixon's administration. The way in which the decision to invade Iraq was foisted upon the British people was, beyond all doubt, Britain's real Watergate – even if the suffix '-gate' is cheerfully appended these days to every petty dispute or infraction as a matter of course. Iraq, though, really was it – and maybe times ten, when you factor in the lives lost as a consequence. But, this being Britain – no impeachment, of course. If Woodward and Bernstein had been British they'd have ended up unemployed, or doing shifts for Press TV, rather than picking up the Pulitzer Prize.

Jack Straw, a decentish enough bloke most of the time, later said that he wished Iraq would just 'go away' as an issue. Well, Jack, luckily it did. Maybe in forty years' time the story will be told, when all the important actors in it are dead or insentient. That's the way we do things here: *All the Dead Prime Minister's Dead Men*, coming to a cinema near you in about 2052.

But back for a moment to that original point: the diminishing power of the individual MP. Parliament itself is of course less sovereign than it once was, with a bunch of powers siphoned off to those enthusiastic democrats in the European Parliament. And politics in general no longer has the force it once had, as the crucial issues, you might argue, are now decided in the boardrooms of multinational companies in Shanghai and New York and Tokyo and indeed London. But individual MPs have become less important even within the truncated importance of Westminster, controlled ever more tightly by the party machines and the whips' office, which seek to constrain even our one remaining forum for genuine debate and investigation, the select committees. Who, today, would be an MP?

So it may be harder to respect our politicians today. But it is also true that respect and deference towards authority have in any case diminished since the mid-1960s. Richard Hoggart saw it, in *The*

Way We Live Now (1995), as a partly commendable dissolution of the sense of 'Them' and 'Us'. The 'Authorities have gone', he argues:

> It would be wrong to assume – and that is common today – that all social changes are, simply by happening, self-validating, to be accepted without question. Much of the old style of authority was mistakenly assumed and adopted, born of the disadvantages of others. Some of it was wrongly applied, the petty authoritarianism of petty people in positions of petty power. Some of it is based on fear, religious or secular.

I think Hoggart, though, minimises the importance of the two key, to my mind, cultural developments in post-war Britain. First, the anti-authority counterculture revolution of the 1960s, during which a host of babies were thrown out with the bathwater. And secondly, and maybe more importantly, the individualistic revolution of the 1980s, when the appetite for collective solutions to national problems was almost eradicated from the public mind, and in its place we had a vaulting personal acquisitiveness and a diminished concept of what constitutes society. If you repeatedly assure the public that government should play a smaller part in their lives, then you cannot but help diminish the respect in which government is held. If government occupies a smaller space in our daily life, then we will naturally be inclined to afford it less deference. And if we are enjoined, over and over again – either explicitly or implicitly – that society as such does not exist, and that it is up to us as individuals to make our mark in the world, then necessarily the amount of respect we have for other people – now viewed merely as competitors – will diminish also.

II

Faux-Left

Like most people of a liberal sensitivity I have been a long-time
inhabitant of the state of conscientious denial.

Andrew Anthony, The Fall-Out

If you are really bored one day and have a computer to hand, you
might find it diverting to play a game I've invented called 'The Long
March Through the Institutions'. I've borrowed the name from the
Marxist philosopher Antonio Gramsci,* who believed that in order
to advance the cause of social revolution, and achieve what he
called 'cultural hegemony', like-minded leftist intellectuals should
seize control of all the institutions that run our cultural life – TV
stations, schools, universities, the cinema and so on. Had Gramsci
been writing today he would have added to his list of stuff that
needed seizing the quangos and the charities and the advisory
boards of everything, and the government inquiries and panels –
the bodies which adjudicate, in very reasonable tones, about everything we do, and by which wc arc run.

If you play my game you will very quickly begin to understand
that what Gramsci advised has, in fact, been done. And all this
despite the very strong evidence that Gramsci was a charlatan. The
seizing control bit, incidentally, has been effected not by shooting

---

* There is some dispute as to whether Gramsci actually used the phrase, even
if his work does embody its meaning. It may have been a hugely irritating
German activist called Rudi Dutschke.

people and waving red flags from the top of burning barricades as the fascist forces and their running dogs move in for the kill, but by the more amenable process of like-minded liberal intellectuals appointing one another to positions of power and authority, perhaps over a cup of coffee and some nice organic biscuits, those ones that have bits of oat in them.

How to play the game? Think of a quango, or a public body, or a charity, or something even bigger, like the BBC, or some inquiry that the government has going at the moment. Google the name you've chosen, and then find out who runs it or advises it. That's easy to do – they're all meant to be transparent now, so the advisory board or the trusts will all be listed somewhere. Then click on one of the names and look up the biography of that person. You will find, without fail, that they are also on the boards of at least five or six other things. At this point you might be surprised, because there will not seem to be a connection at all between the various institutions listed – except that, most likely, they depend upon your wallet for their existence.

So, if you tap in 'BBC Trust' – the people who govern the BBC – and find the name Mehmuda Mian, you will discover that Mehmuda is also a non-executive director of the Independent Safeguarding Authority, a quango of which you may never have heard. The ISA is a body which was set up to make sure children don't get sexually abused by adults, basically. Among other things, it compiles that famous register which you have to be on if you're going to referee a children's football match. Its remit, then, is very different from that of the BBC, which is to make television and radio programmes that people like to watch or listen to. Can one have an expertise in both areas? Does Mehmuda have expertise in either area? Her BBC biog says simply that she 'has spent much of her career upholding standards in public life'. For which many, many thanks. That was kind of you, Mehmuda.

Go on down the list and you'll find Diane Coyle, a former journalist for the *Independent*, and note with a modicum of surprise that she is also a member of the UK Border Agency Advisory Committee, along with a whole bunch of other posts for similarly utterly disparate organisations, including adviser to the Labour Party. Then click on 'UK Border Agency Advisory Committee' and look down the list of members – and next to Diane Coyle you'll find a chap called David Metcalfe, who is a professor at the London School of Economics. Look up his biog and you'll find he is also on the Senior Salaries Review Board. Tap that into Google and see what turns up. What you will learn, if you do this for long enough, until your eyes are popping out of your head, is this:

- The same names keep turning up, over and over again.
- There are more fucking quangos and advisory bodies than there are grains of sand on a beach.
- The people who are members of these boards have, in most cases, either little or no particular expertise in the job they are doing.
- A very high proportion of them are people who *have had their struggles too*.
- There was not, in almost all cases, a due and transparent process for their appointment. In other words, they were just ASKED.
- In almost every case, *you* pay for the work they do, even though (in the majority of cases) their salaries are minimal or non-existent.
- They are all liberals. Without exception.
- Most of them have been honoured – CBEs and the like – for reasons which are not immediately evident.
- The name 'Shami Chakrabarti' will come up an awful lot. Shami is the director of Liberty, and the lady you see every other week on the BBC's *Question Time*, when Mehdi Hasan is

on holiday. Shami's name comes up so often, in fact, that you could play a game which might be even more fun than 'The Long March Through the Institutions'. You could play 'Six Degrees of Shami'. Let's see: BBC Trust takes you to Diane Coyle, who takes you to the UK Border Agency Committee, which takes you to David Metcalfe … who is a professor at the LSE, where Shami was on the board of ITS trustees. Bingo! It's not even six degrees of separation – it's more like three degrees. Not that pop group Prince Charles liked, obviously. Shami is also on the Leveson Inquiry and the board of the British Film Institute, and is the Chancellor of Oxford Brookes University. Such busy, busy, people they all are. How do they find the time?

The important points are that they are all faux-left social liberals, including the BBC Chairman Chris Patten (who has an additional TEN posts, as well as running our most important broadcasting institution), that they are largely appointed, and that there are comparatively very few of them. That's why the same names keep cropping up. They are our new version of the great and the good; where once it was the aristos and the rich who staffed these institutions (when there were a hell of a lot fewer of those institutions, to be fair), it is now this lot: secular, middle-class, *bien-pensant* liberals. There are very few trades unionists on these boards, or for that matter plumbers, cab drivers or arc welders. There are no people known for their strident right-wing views, either, nor many Christian churchmen. There are no people known for their very strident left-wing views, either. It is an impeccably well-brought-up faux-left consensus. We will come back to what I mean by faux-left very soon.

Last year the *Daily Mail* got itself terribly worked up about one tiny corner of this whole business, this charade. It focused, for very pragmatic reasons, on the Leveson Inquiry, and in particular the presence, alongside his noble lordship, or however you're meant to address these gilded monkeys, of a certain Sir David Bell. The newspaper pointed out that Bell, who was supposed to be an impartial arbiter, was previously one of the trustees of another organisation, the seriously fucking pompous Media Standards Trust, which had itself created the organisation 'Hacked Off' – slebs who were pissed off that newspapers kept trying to find out if they were up to their armpits in gak or fiddled with kiddies – which Leveson was duly taking evidence from. Bell as both sort-of judge and witness for the prosecution! The *Mail* also pointed out – across eleven pages – that Bell was a creature of New Labour, and was also wrapped up in another organisation called 'Common Purpose', which has a sort of Moonie ring about it; in other words, the *Daily Mail* sort of played my game, 'The Long March Through the Institutions'. And it was right. But, hell, Dacre – what did you expect? Incidentally, Bell is also a trustee of the Bureau of Investigative Journalism, which also gave evidence to Bell, and Leveson, during the inquiry hearings. Its boss, Iain Overton, told Leveson (and Bell, who must have listened on with much scrupulously impartial pride) that its work constituted 'the gold standard' of journalism. Oh, how we laughed.

Not long after that, it was the Bureau of Investigative Journalism which produced that fantastically incompetent piece of journalism for *Newsnight* about a 'well known senior Tory politician' being involved in serial child abuse at a children's home in North Wales. Unfortunately, the senior Tory politician had not been thus involved and the journalists responsible for the film had not done the most basic of checks. That little nugget of gold-standard investigative journalism resulted in the resignation of the BBC's Director General and the biggest mass issuing of libel writs this country has ever seen. But Bell, a trustee of this witless organisation, is still there, advising upon British journalism and what should happen to it.

As a trustee of the Media Standards Trust he is also, therefore, a sponsor of the Orwell Prize – a bauble given out every year to the sort of journalist George Orwell would have despised.

Go away, Bell. You have done enough. You have given of yourself sufficiently. Now just go away.

I first devised my game 'The Long March Through the Institutions' way, way before any of this stuff happened. I think it first occurred to me when I was having a hugely enjoyable lunch with a really good friend, Samir Shah, who was formerly the head of the BBC's Westminster coverage – i.e. all the politics stuff the Beeb puts out. Samir now runs an independent production company, but he was, until very recently, a member of the BBC Trust. Anyway, at some point in our (on my part) well-oiled conversation, he mentioned the Victoria and Albert Museum, and what he'd been working on there. I sort of perked up. 'What have you got to do with the V&A? You a curator now, Samir?' Turns out he's a trustee, or on some sort of advisory board of the place. Why? Then Samir told me the other things he was on the board of. Loads of them. Chairman also of the Runnymede Trust – check. Chairman of the Medical Foundation for the Victims of Torture – check. Panellist on Joseph Rowntree Foundation inquiries – check. Special Professorship at the University of Nottingham – check. How, Samir? Howja get all that stuff, along with the fucking OBE? He sipped his water (Samir's diabetic; his abstinence from alcohol is medically, not religiously determined. In any case, the dude's a Hindu. His wife, Belkis is a Muslim. They have entertaining debates about the state of the world, the two of them) and said, 'I'm a high-achieving liberal BBC Asian. They can't get enough of me.' This reply is one reason why I love Samir.

In my game, the game I mentioned earlier, you can get from Shami Chakrabarti to Samir in about one move.

You can get from them to Sir David Bell, and thus Lord Leveson, in one move.

You can get to Lord Patten, and Mehmuda Mian, from either of them in one move.

You can get to the former boss of the Royal Opera House and now DG of the BBC, Tony Hall, in no moves at all.

You can get to everything else that matters, that has some sort of culturally hegemonic power over us all, in two moves max, if we're honest.

This is not a conspiracy theory; it's just how things are. I do not think that Samir and Shami and Bell and Patten and all the others are alien lizard creatures bent on world domination and the subjugation and enslavement of the human species, or that they eat live guinea pigs. It's just that this is where the cultural hegemony resides: with a disproportionately tiny number of well-appointed, largely North London – but also, to be fair, West London – liberals, or faux lefties, who are, by and large, in agreement about everything.

What do I mean by 'liberals, or faux lefties'? The description 'liberal' is so ambiguous as to be, these days, almost meaningless. It could mean anyone from the late and enormously lamented General Pinochet of Chile – economically, a classical liberal – to Shami Chakrabarti, who I suspect would not care to be mentioned in the same sentence as the good, if somewhat authoritarian, general. It is a term which has become otiose and pointless, so we shall not use it any more here. Let's use 'faux left' instead, for these particular puppies.

So what do I mean by faux left, then? These are people who consider themselves of the left, or leftish, but whose views are either wholly irrelevant to the poorest indigenous sections of our society, or actively hostile towards them. Their leftism will certainly include a warm embrace for the notion of 'diversity', but when this term is examined in detail it will be seen to explicitly exclude the white working class. You do not hear faux lefties demanding quotas for working-class people in positions of power; everybody else, but not the white working class. Theirs is a leftism which will also warmly embrace environmentalism, especially any policy that raises energy prices – something which, again, has its gravest impact on the poorest in society. They will hold a range of social views which are antithetical to those held by the majority of working-class voters. They will be in favour of immigration, partly because it is nice to be in favour of immigration, and partly for reasons of economic self-interest. They tend to be very soft on law and order, and suffused with sympathy for the criminal, who, nine times out of ten, chooses as his victims the working class. They tend – not exclusively – to be humanist. They will tend to have a high income and be well educated; a large proportion of them will be people who *have had their struggles too.*

In the past, in the early days of the Soviet Union, these people would have been known as bourgeois liberals, and they would have been shot. I am not convinced that this is an appropriate sanction today.

Instead we should simply marvel at the way in which they have achieved total cultural hegemony, to use their sponsor's phrase once again. When their views are challenged, when something is said that is 'politically incorrect', to use the well-worn term, they will react *en masse* with a ruthless ferocity. Or a ferocious ruthlessness, one of the two. You will certainly not be allowed entrance to their *milieu* if you suggest, for example, that large-scale immigration has made life worse for a sizeable proportion of the indigenous population. Or that you don't believe gay couples should be allowed to marry in church. If you say either of these things you will instead be hounded. You certainly won't be invited onto one of those boards they all run, over a cup of coffee and some nice biscuits with oats in them.

When I say that they are 'actively hostile' towards the working class, it may seem a bit of an overstatement. For sure, most of the time they are not 'actively hostile'. They may even, from time to time, occasionally, say mildly sympathetic stuff about a lack of social mobility in society, and isn't it a shame about the great inequalities of wealth we have? But these are not pressing concerns for them. And every so often the mask will slip and you will see what I mean by 'actively hostile'.

Take the journalist Yasmin Alibhai-Brown, for example. Here is what she had to say about the white working class. It was in an article written for the *Independent* in 2009 under the slightly giveaway headline 'Spare Me the Tears Over the White Working Class', which began with Yasmin castigating the 'wretched' self-pity of the white working class, and suggesting that its members were 'crying into their anti-macassars and threatening to vote for fascists'. Then she went on, with heavy sarcasm:

> ... their [the white working class] culture is proud; they are noble. What they believe – however stupid or vicious – must be awesome. Oh and they are never to be called racist, not even the scum who drop shit and firebombs through the letterboxes of asylum seekers ...

And then:

> Working-class white men provoked race riots throughout the Fifties and Sixties; they kept 'darkies' out of pubs and clubs and work canteens.

Lordy, now there's a screed of hatred. Imagine such a venomous *ad hominem* attack being made against another section of society, perhaps a non-white section of society! You'd never work again! Except, maybe, for the Stormfront White Nationalist website. It was of course white working-class men, in the Labour Party and the Communist Party, who did battle with the fascists in the 1930s.

Never mind the grotesque tarring of an entire community with one broad sweep of her lavatory brush. My point is simply that when you rub away at the surface of these people, this is what emerges. They hate the working class. Hell, at least Yasmin was being more honest than most.

Yasmin describes herself as a lefty-liberal who has voted Liberal Democrat the last two times around. Aside from writing this sort of stuff for the *Independent*, where, as I say, it is read by fifteen people in North London, she is also Senior Research Associate at Tony Blair's thinktank the Foreign Policy Centre. And Honorary Fellow at Liverpool John Moores University, Visiting Fellow at Cardiff University and Visiting Fellow at Lincoln University. She has also won – of *course* she has – the Orwell Prize. And been awarded the MBE. Fuck me sideways. All that stuff, just for having congenial views.

It's very easy to play Six Degrees of Shami with Yasmin. The Orwell Prize gets you to Sir David Bell, which gets you to the Leveson Inquiry, which gets you to Shami. There are probably about fifty other routes, too.

That piece of hers which I've quoted from was forwarded to the Press Complaints Commission. Not by me, I hasten to add. I wouldn't forward a rat's ringpiece to the PCC. We have seen recently how stunningly useless it is. More to the point, it epitomises the faux left: it is tendentiously politically correct and uses its offices to further a faux-left agenda. Anyway, as you might expect, the PCC decided there was nothing wrong with Yasmin's piece, and therefore it would not be taking any action. Hilarious, no? Side-splitting.

You can play Six Degrees of Shami with the PCC, too, in a virtually infinite number of ways. Not least via the clients who have signed up to each departed director's PR company – Alder Media, in the case of Tim Toulmin, or Pagefield Consultancy in the case of Stephen Abell.

The faux-left stranglehold bamboozles even the Conservative Party. A few years ago the party re-evaluated its position on a number of issues, at the behest of an adviser called Steve Hilton. The aim was to 'detoxify' the Tory brand. It was this mysterious toxicity which was keeping it out of power, it was argued. And so the party niced-up, by adopting a faux-left position on stuff like immigration and law and order (anyone remember 'Hug a hoodie'?). Cameron was photographed peering at a glacier and feeling bad about some polar bears. The wrong glacier, as it happens, but never mind. A wind turbine was hastily glued to the side of one of his houses – the one in Notting Hill, where there is no wind – to show that he was eco-conscious and greener than George Monbiot's garden. He was filmed cycling to work in an eco-friendly manner, while a car followed behind with his smart work shoes and briefcase in a slightly less eco-friendly manner. And gays were embraced, even if they didn't want to be embraced. This bizarre detoxifying has now caused the party to be split, with working-class Tory MPs arguing, with some force, that the old policies and approaches to these largely social issues were not remotely toxic, so far as their constituents were concerned.

The point isn't that everything the faux left says is wrong. Some of it, to my mind, is absolutely right. I can get very faux-left myself on issues of gay and lesbian equality, women's rights and animal welfare (especially hunting). What gets to me is its utter ubiquity across public life, and the viciousness with which it castigates any transgression from its own amenable positions. There is no alternative. And yet when people are polled on these touchstone issues they very often disagree fervently, immigration being a case in point. Or they are split 50–50 (gay marriage in church). The working class is especially against most of this agenda, so it has no major party to vote for.

This was simply not the case in the 1960s, or the 1970s. My parents were able to vote for a party – Labour, the party of which I am still a member – knowing that it broadly shared their sentiments and aspirations.* That is long gone.

---

* More recently we have heard about how the trade union Unite has been attempting to gerrymander and bully its way into Labour constituencies, ensuring its candidates are selected. Good for them. Rather Unite gerrymandering the process than the Labour leadership, which has been doing so for thirty years.

12

Juristocracy

Where there are too many policemen, there is no liberty. Where there are too many soldiers, there is no peace. Where there are too many lawyers, there is no justice.

Lin Yutang

Should we kill all the lawyers, do you suppose? There are still some people around who disagree with this notion, considering it 'too extreme' and 'an overreaction' and 'illegal'. Of course this last objection somewhat loses its force if we killed all the judges, too – and indeed it is probably the judges with whom I would start, if I had to organise the whole thing. It would take a terribly long time, because there are so many of them – lawyers, judges, solicitors and what have you. And their number has grown almost exponentially these last twenty-five years. At around about the time Britain stopped making stuff, we started breeding lawyers out of the dead ground; lawyers are what we have these days in lieu of a manufacturing base. It is quite possible, at their current rate of expansion, that by 2050 everyone you meet will be a lawyer.

The original imprecation to kill all the lawyers came, of course, from a minor character in Shakespeare's *Henry VI*, a chap called Dick the Butcher. 'The first thing we do, let's kill all the lawyers,' he says to the treacherous Jack Cade, who replies, 'Nay, that I mean to do.' There are plenty of lawyers around who will tell you that Shakespeare meant this as a sort of backhanded compliment to lawyers, that it was implicit therefore, m'lud, that it was only lawyers who stood between Jack Cade and his villainous plans. But of course they wouldn't be able to make this point if they were all dead, and in any case it ignores the various other gobbets of lawyer-bashing in Shakespeare's plays, not least from Hamlet, who takes the piss out of them shortly before he gets his hands on Yorick's skull. He knew his audience, Shakespeare, and even though there were only about seven lawyers in the entire country back then, he knew his audience hated them all.

There are no longer only about seven lawyers in the country. There are apparently a countless number. Of the two figures I have seen recently, one puts the number at 151,043, the other at 128,000. But we can be sure of a few things. First, that they have increased threefold in the last quarter of a century – we have 88,000 more of them now than we did in 1987, and there were too many then. That's using the lower of the two figures I quoted, incidentally. The second is that we have more lawyers than our fraternal European partners France and Spain put together. And we have more than thirty times the number of lawyers per head of population than Japan. So when someone tells you that lawyers are crucial to the smooth running of a modern, developed economy, point them in the direction of Tokyo. They do all right, economically, the Japs, despite their terrible lawyer deficit. We do not have the highest proportion of lawyers per head of population in the world – you can guess which country holds that distinction right now, Bud. But we're in the top five, and we're moving up. Maybe one day we will catch up with the United States. Until then we just have what the philosopher and social reformer Jeremy Bentham called 'a plague of lawyers'. The term 'plague' had even more force in Jeremy's day than it does now.

You may have experienced this lawyer surfeit, the lawyer plague, yourself recently when you received a text message on your mobile phone from the legal profession's equivalent of a pox-doctor's clerk, telling you about the thousands of quid you can claim if you've tripped over recently, and giving you a number to ring. Sometimes they don't just text you, but ring you instead. This is the compensation culture that everyone moans about but nothing ever gets done about it because we're run, these days, by lawyers, as we shall see. The one thing they never do, lawyers, is piss on their chips, to use a phrase which I believe originates in Port Talbot and means the same as shit on your back doorstep. First and foremost, they look after themselves. Anyway, the compensation culture is the reason why your car-insurance premiums are so fucking extortionate. It's at the heart of why fundraisers can't sell pots of homemade jam from village stalls, why your children are no longer allowed to play strenuous games in the school playground, why councils chop down horse chestnut trees, and so on. Everyone is terrified of being sued. The compensation culture has been one of our few growth industries in the last decade or so – although of course it does not actually generate wealth, it just moves it around; into the pockets of lawyers, primarily, and those of the supposed victims, and almost always out of your wallet somewhere along the line.

It is difficult to know the right approach to take when you get one of these importuning texts on your phone. I suppose the sensible answer is just to ignore them. But they rile me, and sometimes I find myself ringing the number they've given and shouting vivid and physically unlikely sexual obscenities down the line. I can recommend this as a therapeutic recourse, even if it is illegal, probably. Better still would be to find out where their office is, and then ring back and register a claim against their own firm for an injury occasioned to yourself as you were delivering a leaflet offering the services of a claims-advice line through their letterbox. A severed finger or something. But that would probably take more effort than you would wish to expend, and in any case the firm probably wouldn't have a problem with suing themselves. They'll be covered.

The compensation thing is typical of our age; a grasping and individualistic approach which would, in the days of our parents, have seemed obscene or simply ludicrous. The quintessential anti-communitarian response to a – usually minor – problem. It has grown the way it has partly for the very cultural reasons I've been exploring throughout this book, but also because we have many more regulations these days, governing how we go about every-thing we do, so that it is almost impossible not to infract them. That's where the lawyers wheedle their way in. And who drafted the regulations in the first place? You see, these monkeys have both ends covered.

The number of barristers has also increased hugely over the last decade. There are now 15,300 of them. I had forgotten about barristers, briefly, but then they suddenly came back to me. I don't wish to leave them out of the story, it wouldn't be right. They are after all second in line for leaden death, after the judges.

One of them, maybe more, maybe hundreds of them, are wondering at this very moment if I can be sued or prosecuted for a hate crime as a consequence of this chapter. Hurry, hurry, you bewigged clowns, because my stockpile of ammunition is building. Rat-a-tat-tat!

But it's not the compensation stuff which is the most worrying, nor which marks the biggest break with how we were before, a few decades back, even though in itself it's pretty significant. It is rather our progression from being a representative democracy to being a fully-fledged juristocracy. Less government by the people for the people than government by the lawyers for the lawyers. You wonder why politicians are such a dispirited and estranged bunch these days? It's because their powers have been usurped, across the board, by the legal profession. There is almost nothing upon which they can adjudicate which will not be countermanded by the judges and the lawyers – either the multitude here at home, or those in Brussels or Strasbourg.

Remarkably, although we live in a parliamentary democracy, even the politicians these days seem to defer to the lawyers when important stuff needs doing. In 2012, for example, the issue of the behaviour of our bankers, and particularly the issue of their humungous bonuses, was very much in the public mind. We were pissed off with the bankers, and the bankers, for their part, did not seem overly worried by this pissedness; their bonuses kept on growing, while the high-street banks decided against lending to small businesses because of their suddenly-acquired acquaintanceship with the notion of 'risk' – something which hitherto had deserted them. So we were cross with the bankers and something needed to be done, it was agreed on all sides. And so the government ordered a parliamentary inquiry into what, precisely, should be done, to be carried out by a select committee of MPs. Labour objected; they wished the whole issue to be the subject of something much more important – a judicial review. In other words, some desiccated and superannuated Law Lord convenes a panel of lawyers and pontificates on the matter, calling witnesses and showboating for the public, at the cost to the Exchequer, and hence the public, of millions and millions of pounds. Because when judges and their retinues are called to sit on these judicial inquiries, investigating some matter for the public good, they do not cease to charge their astronomical fees. They rack it up, day after day.

My animus here isn't directed towards Ed Miliband and the Labour Party, which demanded the judicial review – because it was implicitly assumed by all sides that a judicial inquiry carried more weight, had more substance, was somehow more serious, than an investigation comprised of parliamentarians (who would have done it for nowt, pretty much, it being their job). That's why they called for it. The thing that grates is what is quite explicit in that call. Parliament may make the laws and the job of judges and lawyers may be to administer those laws; but now we have a role reversal. The masters of our democracy are subordinate to the factotums, the beadles, the scullions. A judicial inquiry is now worth more than a parliamentary inquiry. Why should this be? As Jeremy Bentham put it, 'Why should we prefer the opinion of the few to that of the many?' Because even though there are, now, lots of them, they are still comparatively the few. And they are answerable to nobody. You can vote out your local MP at the next election, and you can help to get rid of the government at the same time. Try getting rid of a High Court judge and see how far you get. Try getting rid of a lawyer. They are an unelected and elitist excrescence on the body politic and on the lives of the people, accountable to nobody but themselves, largely insulated from censure, vastly over-remunerated (it's a sort of monopoly, natch), fantastically pompous, always utterly out of touch with popular opinion, insulated from the aspirations of the public by their wealth and status. And yet, as every year goes by, more and more power is ceded to them.

The judicial review or inquiry is one of the horrid motifs of our time, one of the most successful means of wasting money this country has ever devised. Almost everything, today, gets its judicial review. Look back, and anything that has bothered us has eventually had some judge installed in a deathly room, with a politically-correct contingent of the great and the good, mainly lawyers, asking questions badly and coming to the wrong conclusions, or evading the issue. They are nowhere near so clever as they think they are. Remember the Hutton Inquiry, into the death of the government scientist Dr David Kelly and therefore, by extension, the way in which the Blair government misrepresented our security services, and then misled the public and Parliament about the invasion of a sovereign state, Iraq? That was one of my favourites. I suspect that as a consequence of his performance during that inquiry, Lord Hutton would have difficulty securing a part-time job in Tesco's labelling the chickens with sell-by dates. An inquiry shorn of even the mildest interrogative thrust, a whitewash of the government – of course – and, as usual, a victory for vested interests. And then all the others: BSE, the *Marchioness* disaster, Bloody Sunday – two of those, the second one lasting twelve fucking years and costing a staggering £400 million, according to the government – Hillsborough (twice), Harold Shipman, the Leveson Inquiry … hell, it goes on and on. Do they shed light, these inquiries? Only if they are held about thirty years after the event, and even then not much light, not much more light than had already been shed over the intervening years by journalists who might sometimes have had recourse to powers which the likes of the hapless Lord Leveson sought to outlaw.

Again you ask yourself the question Bentham asked: why should we prefer the opinion of the few to that of the many? Because of their scientifically engineered impartiality, the lawyers and the judges, the intimation that they are somehow above the fray, that the law exists in a pristine world, insulated from the ebb and flow of political discussion, and that judges, especially, are beyond the mundanities of good and evil? Hilariously, that is the reasoning, and it is perhaps the biggest joke of all, a joke on all of us. Of course they are not. How could they be? As a consequence of their salaries, or their membership of agreeable clubs, or their gilded backgrounds? They are the chief prosecutors for the establishment, and that much is true no matter which establishment holds sway. The establishment that pays the bills, either way.

Are they at least representative of us, these people, even if we have not actually elected them to represent us? Nope. They are about as representative of the ordinary Briton as is the Marquess of Bath, that gibbering, kaftan-bedecked lunatic with fifty 'wifelets' or something who runs some sort of theme park in Wiltshire. They are, of all the trades and professions, precisely the least representative of us, socially and economically and culturally. It would be more representative of Britain if decisions were made for us by equerries to the Queen. With the judges and barristers and lawyers there is not the remotest genuflection, scarcely even a nod towards the actual make-up of this country. Even more than politicians, our judges and barristers and lawyers are white, privately- and Oxbridge-educated, and largely heterosexual middle-aged men. And that's the way they wish to keep it, thank you.

In the top six categories of judge (they have their gradations, these monkeys) there is not a single black British or British Asian face. Only 15 per cent of High Court judges are women – and that is a better score than in several other senior judicial posts. Of the very top judges, 90 per cent were educated at private schools, and 90 per cent are white middle-aged or rather older men. They urge progressive change upon the rest of us, they demand it of us, and given the opportunity they will persecute us for not being sufficiently inclusive and diverse. They will rail against racism or sexism from their benches – their perniciousness, their wrongness. But it is a case of do as I say, not do as I do. There is not a less inclusive, less diverse, set of people in the country. And they know this. But they are not noticeably unhappy with the situation as regards themselves.

We have these flawed, and pompous, high-earning, white middle-class men telling us what to do partly, of course, because we have laws. The judges are there to expedite those laws, to ensure that they are applied fairly – which, of course, they fail to do, because of who they are and where they are from, because of the political mindset they have, and because of other laws imposed upon us by other white middle-class men from other countries, in Strasbourg or Brussels or Geneva. Other men whom we cannot vote for or get rid of, incidentally.

But let us leave that aside, and concentrate on the laws for a moment. In a sense it is surprising that we don't have even more lawyers and judges, even more than we currently do, because the number of laws we have has expanded at an even faster rate, and shows no sign of stopping – although its rate of replication has at least slowed a little in the last three years. How many new laws do you suppose are made, and at what rate? Would you reckon one a month? One new law for us all to get worried about every month? Maybe you're a really hard-bitten cynic, and you think it's even worse than that. It would not surprise me to learn, you might say, that the government concocted some fatuous piece of legislation once a week – possibly even more. A new law for us to follow and bow down before every single week. How awful would that be? It cannot be that bad, can it?

Oh, if only that was what it is, one new law per week, every week, for every year. If only it could be confined to that.

Under the last Labour government we had 13.8 new laws EVERY WORKING DAY. That's what it broke down to. That was the figure for 2010 – a total of 3,506 laws introduced as the outgoing administration rushed through the last bits of its programme, an astonishing amount of legislation. Is that an anomaly, then? Yes, it is, I suppose. Under the current Conservative-Lib Dem coalition we have only about eight new laws imposed upon us EVERY WORKING DAY, more than two thousand new bits of legislation every year. Two thousand! These are the same Lib Dems, incidentally, who under their last but – oh hell, I forget, two? – leader Charles Kennedy – the nice one, who liked a drink – pledged to repeal one law for every law they introduced. I suppose you can promise to do stuff like that when you haven't got a cat's chance in hell of being elected. Oh, but you were elected, sort of ...

So, even now, two thousand new bits of legislation – minimum – per year, including stuff like the right of local councils to measure the height of your hedge and the right of the filth to break in and have a look at your pot plants. Still unrepealed, by the way, are all the old laws, about not being allowed to fart in front of the monarch and not being allowed to eat mince pies on Christmas Day – both still on the statute book, incidentally. I think you're also allowed to shoot a Welshman if you see him near Hereford Cathedral. Join me in lobbying for an amendment to this law to remove the 'if you see him near Hereford Cathedral' wording. Always keep things simple, I say. Oh, and I forgot – those new laws Labour introduced? They also provide 420 new powers for the filth, or other agents of the state, to enter your home on the suspicion that you've been up to no good in some ill-defined way or another. Just 420, then.

So, plenty of new laws every day. And all of this, by the way, excludes legislation introduced as a consequence of our membership of the European Union. How much more is there as a result of that unquestionably beneficent arrangement? Nobody really knows. The most neutral and authoritative guess comes from the House of Commons Research, which suggests that somewhere in the region of 15.5 per cent of our laws emanate from Brussels, that even more gilded and unrepresentative elite than our own. UKIP, which is not necessarily neutral on this issue, suggest that 75 per cent of our laws now come from Europe; but then they would, wouldn't they? Either way, lots more laws. Nobody knows the total number of laws we have. It's a mystery and an enigma, like Bigfoot and Andy Carroll and Schrödinger's Cat; there is just no knowing, it is beyond imagining.

The dispiriting central point to draw from this is that we are approaching the state of a juristocracy, where it is not the politicians who rule us, but the unelected judges and lawyers. Jeremy Bentham's antipathy to the role played by the judiciary was based upon his entirely reasonable assessment that the judges were a means by which the aristocracy might 'mediate' the nascent demands of a democracy. I put 'mediate' in quotes because I think that in reality it might mean 'thwart'. An extremely reactionary force against the growing and dangerous aspirations of the ordinary people. It is not terribly much different today. Take a look at a fine book by a US academic called Ron Hirschl, *Towards Juristocracy: The Origins and Consequences of the New Constitutionalism*, if you get a moment. Ron is a leftie-liberal. Ron may even be a faux leftie. But for now we will forgive him, because he is conveniently taking my side in the argument, which absolves all manner of people from any form of censure; and furthermore, he is a US faux-leftie liberal, and they are not always *de facto* wrong, as our own faux lefties seem to be.

Hirschl challenges the comfortable idea that these legal elites are there for our own good, to advance progressive (as he would put it) legislation when the political body is unable or unwilling to do so. For him, the judges instead reinforce elites which themselves feel threatened, while the courts do little to advance social justice. In short, the judges and the lawyers insulate political and economic elites from the 'vicissitudes of democracy'. This is Bentham under a different name and in a different century.

Over here, ironically enough, they seem to pursue an agenda which insulates the metropolitan middle class, the faux lefties, the affluent liberals, from those vicissitudes of democracy. Their agendas seem tilted most decisively against the working class; they always were, if we are honest – right back to Bentham's day and beyond. But now they are tilted in that imaginary leftwards direction, so that they will be soft on the burglar who breaks into poor people's homes; they will be soft on the criminal asylum seeker, even if he is a member of Al Qaeda; they will be soft on the antisocial yob who terrorises the neighbourhood of ordinary people; they will be soft on the immigrant rapist, or mugger, or drug dealer. By 'soft' I mean lenient; lenient to an extent that astonishes and appals. Miscreants from abroad will not be sent back to the countries from which they originate because their human rights might be infringed – and that, according to the new elite, the new and loaded and faux-left elite, is a more serious transgression than the possibility or indeed probability that this semi-house-trained scumbag will continue to wreak havoc among the hard-pressed people whose lives he has already made a misery. Not among the upper class, not among the judges and lawyers and solicitors and *Guardian* leader-writers, but among the truly impoverished and the truly struggling. The elite are insulated from his depredations by their wealth, and as a consequence of this by the pleasant neighbourhoods in which they live, where such miscreants do not, on the whole, venture. I often wish that a judge who has just let loose some fucking savage, in the name of faux-left tolerance and decency, should be forced to quarter the bloke for six months – have him in His Lordship's house for a while, see how he likes it. For the liberal agenda of the judiciary regarding crime is derived from basic economic self-interest; the same self-interest that urges upon the general population unsustainable amounts of immigration and the now defeated creed of multiculturalism. When their own lifestyles are threatened, the judges and the lawyers suddenly become rather more stringent, rather less indulgent of crime. In essence, this is no different from how it was in Bentham's day. It is simply that a veneer has been applied over the top, regular brushstrokes, you can't see the join any more.

I suppose you might venture that another reason for the incredible growth in the number of laws, and lawyers, is that they fill a vacuum created by the gradual evaporation of social cohesion. That a smaller proportion of us these days sort of 'know' what is right and what is wrong; that social opprobrium of behaviour that harms society has dissolved, and we therefore need to put it down in writing, and that in the end, having embarked upon this path, cannot stop ourselves until almost everything is transgressive and punishable by the state.

Listen, I know, I know – there are some nice lawyers, some good lawyers. Four, in fact.

13

Cloistered Elites 5, the North 0

The diverse natures of men, combined with the necessity to satisfy
in some manner the sentiment which desires them to be equal, has
had the result that in the democracies they have endeavoured to
provide the appearance of power in the people and the reality of
power in an elite.

Vilfredo Pareto

Huge excitement in about 1975: the suburb in which I then lived was described, in the *Guardian*, as being 'a select area of Teesside'. My family knew this because, almost alone in the place, we got the *Guardian* delivered every day. Everyone else knew about it because the article was Sellotaped up in the window of the local newsagents, Dixons, with the phrase 'select area of Teesside' underlined in red Biro. I can't remember now why we had got ourselves in the national press – maybe it was something to do with our Wanker, still resolutely tugging away behind the miles of privet and acacia, although I don't think so. I seem to recall his strenuous efforts gained little media reward, maybe just a squib in the local rag, the *Evening Gazette*, if even that. People were a little less bothered about alfresco public wanking in those days, for better or for worse. Anyway, it was a marvellous and uplifting thing for us to be described as a 'select area of Teesside', and it made us all feel very pleased with ourselves. It would have been pretty nice if this encomium had been printed in the *Gazette*, or even better in the *Northern*

Echo, but to have it said by a London publication as high-minded and expensive as the *Guardian* – well, they knew 'select' when they bloody well saw it. People talked about this, the 'select' business, for months.

I suppose that Nunthorpe was, and to a degree still is, a select area of Teesside – although without wishing to disrespect my home town, this is a little like saying 'a select area of Mogadishu' or 'a select area of Norilsk'. It was effectively a new town, most of it begun in the 1950s to serve the slightly-higher-paid workers at the vast and expanding ICI plant at Wilton and, despite the much lengthier commute over the river, ICI Billingham. At its heart was a genteel area of housing built, I would guess, in the 1920s; the rest was successively bolted on around it – first the estates of late-fifties semis (which was where we lived), then the squat 1960s chalets with brilliant white woodwork around the windows, and later groves of cramped identikit lawn-fringed cul de sacs, each house with its fenced-in postage-stamp allowance of grass and a Ford Cortina in the drive, these quiet little roads called mimsy confected stuff like 'Mallowdale' and 'Silverdale' and 'Runnymede'.

You get the picture. Just over four miles from central Middlesbrough, attainable in fifteen minutes by a decentish rail service, and with views to the south of what some called the Yorkshire Matterhorn, a photogenically eroded thousand-foot stump of limestone, Roseberry Topping, Nunthorpe was probably an aspirational place to live, if you came from the area, the heavy industry out of sight, if not actually out of scent. For there was always the smog, especially on hot days. In the same year that the *Guardian* casually bestowed its 'select' description, a square mile of Middlesbrough, directly beneath some terrifying and now demolished industrial installation called 'Warner's Chimney', was defined as the most grotesquely polluted spot in all of Europe – including, remarkably, Eastern Europe. But though we might occasionally have cavilled at the rich flatus stench of sulphur, or the somehow more sinister sweetish tang of acrylics ever in the air, we knew that this was how the town made its money, why it existed and even, for quite a long while, prospered. Even more remarkably for a sizeable settlement in the north-east of England, Nunthorpe did not have a pub, as a consequence of some arcane property deed which presumably related to a long-disbanded convent. No pub – that's class for you, that is, fucking class.

But there was a select area of Nunthorpe back in the early 1970s too – a hermetically sealed outpost to which those who lived elsewhere in this comfortable suburb looked with considerable envy and abiding *petit-bourgeois* respect. This was the Grey Towers estate, a smallish agglomeration of larger, almost faux-Georgian houses, constructed, I think, in the mid to late 1960s. Some of these houses had *drives*. Not very long drives, but drives nonetheless. And the sorts of people who lived there? Christ, they had *solicitors* there, and even *doctors*. Even the professional footballers from the fine Middlesbrough side of the time couldn't quite afford Grey Towers: the brilliant centre forward John Hickton made do with a polite 1960s semi, well away from the Valhalla of Grey Towers. I delivered to houses on Grey Towers Drive on my paper round, and did so with cowering humility. It had a Ballardian quality to it, silent and closed, imperious and, I thought, ever so slightly ominous.

So, why not move there?

> A fabulous four double bedroom detached residence of lovely family sized proportions beautifully located within what is still regarded by many as one of Middlesbrough's best addresses. Notable attractions include a good sized well maintained gardens, double integral garage & uPVC double glazing ...

That's the beginning of a description of a large property for sale this week (as I write) in Grey Towers Drive, Nunthorpe. It's an *improved* property. The current owners have even done that conservatory/dining-room thing that Kirstie Allsopp always commends to people on that fatuous and venal property programme *Location, Location, Location* – glassed-in back room looking out to the North York Moors and Roseberry Topping. Well, there's your location, Kirstie – a big house in the most select area of the most select area of Teesside. And the asking price? £399,995.

The average price of a two-bedroom flat in London this year is £465,000. To buy a detached four-bedroomed house with a decent garden and double garage in the capital you would be looking at £2.8 million. And of course, don't expect a view of the countryside for that. There was a single garage for sale in central London recently with an asking price of £585,000, nearly two hundred grand dearer than a large house in the most expensive part of the most expensive part of Middlesbrough.

I know you knew this already, or might have guessed. Middlesbrough is a very cheap place to live, comparatively. You know this by instinct, perhaps, or experience, or even through having seen Kirstie Allsopp's *Location, Location, Location* jamboree top-twenty special where they ranked a whole bunch of towns according to their desirability, and Middlesbrough, Kirstie said, with a sad shake of her fluffy little Tory head, came last. And you knew it more generally, too: for Middlesbrough read Sunderland, or Hartlepool, or Oldham, or Keighley, or Nelson, or Burnley ... the north is cheap as chips, cheap as chips with either gravy or curry sauce on the side, depending upon which side of the Pennines you're living. Always has been.

And sure, that's right – but never quite so staggeringly cheap, by comparison. Never has there been quite such a fantastic chasm between the northern towns – the empty old ports and steel foundries, the red-brick terraces that once hunkered under a yellow chemical haze, the bereft weaving valleys, the pitheads – and our gilded capital. Forty years ago that house in Middlesbrough would have been sold for maybe half the price of a similar residence in

London, maybe a third of the price if you're talking ultra-posh London. Not any more. You can still buy a house in central Middlesbrough – not Grey Towers, obviously, nor really the 'select area of Teesside' for Christ's sake – I mean the scary and skag-headed council estates in the middle, Pallister Park, Grangetown, Brambles Farm, for less than £20,000.

If you're a labourer or an electrician living in Middlesbrough, or Rochdale, or Hull, or Bootle, and having watched Question Time you decide that David Starkey's dad was dead right, and it's time to gather up the family, rent a pogo-stick and bounce to where the work is – how do you do it? How can you possibly bridge that gulf? If you own your house you'll be downsizing to a microscopic studio flat, or a cupboard, if that. If you don't own your home you'll be paying five times as much per week in the private rented sector. And don't even think about the council waiting list in London; there are so few properties left, and those that there are will go to the people with the most pressing need, which, very often, means large families just arrived here from abroad. Don't try to plead your special need with the council; they've got people queuing up from Somalia and Albania who are much poorer than you. Hell, you're from the affluent first world, you ingrate.

What I think Mr Starkey, and before him Mr Tebbit, wants you to do is live like the Poles: leave the family behind, bed down six to a room with your colleagues while working on a three-month contract, send whatever money you can back home, live out of a suitcase – and then when that job's up, move somewhere else and do the same thing again. I've got plenty of friends from Teesside who've done that stuff for almost their entire lives and are not, if we're being honest, hugely happy about it. Not happy about how their lives have worked out as a result. You can imagine what that sort of existence does to your family life, to your marriage. And to you. And I've got one or two other friends from the north-east who look at this primitive, nomadic, hunter-gatherer means of existence and think, fuck that for a game of soldiers, and stay on the dole. I don't blame them one bit for this decision – in terms of what we call social cohesion it's probably marginally preferable to scooting around the country in search of work; but imagine, too, what that mode of existence does for your family life, for your self-esteem.

Of course there has always been a divide between north and south, between the capital and the other stuff in the country, which we might call 'non-London'. But there was also a sort of balance, a sort of quid pro quo. Not any more. The growing disparity has been noticed by commentators on both the right and the left, although they tend to focus on different aspects of it, for reasons of political convenience. There was a fine analysis in the *Guardian*, for example, from the leftish writer John Harris, a native of Wiltshire:

> And so to a couple of very big questions that have jumped into the media over the last 10 days, partly thanks to a cover story in the Spectator titled 'Planet London' that focused on 'the great divide between the capital and the country'. How much longer can Britain go on with our economy, politics and culture – and now, if we're not careful, our public services – in such an unbalanced state? And if what passes for public life increasingly seems to amount to a collection of cloistered elites loathed by the population at large, might all this have something to do with it?

The *Spectator* article to which Harris referred was by Neil O'Brien, of the right-wing thinktank Policy Exchange:

> Londonitis. The politicians, civil servants and journalists who make up Britain's governing class have had their world view shaped by living in the capital and its wealthy satellites. They run one country, but effectively live in another.

The left talks about low incomes and a failure to invest in industry and technology, but doesn't worry itself too much about the liberal social agenda which is set by affluent London for the rest of the country. It doesn't talk about the problems occasioned by immigration, for example – indeed, it pretends that these problems do not exist, or that they are not actually problems at all, and that everybody is terribly happy unless they are untreatable antediluvian racist scumbags. The right, meanwhile, castigates the London metropolitan elite for its 'progressive' social agenda, anathema to the majority living outside the capital, but will not accept that direct government intervention in the economy is needed, and that the false god of the free market needs to be usurped if the growing divide is to be somehow healed. And further, that three decades of right-wing economic policies, and a concomitant culture of perpetual acquisitiveness, have actually exacerbated this divide.

What neither the left nor the right seem to get is that the liberal social agenda is a direct consequence of London's privilege and affluence. Marx was right in this, if in nothing else – the base determines the superstructure. What the London liberal elite dresses up as social concern and progressivism is actually partially-clothed economic self-interest. It likes immigration because it means employees are cheaper, and so are the staples of the metro middle-class elite: nannies, foreign restaurants, electricians, decorators, plumbers and taxi cabs.

But then the elite doesn't have to live cheek by jowl with the lowest-paid immigrants, because of course the immigrants cannot afford to live in the affluent parts of the capital. This exploited workforce lives, instead, among the indigenous working-class communities whose jobs it has gratefully taken. The London middle class does not need to worry about their kids going to a school where English is a minority language, or that's rife with gang warfare, because their kids either go to private school or to the very local posh state school, which, given the cost of housing in the area, is sort of effectively a private school in any case. And they do not have to worry about their area being changed out of all recognition by this brought-in labour force for much the same reason: a high level of immigration means, for them, a more interesting deli at the end of the street and a really rather fab new Ethiopian restaurant where they do this totally amazing bread, sort of flat and spongey, you know, absolutely delicious? They do not, on the whole, suffer the higher crime rates, the shortages of work, the Third World diseases, the drive-by shootings, the muezzin's wail, and the attacks upon single women, the grooming of young teenage girls – all stuff which, rightly or wrongly, the indigenous working class complain about until silenced by the massed ovine bleat from the liberal elite: rrrraaaaaaaaaacccist. I remember one of the soft left's usually most decent, entertaining and perceptive commentators, David Aaronovitch, addressing this question about areas changing as a consequence of immigration. Well, was the gist of his article, areas DO change, time marches on, it's a fact of life, get used to it. And for sure, they do. But is there not a difference in the sort of change imposed upon Keighley or Blackburn or Mile End and the sort of change which has been imposed upon the area in which you live, David – i.e. fucking Hampstead? You know, just the slenderest little smidgeon of a difference, mate? A soupçon? Un tout petit peu?

Again, just in case of any misunderstanding, none of the blame should fall upon the immigrants; Polish or Bangladeshi or Somali. Who would blame them for trying to improve their lot? Or, for that matter, for in some cases cleaving to their traditional customs when, under the forlorn banner of multiculturalism, they have been exhorted to do so by the state? It is palpably not their fault. And the majority of people recognise this. Trouble between the incomers and the indigenous population tends to boil over only when the complaints from the latter are dismissed out of hand for reasons of political correctness, by local or national politicians, the social services departments, or the police.

Immigration is important for a number of reasons. First, it is the perfect example of an issue over which the numerically minuscule metropolitan elite has imposed its will upon the rest of the country. An overwhelming proportion of British people wish all immigration to cease now, including a majority of those who were not themselves born in this country – and a large majority of British people think there are too many immigrants here already. The public has been remarkably consistent on this issue over the last fifty years, although opposition to immigration is now higher than it has ever been – the consequence, one would assume, of the astonishing numbers of new arrivals who have come to Britain since 1997. Second, the most pro-immigration party, Labour, has the most immigration-averse voter base, which has led to large swathes of the working-class electorate feeling disenfranchised from the mainstream political process. This is a consequence of Labour's 'Londonitis', naturally: at the very top of the party it no longer identifies with the hopes and aspirations of the people it was set up to represent. Third, the way in which immigration has taken place – the raw numbers of those who have come in, and the refusal of successive governments to consider how these people might be best integrated, or better still, assimilated – has chipped away at the notion of Britain as possessing a coherent cultural identity, a set of values to which we might all more or less subscribe. It has also necessarily shaken the view we had of our own history. You can argue one way or another as to whether or not this is a good thing. Either way, it is a double whammy in that unequal battle between those two disparate parts of the United Kingdom, London and non-London. London has imposed its minority views upon non-London in a way which non-London deeply resents, thereby exacerbating a growing political divide between these two entities. And further, the consequence of mass immigration has been to loosen even more the ties which bind us together as a nation state.

14

Choice

There is no real choice. They say 'freedom of choice'. You're given the illusion of choice.

George Carlin

At hospitals these days there are questionnaires you fill in to express how much you enjoyed your experience of being ill on a particular ward. That's quite a new thing. It asks stuff like: 'Would you recommend this ward to friends and family?' I don't know if they do it on the terminal wards – I think it's only for patients who leave the hospital without the protection of a wooden casket. So you might argue the survey is already weighted, against the dead. If I were dead, I would feel excluded by this.

Remarkably, though, they really do have the same sort of questionnaire in Accident and Emergency. Would you recommend this ward to friends and family? Yes, yes, I would, I would. It was great. It was so good I'm going to maim my friends and family with a monkey wrench so that they can enjoy the experience themselves. I suppose the NHS managers, of whom there are seventeen million, will tell you that this sort of thing will help them improve the service they offer to customers. And that is how they will put it: a service offered to customers.

The 'customer' business began in the early to mid-1980s (although not, back then, in the NHS), and has continued pretty much unabated ever since. Its inception was, I suppose, a laudable attempt to inculcate a new ethos into state or quasi-state institutions: to encourage schools and British Rail and dole offices and councils and so on to adopt the mindset of commercial organisations and treat the public as paying consumers, rather than as an irritating but necessary encumbrance to their daily lives, who could be treated peremptorily or with contempt because they were at the mercy of a monopoly. It was part of the Thatcher government's consumer-driven economic boom and concomitant disdain for pretty much all appurtenances of the state, which it believed were bureaucratic, ossified, costly and positively hostile to their, uh, consumers, the taxpayers. Its subtext, the philosophy behind it, was that to consume was good, even noble; and further, that an individual could be judged by his ability, or inability, to consume, and that therefore people should be enabled to consume, by being offered choice. As ever with Margaret Thatcher's government, the philosophy was inconsistent: free-market reforms were allied to much tighter central regulation of the very institutions she wished to emulate those in the free market. A strange woman in many ways, riven by contradictions.

Central to Thatcher's consumer-driven economy was the concept of 'choice' for the individual, who was now, happily for him or herself, known as the customer. In a sense, you can't really be a customer unless you have choice. And so the tenets of the free market, with its abiding and deterministic emphasis upon choice, was dragged into any and every walk of life; and where it could not be enforced, a sort of imaginary choice was concocted, to give people the illusion of choice even where there was no choice.

Henceforth, then, you would be given more power over where you sent your kids to school, for example. This choice, when I was a kid, did not exist in practice. We went to the nearest school, and there was an end of it. I attended the nearest nursery school – from which I was expelled for smashing a stool over another boy's head, a boy called Lee – the nearest primary and the nearest junior schools, without my parents giving it a moment's thought: it was just what one did. After passing the 11-plus I was told by the implacable authorities that I would be attending a school six miles from my home: told, and that was that. There was no choice involved. Unless you used the private sector for the education of your children, unless you were one of those people who *have had their struggles too*, then choice did not exist.

Now you can scour the Ofsted reports and quiz the locals. What's the Daniel Ortega Academy like? Is it a fucking hellhole full of crack cocaine, proto-yardies and chavs? Would Olivia be better off at the Mary Seacole Institute three miles away, or perhaps the huge and expanding Hastings Banda Academy? Now you have the right to make that choice for your child. You have been empowered by choice. At the end of the day you decide Olivia would probably be best off at the Cecil Rhodes Church of England School eight miles away, great Ofsted ratings (except for multicultural awareness, where it gets a terrible grade 4), and for which the waiting list is of course full – and open first and foremost to churchgoers. And so, despite having rented a rogue flat only yards from the school gates, and having regularly, these last few months, helped out at evensong and fellated the vicar on several occasions, it's still no go, so it's Hastings Banda for Olivia. Still, you had that choice, illusory though it might have been. And when, in a year or two's time, Olivia is pregnant, you can choose between your various NHS providers as to what sort of care pathway she is placed on. If she's middle-class she can probably have an elective caesarean, or even a home birth in a swirling water bath. But we will come back to that. Such choices, though, such choices.

The Thatcher government's fetishisation of 'choice' was continued by her successor, John Major, and with even greater fervour by his successor, Tony Blair and the New Labour administration, which in many of its policies was unreconstituted Thatcherism with a nice smiley youthful face. The notion of choice is still fetishised: choice is seen, wherever it can be imposed, wherever it can be stapled on, as an untrammelled good. This seems, on the face of it, reasonable enough: if you ask people in an abstract sort of way if they would prefer to have choice, or prefer to be told what to do, they will tend to go with the choice choice. People like the idea, so we are told, of having power over their own lives, the right to make decisions as to what is best for them. But the reality is very different. The reality suggests that too much choice drives them up the fucking wall.

And of course choice wasn't much use to the thousands of parents who tried to get their kids into the Cecil Rhodes Church of England School but have ended up with Hastings Banda. That choice wasn't ever really there, if we're honest, was it? And what of the thousands of parents who didn't try to get their kids into Cecil Rhodes, because they either didn't know about the Ofsted reports or didn't have the time to devote to such investigations, or maybe didn't really care? Do we just write their kids off?

The counter point is that the previous system militated against the poorest children, the kids from the skint families. The middle classes had more choice over where they lived, and thus tended to pick the areas where the best schools were; the poor did not have the financial clout for such a recourse. That is true. But the poor are also largely militated against by this system too, though, which turns school attendance into a competition in which the most articulate, and the best-informed, and those with time on their hands, and those who are able to move house more easily (again), will always come off best.

Under the current system the schools which fail to attract pupils and which fail to get the requisite grades for their students are placed in something called 'special measures', and are then, if they fail to do better after having been harassed for a while by the failed teachers who comprise the Ofsted squad, closed down by the Education Secretary. These schools are almost always in our poorest areas. They are the schools which are as broke as the areas in which they are situated. What they need, you might argue, is more money – for better staff and facilities. Not closure enforced as a consequence of competition and choice.

So that's schools. But this chimera of choice, this encumbrance of choice, is now everywhere, and I hope you are feeling truly bloody empowered by it.

For example, imagine for a moment that you have been diagnosed with a form of cancer. This is not a pleasant thing to imagine, I grant you, so apologies. But right now you have cancer, and obviously you wish for it to be treated, preferably so it goes away for good, or for a good ten years at least. What would you prefer? That your GP, who knows a thing or two about health, refers you to the consultants in the oncology department of your local hospital, who know a thing or two about cancer, and who then recommend for you the best kind of treatment, and where that treatment night be best carried out? That seems to me a sensible option. Or would you prefer to be bombarded with choice, requiring you to know the stage of your cancer and its precise type, and then to start scouring the internet for places that have a good rep for dealing with such cancers – hey, you've found one, in Dundee – overwhelming yourself with a deluge of information which you are not remotely equipped to assimilate or understand?

Would you wish for choice at such a time? Or would you rather put your trust in the experts? Perhaps you do wish for choice; perhaps, even in your current cancerous state, which is not a particularly happy state, you wish to be viewed as an alert and informed consumer of cancer care treatment. Perhaps you feel yourself equipped to make decisions about such things, despite everything else that is going on in your life, despite the horrible stress and the worry and the sickness and the family stressed out for you too and the fact that you got a D grade in biology and know fuck-all about anything health-related. If so, I would guess that you are in a minority. And even if you are confident about your potentially life-or-death decisions, involving all those trips up to Dundee and back, you may still, in fact, be wrong. But at least you'll get to fill in a form when you leave after the op: 'I was delighted with my mastectomy and would recommend it to all my friends and family. It was the best mastectomy I have ever had.'

On a related point, when parents who send their kids to school, and people who suffer an illness, become consumers, become customers, of these respective services does this not have an effect upon their relationship with the teachers and the doctors? We know that the comparative authority of teachers and doctors has diminished over the years; I wonder if this is a partial cause. We no longer consider them to be the experts; they are simply salesmen and saleswomen, plying their wares. They are nothing to write home about. We have their measure.

Here's another one, another choice thing, another chance for empowerment. You wish to travel by train to Sunderland from Exeter sometime soon. Do you wish to be presented with an array of fifty-seven possible ticket prices that will enable you to do this? Do you appreciate the time you've spent working out that it's probably cheaper to buy a single to Bristol Parkway, then a super saver return for the next leg of the journey to Nuneaton, then an off-peak family return between Nuneaton and York if it's mid-afternoon on a Sunday, and then a single from York to Sunderland with Grand Central, your fourth rail company on this particular journey to offer you choice and empowerment? Do you think that was time well spent? Perhaps you do. Perhaps you're grateful for the chance to save yourself ten quid on the most expensive rail service in the known universe. (There's choice and competition at work for you.) Perhaps you will think this even when the utter gumby of a guard – or 'train manager' – tells you, at Mexborough, that your ticket is not valid on this section of the journey and you must pay the full regular fare, which comes to an extra £10.99 sir, please don't take that tone with me, I have a right to go about my job without being called a finagling duplicitous cunt, sir, and if this abuse continues I will hand you over to the British Transport Police at the next stop, which is Selby in exactly eighteen minutes.

Isn't it time you changed your energy provider, you mug, you halfwit? Come on, come on, sift through the lies, the lies, the lies. All those lies from all those competing French and Spanish companies telling you how much better off you'd be with them. Is it cheapest, right now, to buy my gas from the electricity people and my electricity from the water people? Hard to tell. Could go either way. Might have to change again next January. Go on, do the research. It's a marketplace and you are empowered: it is in your hands.

Again, in theory, these choices should be empowering. It has become axiomatic that choice is a good thing, wherever it rears its head. This is because for the last thirty years the free market has, in a way, been the only ideology; we were at the end of history, remember: the free market was the perfect expression of freedom and empowerment and democracy.

I don't buy it. You can have choice, and it can be a good thing. And then you can be deluged with choice, harried by choice, stressed by choice, driven to despair by choice, have your life eaten by choice. Sometimes it's a good idea to trust in the wisdom of crowds, in the things that we decide as a society are right for us, or that the experts think are best for us, because they know more than we do. In a sense, the free market, and this perpetual demand for choice, is another expression of our modern individual narcissism, and our insularity: we alone know best. Alone. And so, empowered, we stand before the counter in a coffee franchise which has arrived here from Seattle, and we ask for a coffee, but that is not good enough – Regular? Medium? Large? Skinny? Macchiato? Extra shot? Vanilla? Latte? Cappuccino? – until we turn into that

Edvard Munch painting, the one that was nicked, and with our hands over our ears we just howl: Enough, enough, enough – I want my children to go to the nearest school, I want a flat price for a rail ticket, a decent local hospital and one energy company to provide me with energy. And I just want a coffee, that's all. The same coffee someone else wants – him, over there, I'll have whatever he had. My life is not measured out by macchiatos. I am not defined by the coffee I drink. These are not the most important things, or even remotely important, these ever more complicated and yet minuscule differences which we are required to learn, to digest. I just want a fucking coffee, Svetlana, to be honest – I'm through with choice.

In the 1960s, when I was a young child, there was pretty much no choice. It was, compared with today, a very straitened world. Straitened in ever so many senses: narrow, perhaps, collectively inward-looking, monocultural, insular, still isolated from the rest of the world by that twenty-odd miles of Channel and the huge cost of air travel. There was certainly no choice about where you went to school, unless you were the offspring of people who *have had their struggles too*. Or which hospital you went to, or where you got your electricity from, or how much it cost to travel on a train. Still less, frankly, about what coffee you wanted, if you were so effete and Continental as to want coffee. Even in the new supermarkets that were springing up all over the place there was less choice: you bought what they offered, and they offered far less than today. Except maybe for biscuits. They had loads of biscuits, long aisles of Morning Coffee and Marie and Nice and Malted Milk and Bourbon and Garibaldi and Gypsy Creams. I sometimes think it was through biscuits, and biscuits alone, that we vicariously experienced the outside world back then, and over which we were allowed to exercise our innate desire for choice. The outside world as something you would savour briefly, twice baked and vicariously, with a cup of tea. Wagon Wheels! Now there was a choice. My parents thought them filthy and decadent. And it is true that in the early days their coating was not chocolate, but something called 'chocolate flavoured coating'. Ersatz chocolate, in other words, like the stuff they had on the outside of Jacob's Club biscuits in the old days, a distant whiff of the war. The war, back in the 1960s and even the 1970s, was never much more than a whiff away. That old *ersatz* – from the German, meaning 'substitute' – chocolate has pretty much gone now. Even tuppenny chocolate mice are made from proper chocolate these days. And I suppose they aren't tuppence any more. But I digress.

The thesis is that choice has made us happier. That this control we now have has given us better lives. Has it?

The British government has begun to measure happiness. I am never terribly sure about this type of thing. It seems to be the sort of trick to which governments resort when everything else is fucked: Ah, yes, we've destroyed the economy and put everyone out of work, but are they happy? At least when we're on the *Today* programme we can tell that bastard Humphrys that while inflation has risen and unemployment has risen and there are riots in the streets, the index of happiness for the country has risen by 2.3 per cent, to 61.9 per cent. That should shut him up. Indeed, as it happens, the index for Gross National Happiness originates from an authoritarian monarchy, Bhutan, where the absolute leader, Dragon King Jigme Singye Wangchuck in 1972 decided that he needed some sort of modernist device to assure his benighted subjects that they weren't merely a viciously downtrodden agglomeration of yak-fucking subsistence-level Himalayan Buddhist peasants. And the Gross National Happiness index is what he came up with. Surprisingly, His Royal Highness Wangchuck was able to assure his subjects, waving his index around, that they were very fucking happy indeed, according to all the available data. And his device has caught on in more secular and developed climes, including Britain.

The latest happiness index stuff is not good news for we people here in Britain, though. We come well down the list, compared to other developed democracies. We are right down at the bottom, the surliest and most fractious and dissatisfied – more than 60 per cent of us complain, for example, that we are subject to 'anxiety'. Apparently the Danes come out top in this happiness index thing, and this is where I have another problem. Perhaps it's simply the case that the Danes, with their cloying pastries and clean wind-swept meadows and pig farms and ever so chi-chi restaurants and pornography are just the most pointlessly fucking smug people in Europe, suffused from top to bottom with a quite repellent level of self-satisfaction. I cannot think of any quantifiable reason for the Danes to be so pleased with themselves. Or perhaps it's just that they are a nation of gullible blond halfwits, mindlessly grinning their way to Valhalla. Or possibly they are in a constant state of euphoria simply because they are not Swedish. That is the problem with such comparative surveys.

Within Britain, the picture is straightforward. People in rural areas are happy-ish, people in urban areas much less so. Here the survey begins to make more sense. Away from the *mélange*, the furore, the transience, people have a certain peace and content-ment, and perhaps they can pretend it is still 1952. The place where apparently everybody is unhappy is, of course, London: they're really hacked off here. But they're also quite miffed in Birmingham and Manchester. So, here's a controversial take: the more multi-cultural a place, the more pissed-off everyone who lives there is. The more transient the population, the less a sense of community, the more pissed-off everyone is. None of this, mind, explains why the people of Rutland should be easily the most self-satisfied in the country. Perhaps because it's very rural and pleasant and leafy and green but they don't have to put up with northerners. Who knows. Rutland is affluent, of course, which may explain some of its people's epic smugness. But London is even more affluent, and so too are the counties of south-east England. And they're not happy. I'm not sure why.

I'm not sure, either, what the point is of comparing happiness levels across countries, seeing as how we judge things so differently, and how people like us in Britain are traditionally somewhat reserved about admitting to happiness, whereas people in Denmark are forever stabbing themselves in the arms with pins and screaming, 'Ya I am very happy, now leaf me alone.' But I suppose there might be some point to comparing them across decades. We judge things differently this way, too, when we're dealing with that strange country which is the past – but not quite so differently, maybe.

The one comparative study which has been done, by NOP in preparation for a BBC documentary in 2006, suggested that we were hugely less happy now than we were back in the 1950s. According to NOP some 36 per cent of us are 'very happy' today, whereas in 1957 more than half of us – 52 per cent – described themselves as very happy. That's quite a big difference. More of us were just a bit happy in the past too. It is not easy to discern why this is so.

We earn more money today, both in real terms and absolutely. Even the poorest of us are financially a lot better off than we were in 1957. We are healthier, less prone to chronic diseases. We live longer, quite a bit longer. We get to visit more places, do more things, consume more stuff. We are more likely to own our own homes, with all the financial security that provides. We travel abroad, we have carports and hummus and Xboxes and delicate creamy unguents which, apparently, defy the ravages of ageing, and little blue tablets which give us a stiffy whenever we want. We are better educated, better fed. Women have had their lives transformed: they are no longer tied to hearth and sink, they can now have careers, without people thinking them weird and dangerous lesbian creatures. We have freedoms we could never have dreamed of in 1957 – financial and sexual and social and technological. We do not have the Bomb hanging over us in Damoclesian fashion, either, in all its scary Einsteinium-producing glory. All that stuff has gone. The Soviet Union has gone, smallpox has gone, rickets has more or less gone. And yet we are much less happy. Why is that?

As I say, I am not sure about these surveys. We may still have been infested with that cheerful notion of 'Keep happy and carry on' back in '57, the refusal to admit displeasure, a certain acquired hardiness. Or we may simply have been delighted that the Krauts were not trying to blow us to hell with their V2 rockets, that we were enjoying a rare peace of a kind, despite the stuff that had been going on in Egypt and Korea and Malaya and Kenya. Who knows what went through the minds of those people, back in 1957, when they were asked how happy they were by these official-looking, posh-besuited monkeys, with their icy diction and their clipboards and expensive black cars? Remember, for better or for worse, people were more mindful of and kowtowing to authority back then – in this case perhaps authority in the simple, pristine form of a questionnaire: Oh yes, of course I'm happy. We're all happy here, guv, go on, 'ave a cuppa tea, rest yer 'ead on me anti-macassars.

Even despite all those caveats, we should be far happier now, and yet seemingly we are not. According to most surveys the UK has followed the USA in seeing a gradual decline in that somewhat indefinable thing, happiness levels, over the last fifty years, and particularly the last thirty-five years. Why should this be?

Who the hell knows. What follows are only guesses, if partially informed guesses. We know, for a start, from numerous opinion polls (usually carried out in the US), that people are happier if they have a religious faith, for example. Or at least they tell people, in a slightly irritating manner, that they are happier. We know too that religious adherence has gradually declined over the last fifty years, both here and in the US. That in itself might explain an erosion of our sense of well-being, I suppose. Certainly, clerics are apt to refer to a 'God-shaped hole' in our lives, a spiritual emptiness and what have you, perhaps the sort of hole that might have been filled by Alain de Botton's superb Tower of Arse, which I mentioned earlier. But I am not convinced; it may be something else to do with religious observance which kept us happy – something which is of more pertinence to this chapter. People, it seems, like simplicity; they like order; they like a clear set of rules; and they like certainties. Perhaps it is this which is missing today, partly as a consequence of the retreat from our lives of God, and partly as a consequence of a whole bunch of other stuff as well.

For example, we know too that stress levels are rising. Stress is now the most common cause for absence from work: a report in the UK in 2012 suggested that 48 per cent of workers are in some way 'stressed'. Higher unpaid workloads, longer hours and a lack of job security were just some of the reasons given for these record stress levels. Doubt and insecurity. Too much work.

We know too that people tend to be happier when they know who their neighbours are, and that far, far, fewer of us know that today. As I have described in previous chapters, these days we move about a lot, we are not settled; we have uncertain existence.

And then there's this. One US psychologist has suggested that we are not terribly happy at being bombarded with a constant stream of information (often contradictory information, of course, the world being what it is). David Spiegel, Director of the Center on Stress and Health at Stanford University School of Medicine in California, suggests that it is harder to 'turn off' this fugue of uncertainty and complexity, that it is 'harder to buffer ourselves from the world' today. Spiegel also cites 'economic pressure', but I am not sure what he means by this. There has not been an increase in absolute economic pressure: we are better off, now, than we were. Perhaps he means comparative economic pressure: we are less content now with what we have, we feel more driven to attain, to acquire and to consume. We look at our neighbours or colleagues – and they are rivals now, in a profound sense. Our position in society is measurable by what we have earned, bought and consumed, by what we have acquired along the way – it is a brusque and arid materialistic individualism, and a lot of us end up alienated, or atomised, or subject to anomie – you choose your favourite pretentious word beginning with 'a', according to which school of sociology you find the most exciting. I'll go with alienated.

And then there's that thing we have in spades, in buckets and spades, these days, the thing we never used to have much of – choice. It has been the mantra now for the last thirty years that this thing, choice, is an unequivocal good, that given the opportunity we would all choose choice. No mainstream politician would dare to advance the counter argument: that too much choice, actually, is a bit of a bugger. It would be deemed to be insulting to the electorate, and worse than that, disempowering of them. (Don't you just love that word, 'disempowering'?)

But there is plenty of evidence that more choice is the very last thing people want. They might like a modicum of choice, a bit of choice here and there, but not the immense, endless superfluity of modern choices, the demand every time you wake up in the morning to make some sort of crucial decision which you are not qualified to make, or only half-qualified to make, about everything, from what coffee you're about to drink to what school your kid should go to. Almost all the evidence suggests that what people actually want is a settled certainty. They do not want doubt, and especially not doubt engendered by their own, inevitably flawed, decision-making.

There have been lots of surveys that have shown how people hate too much choice, and become impaired by having too much choice. These have mainly been carried out in the USA on behalf of the huge supermarkets, which were accustomed to offering their customers an infinite array of choice. The best of them, though, came from a professor of marketing, Baba Shiv, who carried out controlled tests which seemed to prove that people did not always perform best when they were, as he put it, 'in the driving seat'. Sometimes – often – they were much happier being 'in the passenger seat', i.e. being told what to do, or having their decisions made for them. Not merely happier, but better able to function, to carry out complex tasks. Interestingly, Prof Shiv's idea for these tests came from the time, five years previously, when his wife was diagnosed as suffering from breast cancer. The most harrowing part of this experience, he said, was not the diagnosis itself, the reality that his wife had a particularly unpleasant brand of cancer, but the 'horrifying and agonising decisions' that were 'thrust upon' them by the doctors, the countless choices which they were required to make despite their utter and complete lack of expertise. And which they were forced to make because, he concluded, the doctors were 'following the wisdom which has come down the ages', that people need and want choice, and that the more serious a situation, the more that choice is required. Simply not so. Quite the reverse.

For more evidence, if you need any, get hold of Barry Schwartz's book The Paradox of Choice: Why More is Less. Schwartz works in that beguiling and I daresay lucrative area where economics meets psychology. His view, in short, is that despite the perseverance of the paradigm that choice makes us happier – au contraire. It paralyses us, and makes us dissatisfied and unhappy.

I suppose you might argue that this tirade of mine against choice is a railing against the inevitable. That life is more complicated than it once was, and that to eschew choice, those difficult choices imposed upon all of us, is to bury your head in the sand and to pine for the iron-clad certainties of 1952. I don't think so. The fetishisation of choice is a political construct, an illusion. We can choose, given enough time and effort, to make these individual decisions, often based on prejudice and fallacy; but it does not change the whole. The superfluity of choice leaves us angst-ridden and frit. We do not know whether we are coming or going. And that's when the weird illnesses come down ...

15

Hairs, HAIRS, Growing Out of Your Spinal Column ...

> Take a good look at the first two photos below and ponder why a
> person with Morgellons disease would have tissue coming out of
> their body with embossed Arabic numbers on it. This photo is real
> and the sample has not been altered in any way. It is available for
> research and DNA testing. The perpetrators are not beings from
> outer space. They live right here on this planet. This is not the first
> time that numbered pieces of tissue have been found by sufferers of
> this diabolical disease.
>
> Morgellons Exposed website

What's your favourite imaginary illness? I think you'd have to root
around long and hard to come up with something as good as
Morgellons, which, for a while, had thousands of sufferers across
the world, and of course especially in the USA. We, over here, did
not go in for Morgellons in quite such a big way; the Morgellons
Society UK had only a couple of hundred members, including a
family from Dartford, in Kent. I lived near Dartford at the time the
Daily Mail uncovered the story about these people, how the doctors
wouldn't listen to them and implied that they were fruitcakes, and
I was a little worried. However, having checked the copious litera-
ture on the subject, it seemed that Morgellons, while undoubtedly
terrifying, was not contagious, so I could visit Dartford to see
friends with relative impunity. There are always dangers, dangers

in everything we do, of course. But one should not be overly risk-averse. One should always embrace the opportunity to visit Dartford, come what may.

Morgellons in its mildest form – its *mildest* form, mark you – involves tiny, perhaps microscopic, hairs or fibres bursting forth from the skin, all over the body, but especially the back and the arms and the hands. Tiny, nasty, little tough fibres which have somehow burrowed or worked their way into the skin and then popped back up again, causing rashes, cracked and broken skin, and weeping, bleeding sores. Yikes, etc. Where did these fibres come from? Or, more pertinently: *who put them there?* Fuelled of course by the mass, hysterical idiocy of the internet, the number of sufferers grew spectacularly. They could now be divided, roughly, into two camps. There were those – moderates, we shall call them, remembering that all of these sorts of terms are relative – who adhered to the thesis that their unpleasant symptoms were caused by manmade fibres; and then there were the radicals who, having investigated their condition more thoroughly, were convinced that they weren't afflicted by mere fibres, or hairs. They were eggs, tiny little eggs, that hatched into writhing, wriggling little worms, WTF? These must inevitably have come from one of those two reliable conduits of human subjugation and misery: the government or alien life forms from a distant planet. Or, for the real radicals, of course – BOTH, the two being synonymous. So, people now said they felt stuff wriggling beneath their skin, maybe worms, maybe fungi or 'protozoa' – one sufferer likened it to a starfish spread out all the way across his body. Again, you know, I'm like, WTF? As they say. Aside from the wriggling stuff and the itching and the broken skin, the other symptoms of Morgellons included inability to sleep, lethargy, misery, aching muscles and depression. Remember that, because it will come in useful later.

The name 'Morgellons' was appropriated by a woman called Mary Leitao, who lived in Pennsylvania. Mary is the Lister or

Fleming of Morgellons, the main driver behind its enormous popularity and success. She noticed that her two-year-old son had a rash, which was especially bad beneath his lip, and started to investigate with the aid of a child's microscope. She found fibres, she said. And she took photographs of the fibres. She also visited at least eight doctors, none of whom could diagnose any particular allergy or ailment for her kid. A specialist she visited later suggested that Mary would benefit from some form of psychiatric-care programme, nothing too intrusive, mind, not trepanning or anything like that, just a little gentle help from some mental doctor, maybe with a bunch of happy pills. Mary was undeterred. She was a great organiser. She founded the Morgellons Research Foundation, a not-for-profit institution, to investigate this scary and apparently widespread phenomenon.

The authorities were eventually bullied into taking the matter seriously, or at least semi-seriously, and commissioned from the US Centers for Disease Control and Prevention (CDC) a bunch of research costing more than a million dollars. The CDC concluded that there was no evidence of wriggling worms, no eggs, no pathogens or toxins, no disease organisms whatsoever, and that the whole thing was, as you may already have suspected, a case of delusional parasitism – a well-known psychiatric condition, although not one which had been encountered on this scale before. The fibres were just bits of fluff and so on from clothing, or carpets, as you might also have guessed. They were not alien life forms, or the still-glowing detritus from government nuke programmes (also posited), or macabre evil germy things from government biowarfare programmes (also posited).

As I say, Mary Leitao appropriated the word 'Morgellons': she had found it in some journal from the seventeenth century that referred to an outbreak of sprouting hairs within the surely profoundly inbred population of some rural outpost of Languedoc, in France. You cannot fault her for lack of research. It is important, if you are thinking of making up a disease, to tie it to some ancient diagnosis, however fallaciously, so that people cannot come along and say, how come nobody ever heard of this before, you just made it up, you mad old bint. Better still if you do all this subconsciously.

Mary appropriated the term 'Morgellons' in 2002. She discovered the sores beneath her son's lip in 2001. So it has had a good run, Morgellons, even though the research institution she founded has now closed down, and enquiries are directed to Oklahoma State University in Tulsa, Oklahoma, where work on the Morgellons matter is apparently still being conducted by a man called Dr Randy Wymore. Good luck with that, Randy. New cases continue to appear, mind – over here in the UK particularly: in 2012 both the *Guardian* and the *Daily Mail* ran extensive features about the supposed affliction. And not only in Dartford. It's spread beyond Dartford.

You can buy homeopathic remedies for Morgellons. The most usual treatment is derived from thuja, which is a preparation made from various conifer trees. The homeopaths dilute this embrocation to such a degree that there is not a single molecule of tree stuff left in the final preparation – in common with all other homeopathic remedies. If you were being a bit harsh, you might say that there is something fitting in having a non-existent ailment treated by a non-existent remedy. There is a rather winning irony here, maybe.

And another irony. Some of the people, the mainstream medical people, who have had cause to study Mary Leitao, have concluded that she is suffering from a condition known as 'Munchausen Syndrome by Proxy'. This is a distressing psychological condition in which a care-giver – a nurse, say, or a mum – fabricates or exaggerates or induces some medical condition in his or her charge, and may become obsessive about this, falsifying reports and inventing stuff and so on. It was a term coined by a British paediatrician, Dr Roy Meadow, to diagnose the behaviour of two mothers who had supposedly killed their own children. For a while Munchausen Syndrome by Proxy, with its weird and perverse malevolence, was all the rage. Until one of the mums whom Meadow had diagnosed was later cleared of all charges on appeal, having spent a considerable time in prison, and Meadow was suspected of having made a huge statistical error. He was struck off the medical register, although he was reinstated by the Court of Appeal – but Munchausen Syndrome by Proxy was subsequently deemed, by the British and the Australian courts, not to exist at all: it now has no legal or medical entity.

So, in other words, Mary Leitao dreamed up this medical ailment called Morgellons – which, correctly, mainstream doctors insisted did not exist, except as a psychological condition known as delusional parasitism. And to explain away her persistence, her obsession, they saddled her with a medical condition called Munchausen Syndrome by Proxy – which for a while the main-stream health professionals rather liked, but which has now been deemed every bit as fanciful, and non-existent, as Morgellons. I hope that Ms Leitao appreciates the irony here.

But *something* must have been going on with Morgellons, mustn't it? There must have been something badly amiss with these people, the sufferers, even if it wasn't a worm-plague visited upon them by the evil alien reptilian overlords of the Zionist Occupation Government (ZOG), or some half-life shit from the local nuke plant, maybe our old friend Einsteinium. They hurt, these people, they suffered. Across the globe, they suffered, one way or another – largely, it must be said, in highly developed Western nations. And it is one of the little tropes of our time, this sort of thing: the growth within Western welfare-capitalist democracies of the mysterious, debilitating ailment for which there is no known cure; and for that matter no accurate manner of diagnosis and an ambiguous variety of symptoms. This is something which forty or fifty years ago we did not have at all – and while the internet can explain some of Morgellons' rapidly achieved popularity, it does not explain the rest of it, all the other illnesses knocking around. Morgellons is an extreme example, to be sure, and the people who suffer, or aspire to suffer, from the conditions I detail below may be angry that their own ailments are here corralled with what they may well believe are the discredited ravings of mentals – those poor Morgellons sufferers.

As I say, Morgellons is an extreme example of a particular type of modern ailment. But they are all of a similar type, when you examine their pathology, their social pathology: no diagnosis, no cure, an almost infinite variety of symptoms, and a condition which did not – so far as we are aware – exist more than thirty or forty years ago, although claims have subsequently been made for a sort of hastily assembled historicity. Undoubtedly debilitating conditions for which – at the very least – much doubt is occasioned as to whether they are genuine mental or physical afflictions at all, and about which the medical authorities undergo paroxysms of anguish and indecision. Reasonably enough, they do not wish to distress those who claim to be suffering, and may even go so far as to 'recognise' their ailments – which cheers everyone up, and hurts nobody.

So, Yuppie Flu, then. Or Post Viral Fatigue, or Chronic Fatigue Syndrome, or Royal Free disease. Or any one of countless other names – Myalgic Encephapathology, or Myalgic Encephalomyelitis: 'ME', as it has become known. The 'Yuppie Flu' demonym dates the ailment, places you right back where it all began, with those smartly dressed, and affluent, frenetic young people beavering away in Thatcher's consumer revolution, besuited and cool – and then, some of them suddenly suffering this debilitating, unknown thing which somehow laid them low and stopped them going to work, left them helpless. Mid to late eighties, then, for the real upsurge, when it began to impinge. That being said, just like Morgellons, it has its bolted-on historicity, its claim to longevity: the term 'Myalgic Encephalomyelitis' was mentioned in the 1950s, though it was little remarked upon back then. It had no impact or resonance back then. Anyway, just for a while, let's go through the ME checklist:

- No conclusive form of diagnosis – check
- No medical cure – check
- Recent official recognition – check, from both the World Health Organisation and, in the UK, the National Institute for Health and Clinical Excellence (NICE)
- Avid and busy support groups in Western democracies – check
- Diffuse and ambiguous symptoms – check
- Suggestions of possible extra-terrestrial or covert governmental or quasi-governmental roots to the ailment – check
- Allegations that doctors don't take sufferers seriously – check
- Death threats and abusive messages sent to those who suggest a psychological, rather than corporeal, basis for the ailment – check. Double check
- Massive and mysterious upsurge in number of sufferers in the last twenty years – check
- Homeopathic remedies which are of no fucking palliative use at all available from local high-street stores – check
- Suggestions of a vast conspiracy, involving the government, the medical profession and the BBC designed to deny ME a proper official medical existence – oh yay, yay, yay, check

A colleague of mine from the *Daily Telegraph* mentioned in a column he wrote that he had never suffered from ME because, as he put it, 'I am a Conservative'. I think that this is both a funny and an astute comment, perhaps more astute than he had intended. (And for reasons with which he would definitely disagree. If you can be astute without intending to be so. I suppose you can't, really. Oh well. Maybe subconsciously astute, then.) After saying this, though, he had to make one of those cringing apologies, because the switchboards lit up with fury, the emails poured in like bile.

This Yuppie Flu emerged into the public consciousness in the middle of the 1980s, along with Belinda Carlisle, and huge cell-phones with batteries the size of bricks, and very large shoulder-pads. It has had greater longevity than any of those other cultural appurtenances I mentioned.

How does ME affect a person? What are its symptoms? The common stuff, which always occurs, is this:

- Fatigue, not relieved by rest
- Difficulty sleeping; night sweats and panic attacks
- Lethargy
- More fatigue
- Non-fatal
- Depression

One of the societies dedicated to ME suggests that the ailment afflicts one in three hundred British people. In other words, something like 208,803.3333 (recurring) individuals. Others put the figure at one in 250, which would mean – oh hell, you do the maths. Give me a break here.

Almost the first thing you will find about these new illnesses is the intense jealousy and protectiveness with which they are guarded by those who insist that they suffer from them. The flailing paranoia and mistrust and fury. And even more than this, an absolutist determination that their ailment has somehow been imposed upon them by belligerents of one kind or another, or that it is something they have contracted from others, or is the consequence of some undiscovered virus, and that whatever way you want to cut it, the authorities – doctors and the government and the like – would wish to deny them this knowledge, and thus, by extension, the prospect of relief. That their complaint can in no way be something which is neurologically based, because, so far as the old prejudice pertains, that would implicate the sufferers themselves in their own discomfort, rather than a shadowy outside force. So it is a virus, a pathogen of some kind.

You find the same weird and unshakeable conviction among many of those whose kids have been diagnosed with another vaulting modern affliction, autism; this is not a genetic thing because, because, because, that would make us responsible. And above and beyond that, the dramatic rise in cases of autism could not possibly be down to such mechanistic sociology as genetics plus assortative mating, because that would make us responsible too, sort of, in a way. Somehow. Even sharper, more knowing, more sympathetic and scientific diagnoses over the years is not an allowable explanation. It must be mercury in the water supply or the air, or that government-imposed MMR vaccine. With the deeply distressing condition of autism, there are at least clear (if shifting) parameters of what constitutes the affliction; with Morgellons or ME, there are none.

The paranoia, the epic paranoia. Only last year, one woman journalist in the *Daily Mail*, writing about ME, or whatever the hell you want to call it, suggested that there was something spooky and suspect and at the least, you know, questionable, about the way the government was dealing with the issue. She wrote that the official records for incidences of ME were locked away for seventy-five years, whereas you might have expected them to be kept secret for only thirty years. WTF? Alien lizard-type creatures! What are these bastards trying to hide?

Look on the ME support websites and you will see this constant litany: 'Telling GPs the truth about ME', and all those 'They told me I was mad!' stories. It must be awful, thinking you have this mysterious virus thing which is bringing you down and makes you lie in bed all day, and then, after all that, having to deal with the epic disdain of doctors. But then think how difficult it must be for someone who is in the medical profession who has to deal with people who think they are suffering from this virus thing and won't be assuaged, reasoned with or cautioned otherwise.

Take the case of one of the most eminent researchers, Professor Sir Simon Wessely, from the Institute of Psychiatry at King's College, London. Wessely holds that ME is almost certainly a psychiatric condition, and said as much during an interview on the BBC *Today* programme in 2011. Yo, bad move, science boy. Cue the death threats from the ME people, who one assumes suddenly found themselves able to be a little more active, a little more vigorous, than usual. Maybe they were suddenly in remission. Death threats, then, and menacing phone calls. And, here and there, suggestions that Wessely and the *Today* presenter, Sarah Montague, and the BBC and the government were all somehow in this together, in a conspiracy to do down the people who suffered from this condition (or 'PWME', as the ME support group likes to refer to them), and that the interview was a con, a joke, a piece of anti-ME hatred, whatever.

When I wrote up what had happened to Wessely for the *Sunday Times*, the ME people didn't respond merely by insisting that I was wrong, and that Wessely had been wrong: some of them demanded that I be brought up before the Press Complaints Commission (fat lot of good that'll do them, mind – it's the regulatory equivalent of homeopathy), and some suggested that I should be prosecuted by the police for 'hate crimes'. It all led me to suspect that if ME was indeed a psychiatric condition, which it seems to be, then it was actually the least of its sufferers' psychiatric concerns.

Not all of the people with ME reacted in this way, it should be said. Another researcher, Professor Myra McClure, came to the same sort of conclusions as Wessely, but, given the death threats and the menacing phone calls and the generally bad vibe associated with such research, she decided to give the whole thing up and go research something different instead. She left the job. That's a good thing, according to the ME website, because as a researcher she wasn't up to much anyhow. So that's you told, Myra, you besom.

At the time of the Wessely interview and my write-up for the *Sunday Times*, the ME people, the PWME community if you will, put their faith in a study that was due to come out quite soon, and which they confidently declared would prove Wessely and McClure and Montague and Lord Reith and me and all the rest of them to be saps and dupes or agents of the alien lizardy beasts, etc. This was a study carried out at Columbia University in New York, into a possible link between ME and the unpleasant retroviruses XMRV and P-MLV, which have a distant relationship with HIV. Well, since then the Columbia people have reported their findings. They have discovered no link whatsoever between XMRV or P-LMV and ME – and have gone further, to suggest that there is no link between ME and *any* virus. The notion that ME is caused by a virus of any kind should be written off 'for once and for all', they concluded. Did the PWME community react to this expensive and important research with gratification and relief? Go on – take a wild guess.

Meanwhile, Professor Wessely has confessed himself to being utterly bemused. Why would these people, who are clearly suffering, who are clearly not happy, wish themselves to be afflicted by a weird, scary and possibly lethal retrovirus (such as XMRV) rather than a psychiatric condition which can be at least treated and ameliorated? And not merely wish themselves to be afflicted by the virus, but be terribly and sometimes violently averse to the suggestion that their illness might have any other possible cause? It's all a bit of a mystery.

For don't forget, whichever way you look at it, ME is an illness. One way or the other, that's what it is. Just as is, by way of handy comparison ... Fibromyalgia.

Uh-oh. Uh-oh. And now we have mentioned the f-word.

Fibromyalgia is another illness which simply did not exist a while ago, maybe twenty, maybe thirty years ago. Or if it did, it did not have a name. Fibromyalgia means an aching of the muscles and the fibres, from the Latin. The various support groups suggest that 'as many as one in twenty-five' people in Britain suffer from this ailment. That means about two and a half million people, if we believe their estimates. You know that checklist I did above for ME? It all applies here, every bit of it. Impossible to diagnose, impossible to cure, ambiguous symptoms, non-fatal, didn't previously exist, except that recently its promoters have suggested that it was known back in the seventeenth century. One early researcher of the thing, whatever it is, a man called Frederick Wolfe, suggested that 90 per cent of all clinicians and sociologists who had had cause to look at the illness considered that it did not remotely exist. There are no clear boundaries, for example, between Fibromyalgia and ME, for a start. They merge indistinguishably. Its symptoms include:

- Muscle pain and aching
- Interrupted sleep
- Lack of sleep
- Torpor
- Lethargy
- Depression

If you're unlucky and you have Fibromyalgia, you might also have Irritable Bowel Syndrome (IBS), which is closely associated with this imagined ailment. It's highly doubtful whether IBS exists either, other than as an agglomeration of other symptoms which might be a consequence of bad diet, or alcohol abuse, or constipation, or eating seven pies before sitting on the sofa to watch a box set of *Midsomer Murders* with a bottle of Jack Daniel's. I mean the old *Midsomer Murders*, the one that had John Nettles in it and no black folk.

People with Fibromyalgia say that in the past the illness was diagnosed as a form of rheumatism. That is their way of telling you that it has history, it has tenure, as a physical rather than a purely psychiatric condition.

The homeopaths have plenty of treatments for Fibromyalgia too. And so, actually, does Big Pharma, the extremely rich drugs companies. It is not merely bullying or pleading from one side, the suffering side, which results in an illness being officially designated as an illness. The drugs companies are very much in favour. For more information on their approach to illnesses, real or imagined, I would direct you to Dr Ben Goldacre's two books on the subject.* I ought to point out right now that Dr Goldacre may well not share my views about ME and Fibromyalgia; he may have very different views indeed. I mention that just in case you've started to cc his name into the hate mail you're about to send me.

You can see what I'm doing with the lists of symptoms for these illnesses, I suppose. Depression, lack of sleep, indefinable aches and pains, lethargy – the same in every case. I suppose in some ways this is not a surprise. After all, anyone who is suffering from an illness – whatever it might be, even one that actually medically exists – will probably tell you that they have aches and pains, and that they are feeling a bit down in the dumps, and not sleeping too good. Those are sort of the symptoms of every illness. I'm not a doctor or a scientist, so I'm not going to wander blindly down this path any more. It's simply that we have seen a plethora of these vague, non-lethal, muscular achy languorous illnesses which in the

---

* *Bad Science* (2008) and *Bad Pharma* (2012).

past did not exist at all, or if they did exist, had somehow managed to evade the public consciousness entirely.

And then there's stress. As I mentioned before, stress now accounts for the single largest number of days people take off work in the UK. There are lots of different statistics around, but the Health and Safety Executive puts the figure at 105 million days lost per year, at a cost to employers of £1.24 billion. The number admitted to hospital with this thing, 'stress', is rising too: there were 6,370 admissions in 2011, almost all of them people of working age. Another survey suggested that 75 per cent of British people suffered stress on a daily basis – however, this was conducted by the manufacturers of Kit Kats, and I haven't checked out what questions they asked or what was the methodology, so it may well be a crock of shit. Beware of these corporate-sponsored surveys that festoon our newspapers.

Stress is, again, difficult to define, almost nebulous and ungraspable in a clinical context. The list of possible symptoms is almost infinite, too – although it does of course contain within it our old friends loss of sleep or inability to sleep or relax, aches and pains, moodiness, and so on. We know that prolonged stress can lead to very serious medical conditions which are most definitely definable in a clinical context, such as high blood pressure, to give just one example.

My point isn't that all of these illnesses are effectively the same thing – as I say, I am not a doctor. Although it would seem, to an untrained person such as myself, that there are many similarities between them – clinical, psychological and social. Clearly there has been an enormous rise in this sort of affliction over the last twenty to thirty years, even if you take at face value the claims for historicity from the societies representing their sufferers. Something, then, appears to be going on. The swift rise of the sort of affliction which is at best nebulous in its presentation, hard to define, impossible to cure and sort of painful – sometimes very painful, sometimes crippling – must be an expression of great dissatisfaction and unhappiness. I do not mean by this definition to devalue, to under-play, the suffering occasioned to those people who claim to have ME, or Fibromyalgia, or for that matter stress, or the more reliably bonkers ailment of Morgellons. As I say, they clearly hurt, they are in pain, and a good many of them feel excluded and alienated by a refusal on the part of society to take their illness seriously. And we certainly should take them seriously, because not only do they patently occasion distress, they are growing very rapidly in number, and are as defining of our times as a blog page or an Xbox or a politician with his hand in your wallet. We simply did not have them before. And you will note that in all cases there is a frustra-tion and annoyance – or, in extreme cases, a pure loathing – of society or the stuff of society. Even with stress, which is most popu-larly assigned to an imposition placed upon the sufferer by an external agency, usually the employer. Perhaps it is too glib to suggest that what those suffering from ME or Fibromyalgia or even Morgellons are actually saying, when they insist that it is a virus to blame, or mercury in the water, or mobile phone masts, is: 'Something has imposed this horrible disability, this pain, upon us. We do not know where it has come from. We do not wish to be like this, we would like it to go away.'

One commentator, I forget who, suggested rather callously, when presented with a list of the symptoms of ME, that these people were suffering from nothing more than 'life'. Well, indeed. If that is the case, and ME is not the consequence of a retrovirus – which, by now, we can be pretty clear it is not – then we have got life wrong. Not just those who suffer, but all of us. Even the man who does not suffer from ME because he is a Conservative. Perhaps especially him. If it is life the way it is lived today, then this life is making people sick. It is in some way unhealthy. It is not bad diet, or failing to go for a nice jog every now and then. It seems to be something more intrinsic, and far less easy to grasp. An atomised existence, full of insecurity and the constant intimation of failure, an aversion to authority, a suspicion that you are on your own against a hostile world.

A friend of mine, a doctor, was recently working in her hospital's Accident and Emergency department in central London. It was a fairly grim time for her: the gunshot wounds and the stabbings and the abusive drunks and the much-needed litres of blood and the clamour and the chaos and the frequent hostility, even from the sober. What was the worst of it, though, the stuff that really got her down? It was 'the worried well'. The rank upon rank of perfectly OK people who sat there in that racked and suffering bedlam, sometimes till long past midnight, waiting for some sort of treatment, some sort of assuaging, some help. Help with something. People with no real illness or contusion or disability, who took up the time of the medical staff when they should really have been treating the black kid with his guts spilled on the floor after a gunshot wound in a nightclub. The worried well. They comprised slightly less than 50 per cent of the people waiting for treatment, sitting there patiently on their plastic chairs, hopeful that someone might take a look at them and maybe get out the stethoscope or that inflatable blood-pressure thing, anything really, to explain away their discomfort or dissatisfaction, someone in a white coat to do it please, someone properly qualified, because there's something wrong with me. There's something wrong with me.

And there are millions like this. Three million people in the UK alone, for example, suffering a wholly imaginary food intolerance. One in four visits to a GP are from people who have – clinically – nothing whatsoever wrong with them, just this anxiety, this worry, this fear, this expression of what it is to be alive today. And then there's depression – the latest survey (2014) suggests that half of the adult population suffer from this affliction; not perpetually, maybe, but on and off. Fifty per cent of the country.

They work long hours, the doctors in A&E, long, long hours,

and maybe their sympathy can get stretched so far that sometimes it snaps back, like an elastic band. My friend treated a woman there who had been sitting for ages on one of those plastic chairs, waiting for her turn with the doc. 'What is the matter with you?' 'I'm tired,' she said. 'I'm really tired.' Next.

16

The Muon and the Elephant in Your Sitting Room

To live is to war with trolls.

Henrik Ibsen

I sometimes wonder how my parents would have got on with the internet. My mother died before anyone had a computer at home. My dad died when the internet was just up and running, and I had commended to him its wonder, what it might do for us all in the future, its astonishing breadth and infinite potential. He did not seem convinced back then – in about 1999, I guess this would be. This was a man who had never quite recovered from the terrible failure of Betamax; he thus felt hoodwinked by technology, considered himself the victim of a con and became distrustful of all new such developments, of which, he supposed, the internet was simply yet another, yet another. A six-month wonder. You see, he had also gone for those eight-track in-car music cartridges that were popular for about six months in the mid to late 1970s; so you can forgive then his general sense of disillusionment with this stuff being relentlessly urged upon us, stuff we had to buy and quickly adapt to. Technology advances rapidly when money is to be made, and the older you are the harder it is to be patient with both its breathlessly gasped promises and its irritating regimens – and the much harder you find it too to separate the wheat from the chaff.

Neither of my parents experienced the internet, sent an email or joined a web community in their lives. I do wonder what they would have done with the internet if it had been there all along, if it were something with which they were familiar and comfortable. Would my dad have been up in the small hours of the morning, wanking away to the inexpert film of some rather hard-faced post-Soviet babe being fucked in a field by an Alsatian? Obviously, I would prefer to think not. And yet we are told that pornography is the main driver of the internet, the thing most men want when, Scotties to hand and the wife asleep in bed, they surreptitiously log on. And 'Ukrainian Dog Witch' was very popular for a while, back in the relatively early days. Worse still, would my mother have been a member of the Milly-Molly-Mandy Mumsnet community? Christ, I hope not. I think I'd prefer the Ukrainian dog stuff. It is possible, though. Knowing my mum, it's just as likely she would be a valued member of the League of Odin, or would frequent some radical socialist website, or be the progenitor of a blogsite which posited that dowsing could provide the answer to mankind's fears and worries. She was eclectic and unpredictable in her interests, my mother, and not terribly scared of extremes. I'm not kidding about the dowsing thing, either. She was into that. She had a pendulum, and she used it.

The means by which my parents got their information was of course simpler than it is today, and close to binary; so simple that one suspected there must surely be other views out there, ones not being heard. My father, in fact, sometimes contradicted the news-reader on the BBC, arbitrarily and for no good reason. 'The US Army today launched a new offensive against North Vietnamese forces,' Peter Woods or Kenneth Kendall would say, and my father, sitting in that armchair, sipping a cup of tea, would reply with quiet authority, 'No they didn't.' There was no reasoning behind this, other than a wish to be contrary, and the faint conviction that one should believe pretty much nothing anybody tells you about anything, especially if they are in a position of power. Rather like the case of that German newscaster from a decade or so back who was caught with his mic still on, and the cameras still rolling at the end of his bulletin, saying over and over, 'It's all lies, lies.' I don't think my father thought that it was all lies, or didn't believe that the Americans had launched some punitive reprisal; I think it just comforted him to know that there was someone out there ready to cast doubt on all this stuff, i.e. himself, even if it was from a position of utter and complete ignorance. I think he yearned for a different view. For there was no other means of finding out about the latest US military manoeuvres than to make your own way to the Cambodian border and have a look.

Other than the TV, my parents – and I, of course – found out about things through the bland and emollient chirruping of the radio, and the newspaper delivered every day – the *Guardian* from Monday to Saturday, the *Observer* and *Sunday Mirror* on a Sunday. Later in life, after my mother had died, I visited Dad one time and saw a copy of the *Daily Mail* on the little mock-wood melamine-topped table next to his now sunken and destroyed armchair. 'What the fuck's that doing there?' I asked, pointing at this excrescence. At that point in time I was very averse to the *Daily Mail*. It couldn't have been more shocking if I had found him wearing a dress, or rubbing himself up against a goat. He said he'd cancelled the *Guardian* because he was sick of it, especially Polly Toynbee and Peter Jenkins, with their endless, witless, bourgeois, pro-SDP mithering. I got that, sure. Anyone would understand that. But the *Daily Mail*, Dad, I asked. Really? He picked up the newspaper from his table and looked at it for a moment. 'I feel like I've come home when I read it, Rod. I feel like I've come home.' He said it like people say it when they've had a sex change they've been waiting for all their lives.

That was what you did, back then, for a change of view: cancelled the paper, and ordered a different one. This is, I know, belabouring the obvious. The fact is that back then the world was presented to us in binary terms, less complex and so much easier to understand, and the information we got was rationed and scant by comparison with today. It was a more obviously binary era politically of course, both domestically and abroad; there was, in both cases, just left or right to worry about. If you were to challenge orthodoxies you needed to do serious work, you needed to go places, you needed to research stuff, you needed to immerse yourself, you needed to devote time.

Not any more. You can challenge an orthodoxy now with a simple click of a mouse, and register your protest against it without ever having understood how that orthodoxy came about, or what it really is, or why it became an orthodoxy, etc. You can join the 38 Degrees website and click on a different issue every day, even if you know less about it than I know about grand opera or the mating cycle of the fucking ant lion, and feel sure that people take note of your impeccably *bien-pensant* opinion, because it's there as a registered protest which will go to Downing Street or the BBC or the United Nations. Click democracy. Suddenly you are an expert and you count, for which congrats.

And, I ought to add, it's the same if you wish to support the prevailing orthodoxy too: you read four lines some unknown idiot has written on a blog you like, and you sail off across the ether, across cyberspace, depositing your noisome little turds of quarter-baked fuck-brained idiocies here, there and everywhere, demanding this or declaiming that, eviscerating your opponent or stamping your little cyberfeet – with exactly the same basis in fact and reality as my dad putting Peter Woods right about the Vietnam War: 'No they didn't.' Except, unlike my dad, you think you're dead right. You're utterly convinced of that, because of your own prejudice, and because of those four lines you read by some other fucking halfwit.

Mea culpa. You know, I'm no better. I think I'm right, too. Hell, we've all done it, contributed to the moronic inferno – a term coined by Saul Bellow before the internet was a reality, as it happens. We've all weighed in with our tuppenceworth of unmitigated shit which will shed no light whatsoever on some vitally important issue of the day, but so long as we get our word in then the ignorance doesn't really matter, we've scored a goal for our side. And this inferno, this dismal fugue, surrounds us, jabbers at us, its cretinous tweets burrowing like weird polyester fibres beneath our skin, its imprecations arousing us, everything convincing us to dive in with our own little puked-up gobbet of fucknuts – that Israel's dead right to blow the ragheads to hell; or that the Antarctic ice sheets are growing, not receding; or that Hitler had a point about a few things, frankly, when you look at his policies – the sort of conversation you might overhear if they opened a really horrible bar in Rampton. Half-digested shit sprayed from wall to wall forming one single, dark-brown graffito: I am, therefore I must be heard.

Which is fine. Be heard. Fill your boots.

None of which is to let the journos off the hook, mind. This is not a flailing MSM deadwood rant against the usurpers; far from it, we deserve a bit of usurping. Our job has certainly been made easier as a consequence of the internet – we can now write authoritatively facile articles on any subject you care to mention, the information right there at our fingertips. Better still, we need not even go near the source materials, when there's Wiki to give us a handy and cheerfully inaccurate cut-and-paste assessment. There is a truth in Slavoj Žižek's observation that the internet 'provides reality deprived of substance'. The substance is there, of course, but being the creatures we are, we are not terribly interested in it. Obviously this is not something for which we should blame Tim Berners-Lee: the fault is not the technology but our use of it. We are much the same with television; an astonishing medium, unlimited potential, etc. etc., and you will find, tucked away within our 550 channels, rarely, something genuinely illuminating and arresting. But the vast majority of it is some air-headed tart with enormous baps being forced to eat beetles by two gurning Geordie munchkins in a mocked-up jungle.

Likewise with the internet. It is a medium which accommodates itself perfectly to our almost infinite narcissism, our big-I-am willy-waving and relentless solipsism. Its apogee was back in 2006, when *Time* magazine chose its Person of the Year, and guess who won? Yes, it was You! Yes, You! Every one of You, everyone in the world sat behind their little screens tap tap tapping away, You've won! All the people beavering away at their blogs, their take on the world (comments: 0), all the monomaniacal communities. Congratulations – You are the most important person in the world. Hell, shucks and so on – be honest with Yourself, You always were. As if it needed *Time* magazine to tell You that.

I suppose I should concur that we are now more widely informed and more readily informed than was ever the case in the past. But it is hard to argue that we are better informed or more deeply informed. You might counter that this tirade misses the good stuff which has come as a consequence of the internet, and you'd be right. I haven't devoted any time to those brave souls who helped foment dissent against tyrannical leaders in that somewhat questionable 'Arab Spring' we have all so much enjoyed. That's because these acts of defiance are as nothing when compared to the rest of it. They are not a fraction of a fraction of a fraction of what the internet is more usually used for – you would need those monkeys at CERN to calculate just how fantastically minuscule, how sub-atomic, is the proportion of those brave and righteous blogs and posts. A muon placed beside an elephant, perhaps. Most of it is men wanking to women being fucked by dogs. Or films of people getting hurt, or a woman taking a dump in an aisle of Tesco's, or the views of an idiot broadcast only to his own right hand. I am talking about the internet in its generality, in its broad sweep.

Because there is some good stuff, of course there is. There are roses there among the pricks. Earlier I mentioned 38 Degrees, a very clever website set up by some middle-class lefties to advance a middle-class leftie agenda; basically it gets its members to sign petitions, petition after petition: against the cuts, against NHS reorganisation, in favour of gay marriage, and so on and so on. I joined it myself to sign a petition against the selling-off of Forestry Commission land to private owners. And for sure, the campaign was successful, the policy was dropped forthwith.

That was partly because government, and the establishment in general, do not yet understand how to quantify such protest, what weight they should give to a petition signed by 100,000 people. Twenty years ago, a hell of a lot of weight, I would reckon. But today, when everyone is at it? Anyway, the forestry campaign thing was successful, and I received an email from 38 Degrees thanking me for my participation in this successful campaign and noting its previously successful campaigns, such as the one to stop Rod Liddle becoming editor of the *Independent*. Ha, I suppose I should thank them personally for that, seeing how the paper has gone since.

But this is a digression. I was probably wrong earlier to single out 38 Degrees for even mild ridicule. It has moved away a little from the mob-rule bullying-petition business, and now has local groups of people across the UK discussing complex political issues in depth and, you know, in person, in the flesh. I went to one of their local meetings, and the level of debate was astonishingly high, well beyond my background knowledge of the subject (NHS changes). Then they all went out and did stuff to advance their cause, involving considerable levels of hard work and organisation. Local grassroots democracy in action – yowser! You cannot possibly argue against the value of that sort of thing, the internet as a noticeboard bringing together communities of like-minded people who then do real stuff in the real world. Even if you don't like its agenda, you must at least admire the conceit, the aspiration. But still, when compared to most of what goes on out there in cyberspace, we are still in the territory of the muon and the elephant.

Back to that *Time* magazine award which You won back in 2006. Congrats, again. Slavoj Žižek suggests – of course he does – that the You who appears in cyberspace is not the you who is actually sitting in front of the screen. A reflection of a reflection, maybe, or a refraction of the real you; an ideologically-sound nod to Derrida and Lacan. Well, I hope he is right, old Slavoj. Because the You that emerges from those hard drives is in essence a fairly repellent creature; you sort of hope that it isn't us, but then again you suspect that it is a sort of stripped-down, concentrated version of us, at the least.

It's not so much the dog–woman wanking stuff that bothers me, as the utter hatred. The fury and the loathing and the desperate desire to mete out punishment – and the equally desperate desire to be outraged and transgressed. The internet seems to me a convocation of a billion balloons too copiously filled, the skin of each stretched so painfully taut that it will burst at the slenderest indiscretion. So many – countless – sensibilities hungry to be offended and then to respond, not with disagreement, not with a countering of the points of objection, but with a sort of nihilistic rage that such things could even be said, and a feeling that whoever said them has to be somehow punished: get the police involved, kick them out of their job – whatever it is – beat them down with whatever weapons come to hand until they really, really, fucking regret having dared to say something with which others might possibly disagree. Destroy them.

Recently there was a kid living in a village near me in Kent who posted an image on Facebook of himself setting fire to a poppy on Remembrance Day. You may remember the story. You may not, because there is so much of this stuff, a new story every day. I say he was a kid – actually he was nineteen years old, but that's not terribly far from being a kid when you're my age. His name was Linford House, and he lived in the old and rather frowsy former mining village of Aylesham, a few miles from Canterbury. Local people were at pains to insist that he had been well brung-up, good family, what have you. So anyway he posted this picture – which was, to be sure, provocative and maybe a little silly. But I understand the point of his protest. I can comprehend why people, especially young people, might think the whole poppy business has the whiff of hypocrisy about it, glorification of war and all that. I don't actually *agree* with this sentiment – just in case the fucking maniacs are reading this book and are poised by their 'send' buttons. But I get it, I understand. And I think that in a rational face-to-face discussion, in real life, in the flesh, most people would probably understand too, while agreeing to disagree with young Linford.

'Burn that little cunt.'

'I would love to stick hot pins in his eyes.'

'He should be hung [sic].'

'Arrest the cunt.'

Those were some of the comments posted on a Facebook page entitled 'Linford Linny House Poppy Burner – Prick'. They are not, I ought to add, unrepresentative. I have not cherry-picked this stuff. They were the first I saw. A screed of violence and hatred, threats and the inevitable demand for punishment: arrest the cunt.

Anyway, the cunt was arrested, as per the instruction, as happens these days. That's one of the things with the internet. If it just existed out there alone, with no connection or relationship to the real world, like one of those virtual-reality games played by quite unhappy people, where you create a virtual life for yourself away from the debilitating stuff of reality, then it wouldn't matter. But increasingly – and for reasons which I do not understand – it is considered part of the living, everyday world. So Linford House was arrested and held overnight in a police station, in the cells, and then released on bail. Arrested for burning a poppy? He was held under the draconian and to my mind obscene Malicious Communications Act of 2003, under which you can be peremptorily banged up for saying something which others take offence at. Linford House was arrested for having annoyed people, for having provoked imbeciles beyond the limits of their endurance. That's another thing with the net – so many imbeciles, so little endurance. Here we are dealing with the elephant, not the muon. This is actually how it is. Cyberspeak designates these people as 'trolls', but it is a delusion. This is how we are, an awful lot of us. Arrest the cunt.

Linford House then disappeared for a while. At the time of writing I don't know what's happened to him or if he will face charges either for annoying maniacs. I spoke to a Labour councillor in Aylesham, a nice old bloke who knew Linford's family. He was plainly terrified that his community would be next, his village designated poppy-burner central, all manner of misery visited upon it, as if it were Luton. 'Just let it be known we have a lot of army people here,' he said, craving absolution from a crime which was not his, nor was really a crime.

Luton, then, where poppies also got burned, by extremist Muslims who object to the war in Afghanistan. Arrest the cunts! So they were arrested. It was the idiotic gobshite Anjem Choudary's lot, in one of their new incarnations – Islam4Uk or ICan'tBelieveIt'sNotJihad.com. Let them burn their poppies, if that's what they want to do. But when the twittering gets going, when the Facebook pages start up, the Old Bill feel they have no choice: they have a vast array of anti-hate-crime legislation under which they can now arrest someone for exercising their right to freedom of speech. None of this would be happening were it not for the internet – the irony being that a medium designed to enhance and expand freedom of speech has actually had the effect of curtailing it.

You might suspect a certain self-interest in what I'm saying here. It's true that I get threatened with being reported to the police at least once a week. Two recent occasions have been on the diverse subjects of cats and ME. With the cats thing, I had written a long article which began with a description of how I had caught a cat in my garden, subjected it to a summary trial, and hanged it from a gibbet I had constructed while several fieldmice looked on, knitting and cheering. It is true that I am not especially fond of cats, but this particular story was not, as my accusers imagined, a case of straight reportage – it was what we in the trade call 'a joke'. I thought I had signalled the joke thing with the knitting fieldmice, apart from anything else – but no, no. The ME people got annoyed about a mock-doctor column I wrote for a *Spectator* blog. Entitled 'Dr Liddle's Casebook', it divided a bunch of ailments into two categories – illnesses and not illnesses. Under illnesses I had 'most forms of cancer' and 'being blind' and 'having a bad cough'; under the stuff which wasn't illnesses came 'wearing spectacles' and 'being a bit mental' and, of course, ME. On both occasions the police were alerted and instructed to prosecute me, in the first case for animal cruelty, and in the second for 'hate crimes' against people with ME.

In the second case one woman reported on her community's website – which was of course all of a lather – that her local police in Derbyshire had asked who had made these comments, and when she replied 'Rod Liddle,' apparently told her that the man was a well-known 'arsehole' and it was best just to ignore him. So common sense still exists in at least one constabulary, then. I particularly enjoyed the contribution of another woman who told her web community that she would be writing to the General Medical Council to have me struck off as a doctor, not to mention the others who suggested that I probably wasn't qualified as a doctor at all.

The obvious conclusion is, I think, the wrong one – that these people are all very, very stupid indeed. They cannot all be, surely.

I think there is a real thirst, a genuine desire to be hurt and outraged, so that this animus can be channelled into vengeance and the possibility of punishment, and that this monumental drive occludes their vision. And of course there is something in the instantaneous nature of the internet – of the email and the tweet and the blog and the post – which obscures nuance and meaning and almost defies a rational approach. We have never been so hair-trigger sensitive before, so ready to be inflamed, so furious as to fly off in a swarm to threaten the object of our dissatisfaction, and to get on the blower to the filth and the United Nations and what have you, urging that something be done about it all, arrest the cunt.

Arrested for burning a poppy. We used to pride ourselves that here in Britain we didn't get terribly worked up about people being unpatriotic, or anti-patriotic. Not like the Yanks, who would foam at the mouth whenever Old Glory was set on fire by long-haired protestors. Well, that's all gone. But then, we have also started banning certain political groups whose views we find offensive, such as the idiotic Choudary's lot, who I mentioned above. Are they really that much of a threat to us all? As a kid I was a member of the Socialist Workers Party, which had as one of its stated aims the violent overthrow of the government and its replacement with workers' councils comprised of dour Scotsmen and screeching harridans. We were also supporters of Sinn Féin/IRA (which we pretended was a Marxist, rather than Catholic-Nationalist, bloc), which had been cheerfully blowing people up in London and Birmingham. Nobody suggested that we should be banned; there would have been absolute outrage if such a thing had been so much as mooted. It never was. The same went for the Communist Party – which was, as we knew then and know still better now, working on behalf of a hostile superpower that had several thousand nukes targeted at our country. But nobody called for the commies to be banned: people simply realised that they were fucking useless and of absolutely no account. Arseholes, best just to ignore them.

It is not just the internet which has hastened our shift from a position of benign tolerance to one of quite remarkable, thin-skinned intolerance. But the internet is in there, somewhere. In its immediacy and universality. Suddenly the *bien-pensant* left hear views with which they fervently disagree – gypsies can be a bit of a problem, immigration should be curtailed, Christian guest-house owners should be allowed to bar homosexuals from their premises, and so on – and they do not stop at countering these opinions. They do not stop at the quick rebuttal. They call in the police, or the Press Complaints Commission, or they hector the employers of whoever has been so rash as to say something with which they dis-agree and demand 'action' against them. I would guess that this remarkable facility for hair-trigger sensitivity and wallowing in outrage has always been with us, but has recently been facilitated by technology. It was there all along, but largely dormant. It's one of the scarier developments of our age. Suddenly the liberal left can hear what the majority are thinking, and they don't like it one bit.

17

Deutsch–Amerikanische Freundschaft

I don't subscribe to the theory that we only become 'truly adult'
when our parents die. I don't think we ever become truly adult.

Michel Houellebecq, Platforme

In the end, we do what we think we can get away with. The consequences, however injurious, we either deny outright or retrospec-
tively justify in the name of freedom.

My dad once plotted his family tree, back in the 1970s, when he
was in his late forties. This is often seen as a mild symptom of the
mid-life crisis, the sudden wish to burrow back and find for yourself a sense of place and belonging, once your limbs begin to creak
and you first espy death flapping its big black wings somewhere in
the middle distance. Also it was a time when all of his older relatives dutifully shuffled off their mortal coils, beginning with his
mum in late 1971, and then the rest – the Berthas, the Ediths, the
Arthurs, the Josephs – one by one, with the same ham sandwiches
and vol au vents provided by the Co-op, the same flowers in the
same vase, the same singing of 'The Day Thou Gavest, Lord, has
Ended' in dour Victorian red-brick County Durham Methodist
churches, the congregation with each successive passing slightly
diminished, so that you wondered if anyone would be left to mourn
the next generation. Indeed, my dad's funeral was sparsely
attended, and hardly at all by his direct family, of which there was
little left.

Anyway, this family tree – etched in blue Biro on a fantastically hideous roll of 1970s woodchip wallpaper – stretched back to the beginning of the nineteenth century, and the thing that most grabbed you, reading it, was its manifest monotony. For the first seventy years all the men were miners and called John. For the next seventy years all the men worked on the railways and were called Joseph. All of them married just once, had two or three children who like their fathers and mothers were stoic Wesleyans, and they all lived within ten miles or so of each other, in a sort of triangle centred upon Darlington. The women – the Tallantyres, the Atkinsons, the Bowsers – lived slightly longer than their husbands on average, apart from those who died in childbirth. In truth, the trunk of that family tree shows a gradual, at times imperceptible, emergence from abject poverty to a sort of respectable working-class comfort, the gradations of discomfort invisible to the naked eye.

Methodism is sometimes held responsible for having inculcated a political quiescence within the British working class, its promise of a rewarding afterlife and the necessity of working hard and saving down here on earth distracting the labour force from what it really should have been doing, which was manning barricades and killing the rich. Perhaps. Certainly the years of political upheaval in Europe, of societies being turned on their heads – 1848, 1917, 1933 – would not remotely have impinged upon the Liddles. Theirs was instead a placid continuum: wars came and went and they fought and died in them, duty to the state and to their fellow citizens demanding a loyalty which came maybe a solid third to those other immovable loyalties to Church and family. They would have been, in the main, muscular and unsentimental leftists; pro unions, voting first Liberal and then Labour, happy to improve their lot gradually, dismissive of such exotic political creeds as dialectical materialism, loathing the godless and to their minds cruel social Darwinism of the radical right. Their lives were filled with certainties, immutable codes of conduct which descended from society, civil life, the state, the family and God. Not always pleasant certainties, and probably very rarely exciting certainties. Their credo, the stuff they believed in or adhered to, or thought important, changed very little over two hundred years. That, I suspect, is both the way in which we best cope with change as individuals, and the way in which society is best able to continue to cohere. One imagines that they too, the Johns and Josephs, did what they thought they could get away with. But the fact is that, for all those reasons I've listed above, they couldn't get away with very much. And now they've gone.

What I've tried to do in this book is examine the forces which led to this continuum ceasing to continue. They are many and varied, both political and to all intents and purposes politically neutral. It is difficult, therefore, to gauge the extent to which we have renounced the past as a conscious act, or have merely been led to do so – willingly enough – by an elite, or elites; how the old virtues by which we used to put such store are now seen as laughable. It is fairly clear to me that we are no happier for having done so – as I've pointed out, measurements of happiness (a tricky thing to pull off, incidentally, and one in which I do not set too much store) suggest that we are much less content now than we were in an age that contained more privation, but also more certainty. But it does seem to me that my generation, the people who escaped the horrors of the Second World War, have somehow rather conveniently bought into two pernicious schools of thought which, while politically antithetical to one another, when merged in the human mind become an especially toxic cocktail of philosophical self-interest.

Frankfurt and Chicago are glass-and-steel second cities, post-industrial landscapes located near the geographical centres of the two continents which comprise most of the First World. From Frankfurt we got the ephemeral cultural Marxism of the (New)

Frankfurt School, which many on the right, and particularly the US far right, would insist has fatally undermined our various institutions, and indeed the entirety of our civilisation. The splenetic objections from American conservatives to the works of, particularly, Jürgen Habermas and Herbert Marcuse and, before them, Theodor Adorno, seem to stem largely from the fact that they are 'Jewish', which is not a disposition sane people would share. Nor am I so certain that the excesses of 'the sixties', that familiar *bête noire* of the right, can be laid simply and firmly at the door of Marcuse *et al*. Schools of academic thought permeate a lot less deeply than the bloody academics think that they do; and, further, they do not spring fully formed out of the ether, apropos of nothing. They are as much products of their time and place and contingencies as a Ford Escort or a lava lamp, as Marcuse would be the first to agree. Still less am I certain that the practical changes wrought in the 1960s, from the abortion and divorce Acts to the upheaval of our education system, the sudden delightful appearance of rights without responsibilities and the imbecilic championing of yoof culture, plus everyone shagging away like there's no tomorrow, is directly a consequence of Herbert Marcuse sitting down one day to begin writing *One-Dimensional Man*. The students on the barricades in Paris in 1968 may have had their heads filled with inept distillations of Adorno and Marcuse and Horkheimer, but as is ever the case, these thoughtful and deeply pessimistic post-Marxist analyses of history were reduced to broad-brush and, frankly, elitist slogans and expressions of fatuous moral relativism. The state is a false totality. All forms of authority are repressive and bogus. Man has become nothing more than the stuff he makes. Bourgeois decency equals hypocrisy! Express yourself! Stick it to da man! Let it all hang out. And so on, adfuckinginfinitum.

Condensed still further, this became simply an eschewing of responsibility and an undermining of authority, allied with the notion that what anyone has to say on any particular matter is equally valid, which of course it is not. And so why it may well be that neither Shirley Williams nor Lady Plowden had so much as heard of poor old Adorno when they banjaxed the British education system for three generations, the Frankfurt germ, or meme, however distorted or reduced to a travesty of itself, was somehow working its way inside their skulls. That's about as much as we can say. They moved with the fashion. The fashion took them, just as it took the rest of us, or most of the rest of us. And the fashion was with Frankfurt. More esoterically, we can directly blame Frankfurt for affording credence to artists such as Emin and Hirst, composers such as Stockhausen and Schoenberg: only with the dissolute and the avant garde can our misery and alienation be truly realised, we were assured. Thanks a lot for that, Germany.

The best that one can say about Chicago these days is that it is not quite Detroit. It has had a less happy time, post-1945, than the city of the vanquished, Frankfurt. Racially divided, often politically corrupt, rust-belted and crime-ridden, it still claims to be America's second city, despite a declining population, and especially a declining white population, which has decamped to more salubrious satellites. It still packs a punch with its GDP; it is still at heart a post-European blue-collar city, with its river dyed green on St Paddy's day for the Oirish and its plethora of Central European accents and its vast diaspora. And it has always been insulated, geographically and viscerally, from the effete m'kay liberalism which attends to the coastal cities of Boston, New York, San Francisco and to a much lesser degree, Philadelphia. Even its solidly Democrat mayors have been dubious and sometimes brutal bastards, not least the Daly clan. If there was ever going to be a city which would spew forth an economic mantra of unenlightened, insular, anti-communitarian self-interest, then it was going to be the Windy City.

And so from the University of Chicago, via Milton Friedman, we got the spurious scientism of monetarism. We ought to be clear at this point that economics is a science in much the same way as astrology or homeopathy is a science, and that ol' Milt should have been convinced otherwise is scarcely our concern, except to say that the more economists (or sociologists) clothe themselves in starched white lab coats, the less we should believe them. As it happens, Friedman was writing at about the same time as Marcuse and Habermas were beavering away in Frankfurt, but monetarism had about it a latency. Its time had not come. Indeed, as a creed it would have seemed patently absurd at any point in the first two decades after the Second World War. Strict control of the monetary supply, no government intervention, slash taxes, inflation the sole demon to be extinguished – how would that have looked in Britain, or Germany, or France, in 1960? There would have been no recovery without state intervention, no *Wirtschaftswunder* in Germany, no rising living standards here, no social mobility, no new Europe without the profoundly un-monetarist Marshall Aid and huge amounts of direct investment from the domestic governments in what were then called 'public works'. It had a slightly greater purchase back then in the US, which had been bailing out Europe and where there persisted a much more potent mistrust of Big Government. And so it was that the rather agreeable if somewhat right-wing maverick Republican senator Barry Goldwater contested the 1964 presidential election on a monetarist ticket and with Milt installed as his adviser. Luckily for the Americans, he was hammered out of sight by Lyndon B. Johnson, and monetarism went into a sort of hibernation.

Only later, as the unions got arsey in the 1970s and inflation flew into the sort of humiliating double figures we had previously associated with hysterical Latino banana republics, was the, uh, 'science' of monetarism suddenly palatable to politicians any place beyond Illinois; an ur-economic philosophy which, as it happened, had been disinterred by Milton and his later acolytes from somewhere round about the sixteenth century.

It was taken up by the Reagan administration in 1980 and, with even greater avidity, by Margaret Thatcher's new government in Britain in 1979. Oh, and also by that lovable little squirrel, General Pinochet in Chile. In Britain the driving forces were the profound oddities which were Sir Keith Joseph and Thatcher's friends and sometime advisers Sir Alan Walters and Sir Alfred Sherman – both of these latter having communist-influenced backgrounds, strangely enough.

What monetarism did, in broad-brush terms, was fetishise money: it ceased to be a means to an end, and became instead an end in itself. It necessarily diminished the notion of a public good, something which we could all buy into, in favour of a strictly individualistic approach. It ignored the needs of communities, scarcely even recognising their existence; no bail-outs, low taxes, what must be preserved above all else is control of the money supply. The central core of monetarism remained Britain's economic policy even after Margaret Thatcher – and later the Conservatives – yielded power. Only now, with Europe in the grip of a vicious recession, are its primitive stratagems being questioned in the UK (they have long been jettisoned, or bypassed, in much of Europe).

Much as with the Frankfurt School, it would be egregious to lay the blame for the vaulting greed and acquisitiveness of the 1980s (and beyond) solely at the door of the Chicago School. In fact, the ruinous move towards fast and absurdly easy credit, which has left us with mind-numbing levels of personal debt, would have met no firmer adversary than Milton Friedman. But the orgy of deregulation of financial services and the stock exchange; the privatisations performed solely for ideological reasons (the utilities, British Rail); the disdain shown towards taxation and government intervention in the economy, regardless of the misery this caused; the relentless consumer-driven acquisitiveness; the transformation of a house from a home to a means of collateral; and above all the elevation of money onto a pedestal it did not deserve to occupy – well, that stuff can be traced back to Milt and his friends in Chicago.

And taken together, the two schools create a poisonous cocktail. Oddly enough, despite the fact that they emanate from opposing political poles, they have much in common. They were both attempts to grapple with that unexpected thing, welfare capitalism – a development which, for Adorno *et al.*, had left much of traditional Marxism an irrelevance. Both, as a consequence of this grappling, arrived at a point which elevated the individual over society and tore down authority; in the case of the Chicago School this was simply a refusal to countenance any form of intervention in the economy or regulation of private financial transactions from the very authority which had been elected to do just that – i.e., the government. From Frankfurt we learned to be culturally and socially *laissez-faire*, under the guise of despising bourgeois morality: we should do what we want. From Chicago we learned to be financially *laissez-faire*, beholden to no one, masters of our own destiny, owing nothing to the wider society: we should do what we want. And this is why we bought into these supposedly conflicting schools of thought. They are not really so terribly conflicting after all. They say to us: There is pretty much nothing you cannot get away with now. Go for it. Yes, I'm lovin' it. And if this seems a travesty of what both schools of thought actually stood for – well, it doesn't really matter. What matters is what we took from them.

Or, at least, what some of us took from them. For we have been led, since the middle of the 1980s, by an elite which increasingly bought into the secular social liberalism and moral relativism of the 1960s and the *laissez-faire* economics of the Chicago School. And while the rest of us followed along more or less willingly, it was the metropolitan bourgeoisie that gained the most.

I realise that I return to these people, the liberal metro elite, perhaps too often for comfort, that it is beginning to seem an unpleasant obsession. But who gained the most from the absurdity of the property boom? The homeless, the poor, or the people with two homes? Who gains the most from lowering the top rate of tax, from protected inheritances, from cheap labour? The elite cared not that education standards were falling in the state sector, because by and large they had no connection with the state sector. For the most part they had private health insurance too. And in a sense the economic shibboleths of the 1980s paid for these people to live the less *dirigiste* social lives made possible by the new freedoms of divorce and separation. The poor, as we have seen, still cannot afford to divorce. When they do, the misery – economic and social – is boundless.

I do not want to kill these people, the metro liberals. I thought I ought to point that out, in case you got the wrong idea. I am not Pol Pot, or Chairman Mao, not even at night in the fevered and bitter outposts of my imagination. I am not sure what I want done with them, if I'm honest. Perhaps it is enough simply to recognise who they are, and what they have done.

More to the point, identifying who was at the vanguard of this great change, and the people who benefited most from it, does not entirely exculpate the rest of us from following happily along in their wake. As I've pointed out, while the poor cannot afford to divorce, that does not remotely stop them doing it. Presented with new alleged freedoms, social and economic, and the new absence of the old, discredited repositories of moral authority, we did not flinch or cower. For the most part we reached out with both hands. As we always will, we did what we thought we could get away with. And now it transpired that we could get away with an awful lot; we could get away with stuff we hadn't dreamed of before. The thought that along the way we got rid of those controls that made our lives more pleasant, more coherent, better for children, more peaceable and communitarian, did not seem to occur. We thought we liked this new way we were, these new deregulated humans, fearful of nothing. But I think that we have deluded ourselves. We have filled our boots, and deluded ourselves.

The End

The sky whitens as if lit by three suns.
My mother shades her eyes and looks my way
Over the drifted stream. My father spins
A stone along the water. Leisurely,

They beckon to me from the other bank.
I hear them call, 'See where the stream-path is!
Crossing is not as hard as you might think.'

I had not thought that it would be like this.

Charles Causley

To be in your fifties is discombobulating, it gnaws at the psyche and maybe warps one's vision. I mention this partly as a get-out, as an excuse for what went before, in those previous chapters. You have been in the custody of an unreliable narrator, a narrator who was always unreliable but has perhaps become more so of late; more contrite and not hugely suffused with optimism. Or indeed vigour; the rueful memory of vigour, certainly, but not actually vigour itself. That's fucked off somewhere else. And – these days niggles and aches are not easily dismissed with the certainty that they will, within a few days, disappear. They linger and become harbingers, a real or imagined chequered flag, a frank indication that there is not that long to go. A feeling exacerbated when contemporaries succumb suddenly or after that frightening obit euphemism 'the long illness'. John Updike put it well – in the mouth of a character – 'We're getting within the Big Fella's range.' But I prefer the phrase used by an old school mate of mine, Pete Richardson – known as Big Pete when we were kids because he was, frankly, both huge and fairly terrifying – who commented when a classmate of ours had recently died: 'He's pickin' 'em from our pen now, Rod.' When he said this, I saw us suddenly as oblivious sheep, plaintively bleating, huddled together on some damp barren moorland just outside Guisborough, the town where we went to school, the pen to the right of us pretty full, the pen to the left of us now nearly half empty, and ours gradually depleting. Apologies that this is not a particularly cheering vision, but I can't help that. My point is that it impinges, it increases the sense of dissatisfaction, it gnaws at the psyche and warps one's vision. Paradoxically, you might think, it is a state of mind not entirely dissimilar to the fervid radicalism of youth, with its epic mistrust and disillusion. All that's missing is the blithe confidence that things might get better. Truth be told I feel a greater kinship now with myself as an unwashed, dissolute, gobshite sixteen-year-old, full of piss and vinegar and half-arsed rebelliousness, than I do with the supine me at any later stage in life. The knuckling-down years, the doing-what-has-to-be-done years, the working hard, keeping your head down and bringing home the bacon stuff.

An ambulance came round to the house not so long ago. My wife called it because I thought I was having a heart attack. I can't explain to you how terrifying it was, the dizzying symptoms, the fizzing away just beyond my eyesight of coma, maybe permanent coma, the nausea, the shortness of breath, the sweating and palpitations, the dread. It wasn't a heart attack. It was a panic attack. Panic at what? I haven't a clue. Panic at something, leastways.

Back then:

My dad looked at me one time as I was going out for the evening, earring in one ear, ripped trousers with 'Fuck off' written on them in Magic Marker, bright-red SWP badge displayed proudly on the lapel of a filthy second-hand jacket I bought because it looked like the one Neil Young wore on the cover of *Tonight's the Night*. 'Christ, you can't sink any bloody lower,' he commented. Oh, just you wait, just you wait. I promise you I can. We all can. He approved of the knuckling down, during the knuckling-down years, though. Parents do.

He died in a nursing home, where he had taken himself – he said – temporarily, not feeling too hot, Rod, he said, down the phone, it will just be for a while. I was away at the time. And then. One moment he was there. The next he was gone.

Left behind, in a large dark-brown wooden attaché case which had been made by his father, were his details, his stuff: every financial transaction, every bank statement, every bill receipt, for fifty years. It showed a modest accretion of wealth, about forty grand, which had been meticulously acquired, the consequence of hard work and frugality. He had been cheated of university, of being the first in his family to be educated past the age of fifteen, by the war. But society had not been bad to him, post-1945; his background had not noticeably held him back, his standard of living had improved with pretty much every year that passed, perhaps aside from the first few years of my existence, when the family presumably needed to economise. During his working life the Empire dissolved, the Church began its long and dismal retreat from the world (or, more properly, the world began its long and dismal retreat from the Church); what had previously been certainties, invariables, of British life became much less sure. Was this still a great and strong country, of which one could be justifiably proud? The war, I think, confirmed to him that it was, despite Britain's emergence at the end of it more weakened than perhaps any of the other principal protagonists, skint and rapidly stripped of its colonies. But the vestigial tail of Britain's greatness, of its sense of civilised decency (however misplaced this might be) still wagged away inside the minds of my father's generation. Job security, a semblance of social mobility, steadily rising living standards and a kind of permanence of things, of values and mores, helped to convince him that he was doing the right thing, and that doing the right thing would be rewarded, even if not extravagantly rewarded. Rewarded moderately.

What we have now, instead, is a chaos of change, a transience and an impermanence, and a country which has been denuded of those things which bind it together as a whole. We have competing groups, each vociferously proclaiming their sense of victimhood, their grievances. And doing so with such rapidity! The internet and, before it, twenty-four-hour news channels, have given us conduits for the immediate expression of outrage, fury, disappointment – reactions devoid of more than a nanosecond of thought and reflection. That furious yapping you hear is the fugue of our times, a billion dogs furiously chasing their own tails, turning circles in paroxysms of suddenly occasioned anger. Each demanding to be heard. It is not 'I think therefore I am,' it is simply 'I am' – there is not much in the way of thinking at all. Our narcissism has been partly occasioned, one supposes, as a defence mechanism against a lack of real power over our lives. We demand to be heard because we know that underneath we count for less than we once did.

The glue which bound us all together has more or less dissolved, the idea that as a nation state, a territorial entity cohered around a thousand and more years of a common culture, we shared certain values and norms. That seems to have gone, no?

Undoubtedly, there are things we do better now: we are more tolerant of diversity, there is far less discrimination against people from ethnic minorities, women, disabled people, homosexuals and those who are transgendered. This, I think, is a good thing. But the moral and political and social upheaval which accompanied this sacking of the old order has left us fraught and clamorous, unhappy, isolated and averse.

Rod Liddle, Canterbury

Kind permission has been granted to quote from the following: 'Home is So Sad' by Philip Larkin, reprinted by permission of Faber & Faber; 'Bagpipe Music' by Louis MacNeice, reprinted by permission of David Higham Associates; 'Freud Lives!' by Professor Slavoj Žižek, reprinted by permission of the London Review of Books; 'Western Parents Need to Chill Out About Their Kids' by Frank Furedi, reprinted by permission of the author; Brief Interviews with Hideous Men by David Foster Wallace, published by Abacus and reprinted by permission of Little, Brown; The Way We Live Now by Richard Hoggart, published by Chatto & Windus and reprinted by permission of the Random House Group Ltd and Curtis Brown Group Ltd; 'Eden Rock' by Charles Causley, reprinted by permission of David Higham Associates.

Index

homeopathy, 196, 199, 202, 205, 228

homosexuality: and hate crime, 61

Horkheimer, Max, 226

hospitals, and choice, 177

House, Linford, 217–19

house prices, 47–50, 170–1, 231

Humphrys, John, 185

Hunt, Tristram, 138

Hutton Inquiry, 160–1

hydrogen bomb, 15

illiteracy and innumeracy, 92

immigration, 47, 150, 153, 166, 173–6

income tax, 59

Independent, 145, 151–2, 216

Independent Safeguarding Authority, 144

Industrial Revolution, 79, 127

internet, 88, 210–11, 214–19, 221–2, 236: social networking sites, 62; and spurious diseases, 194, 198

Iraq War, 140–1, 160

Irritable Bowel Syndrome (IBS), 204–5

Islam, 61

Jackson, Glenda, 138

Jenkins, Peter, 212

jihadists, 18, 22

Johnson, Lyndon B., 228

jokes, 67, 220

Joseph, Sir Keith, 229

journalists, 118, 121

judges, *see* lawyers and judges

judicial inquiries, 159–61

Kampala, 117

Kelly, Dr David, 160

Kennedy, Charles, 163

Kenya, 188

Keynes, John Maynard, 28

King, Martin Luther, 132

Korea, 188

Labour Party, 9, 31, 101, 145, 151, 159, 224: 'Blue Labour', 127; calibre of politicians, 137–9; and immigration, 175; loss of support, 135–6; New Labour, 108, 147, 179; and new laws, 163–4; party conferences, 139–40; and the working class, 126–7, 129, 137–9, 153–4, 175

Lacan, Jacques, 62, 217

Laing, R.D., 62

Lasch, Christopher, 63

Laurence Jackson School, 124–5

Lawlor, Sheila, 109

laws, numbers of, 162–4

lawyers and judges, 155–62, 164–6: divorce lawyers, 10, 75–6

Leitao, Mary, 194–7

Lenin, Vladimir Ilyich, 107, 132

Leveson Inquiry, 146–8, 152, 161

Liberal Democrats, 136, 152, 163

Liberal Party, 135, 224

linoleum, 35

Lolita, 83

London Olympics, 127

Lord of the Flies, 6

Luton, 219

Lydon, John, 29

McClure, Professor Myra, 202, 203

Major, John, 179

Malaya, 188

Malcolm X, 8

Mandelson, Peter, 138

maps, 9
Marcuse, Herbert, 226, 228
Marshall Aid, 228
Marx, Karl, 95, 173: *Das Kapital*, 113
maternity leave, 108–9
Meadow, Dr Roy, 197
Media Standards Trust, 147–8
memory, 6–7
meritocracy, 121–2, 130
Metcalfe, David, 145–6
Methodists, 23, 37, 101, 223–4
Mian, Mehmuda, 144, 149
Middlesbrough, 7, 32, 44–5, 47–8, 80–1: jobs in, 42, 102–3; Midland Bank, 101; pollution, 168; property prices, 48, 170–1; schools, 89–91, 102–3, 124–5; 'select area' of, 167–71; SWP branch, 131–2; unemployment in, 72–3, 75; *see also* Nunthorpe
Middlesbrough FC, 169
Miliband, Ed, 126, 159
Mill, J.S., 18
mince pies, 163
minimum wage, 30
MMR vaccine, 201
Monbiot, George, 153
monetarism, 228–30
Montague, Sarah, 202–3
Moore, Charles, 117
Morgan, Joe, 102
'Morgellons', 193–8, 201, 207
mortgages, 33, 37, 49, 125
motorways, 35
Mount, Ferdinand, 128–9
multiculturalism, 166, 174, 186
multinational companies, 59, 141
Munch, Edvard, 184
Munchausen's Syndrome by Proxy, 196–7

Myalgic Encephalomyelitis (ME), 198–205, 207, 220

National Health Service, 112–13, 177, 179, 216
nationalisation, 127–9
Netherlands, 41, 96
Newsnight, 119, 147
Ngo Dinh Diem, 134
Nixon, Richard M., 141
Norway, 9, 41
nuclear family, 79–80
Nunthorpe, 167–9
Nunthorpe Wanker, the, 45, 167
Nuttall, Jeff, 134

obesity, 57–60, 62, 85–9
O'Brien, Neil, 172
Observer, 212
Office for Budgetary Responsibility, 28
Oliver, Jamie, 85, 89
Orwell Prize, 148, 152
Osborne, George, 28, 86–7, 117, 127
Overton, Iain, 147

paedophilia, *see* sex abusers
party conferences, 139–40
Patten, Chris, 146, 149
physics, women and, 114
Pinochet, General Augusto, 134, 149, 229
Plowden, Lady Bridget, 227
Poles, 41–2, 171
polio, 10
politicians, 136–41: and lawyers, 158–60
Port Talbot, 157
poverty, relative, 85
Prescott, John, 113